linking civil society and the state

the pennsylvania state university press
university park, pennsylvania

linking civil society and the state

urban popular movements, the left, and local government in peru, 1980—1992

gerd schönwälder

Library of Congress Cataloging-in-Publication Data

Schönwälder, Gerd, 1958–
 Linking civil society and the state : urban popular movements, the Left, and local government in Peru, 1980–1992 / Gerd Schönwälder.
  p.   cm.
 Includes bibliographical references and index.
 ISBN 0-271-02180-2 (cloth : acid-free paper)
 1. Local government—Peru. 2. Urban poor—Peru—Political activity. 3. Democratization—Peru. 4. New Left—Peru. 5. Social movements—Peru. I. Title.

JS2667.A2 S36 2002
320.8'0985—dc21
                                    2001055955

Copyright © 2002 The Pennsylvania State University
All rights reserved
Printed in the United States of America
Published by The Pennsylvania State University Press,
University Park, PA 16802-1003

It is the policy of The Pennsylvania State University Press to use acid-free paper for the first printing of all clothbound books. Publications on uncoated stock satisfy the minimum requirements of American National Standard for Information Sciences—Permanence of Paper for Printed Library Materials, ANSI Z39.48–1992.

Future events . . . will depend, not on academic predictions, but on collective action guided by political wills that make work what is structurally barely possible.

—F. H. Cardoso and E. Faletto

I am convinced that if we had not learned from Marxism to see history from the point of view of the oppressed, gaining a new and immense perspective on the human world, there would have been no salvation for us.

—Norberto Bobbio

contents

Acknowledgments ix
List of Abbreviations and Frequently Used Acronyms xi
Introduction 1

PART ONE

1 Urban Popular Movements in Latin America: Identity, Strategy, and Autonomy 9
2 Decentralization and the Participation of Urban Popular Movements in Local Government 35

PART TWO

3 Urban Popular Movements, Political Parties, and the State in Peru 61
4 The Peruvian Left and Local Government in the Early 1980s 89
5 The Barrantes Administration of Metropolitan Lima, 1984–1986 113
6 Revolutionary and Radical-Democratic Approaches in Conflict 153

Conclusions and Epilogue 185
Appendix: List of Interviews 205
Glossary of Frequently Used Spanish Terms 209
References 211
Index 233

acknowledgments

As is the case with most studies, many people have contributed to this one, and I cannot possibly name them all. First, my thanks go to all those who were willing to be interviewed. I thank them for sparing some of their precious time, for their warmth and friendliness with which they welcomed me in their midst, and for their patience in answering my questions and in explaining, often repeatedly, the more complex aspects of their various activities. I came away from my research with a deeper understanding of the adversity many of them face on a daily basis and a greater appreciation of their achievements under these difficult circumstances.

Furthermore, I would like to thank the Centro de Estudios para el Desarrollo y la Participación (CEDEP) for offering me a home base during my research stay in Lima. I am grateful to everybody at CEDEP, not only for letting me use the facilities of the Centro and their help in collecting research materials, but also for making my stay a fruitful and pleasant one. I would like to express my special gratitude to Eliana Chávez, who was instrumental in opening CEDEP's doors to me and who later facilitated vital contacts all over Lima and supported my research every step of the way. Carlos Franco likewise deserves special thanks for his willingness to share his immense experience and knowledge with me, as well as for his help in organizing a seminar on my research at the end of my stay in Lima. Eddy Márquez, for his part, proved to be, not only a superbly efficient research assistant, but also a witty and lively conversation partner who enlightened me on many a mystery of Peruvian politics and culture during those seemingly interminable waits between interviews. I should not forget to mention my office mates, particularly Edmundo Beteto, Juan Chacaltana, and Lola Castro, who introduced me to the depths and finesse of *limeño* humor, which I have sorely missed ever since. Finally, I would like to thank Juan Miguel Zegarra and Raúl Haya de la Torre of the Centro Constitución y Sociedad in Lima for their help in setting up some important interviews, as well as for the discussions we had about common research interests.

At McGill University in Montreal, I am especially indebted to Philip Oxhorn, my supervisor when this book was still a doctoral dissertation. Henry Dietz of the University of Texas at Austin likewise provided valuable advice, as well as encouragement. I would also like to thank McGill's Center for Developing Area Studies (CDAS) for providing office space during my time in Montreal, Cara Murphy and Iain Blair of the Documentation Center of CDAS for their assistance in collecting research materials, and all other members and visitors of CDAS, particularly Gleema Nambiar, for the animated discussions we had, either at fellows' seminars and presentations, or simply over lunch or coffee. I am also thankful that the staff of McLennan Library and especially its Interlibrary Loan Department remained unperturbed even by my more obscure requests. On the way from thesis to book, the editorial staff of Pennsylvania University Press deserve credit for their professionalism and efficiency. The two anonymous reviewers contacted by the Press provided invaluable comments and advice, helping to distinguish the manuscript from earlier drafts and to draw in more recent debates. As always, though, responsibility for any errors or omissions rests with me.

Funding for this study was provided in part through a Government of Canada Award from the Department of External Affairs and a research grant from McGill University, which is gratefully acknowledged.

Last but not least, I want to express a special thank you to Janet Dorozynski for putting up with me all this time and for taking the time to help me through some of the more difficult passages of this project.

abbreviations and frequently used acronyms

AP	Acción Popular (Popular Action Party, center-right)
APRA	Alianza Popular Revolucionaria Americana (American Popular Revolutionary Alliance, center-left)
CEDLA	Center for Latin American Research and Documentation
CEDYS	Centro de Estudios de Democracia y Sociedad
CELATS	Centro Latinoamericano de Trabajo Social
CENCA	Centro de Capacitación y Asesoría (NGO operating in the district of El Agustino)
CENDIPP	Centro de Investigación y Promoción Popular (NGO operating in the district of El Agustino)
CG	Comité de Gestión (Management Committee)
CIDAP	Centro de Investigaciones, Documentación y Asesoría
CTIC	Comité Coordinador Técnico Intercentros (coordinating committee of the three main NGOs operating in the district of El Agustino)
DESCO	Centro de Estudios y Promoción del Desarrollo
D.L.	Decreto Ley (Decree Law)
FODECO	Fondo de Desarrollo Comunal (Communal Development Fund, provided funding for the MIADES in the district of El Agustino)
FOVIDA	Fomento de la Vida
FFE	Fundación Friedrich Ebert
GREDES	Grupo de Estudios para el Desarrollo

IEP	Instituto de Estudios Peruanos
IFEA	Instituto Francés de Estudios Andinos
INVERMET	Fondo de Inversiones Municipales (Municipal Investment Fund in Metropolitan Lima)
IPADEL	Instituto para la Democracia Local
ISS	Institute of Social Studies
IU	Izquierda Unida (United Left)
MAS	Movimiento de Afirmación Socialista (Movement of Socialist Affirmation, leftist)
MIADES	Micro-Areas de Desarrollo (Micro-Areas of Development in the district of El Agustino)
PMR	Partido Mariateguista Revolucionario (Revolutionary Mariateguist Party, leftist)
PUC	Pontífica Universidad Católica del Perú
PUM	Partido Unificado Mariateguista (United Mariateguist Party, leftist)
SEA	Servicio Educativo de El Agustino (NGO operating in the district of El Agustino)
SINAMOS	Sistema Nacional de Apoyo a la Movilización Social (National System for the Support of Social Mobilization, created by the Velasco government in 1971)

introduction

Local politics in Latin America has been attracting a great deal of scholarly interest of late (see Fox 1994; Nickson 1995; Reilly 1995). This interest can be attributed in part to the simple fact that over the past two decades, the institutional weight of Latin American local governments has continued to grow, spurred as much by the popularity of decentralization policies as by the seminal crisis of the central states in the region. Faced with shrinking resources and painful structural adjustment programs, central governments were often left with no other choice but to divest themselves of responsibilities they could no longer meet.

Even more important, local governments in Latin America have aroused the curiosity of social scientists and other observers because they seem to be situated at the confluence of two other seminal trends: the resurgence of civil society, particularly in the urban realm, and the democratization of formerly authoritarian regimes. When viewed from this angle, local governments appear to provide a crucial meeting ground for the myriad social movements and groups that emerged during and after the transitions from authoritarian rule to focus on such issues as the improvement of urban services, women's rights, nutrition, and public health (see Eckstein 1989; Escobar and Alvarez 1992a), and the still feeble political institutions of the new democratic regimes. Some authors writing on decentralization and on social movements are particularly enthusiastic, hoping that the coming together of these two trends will release important synergies whose repercussions potentially could transcend the local realm (Slater 1985; Ballón 1986c; Boisier 1987; Castells and Borja 1988). Most important, these authors believe that an increase in popular participation[1] at the local level could improve the institutional performance of local governments, which would help demonstrate the viability of democratic institutions at other levels as well, and exert a democratizing impact on local political institutions, thereby promoting the consolidation of democracy as a whole.

In the meantime, however, it has become clear that many of these authors have been overly sanguine about the prospects of local democracy, often assuming that it would flourish if only the appropriate institutional preconditions could be put in place, namely the devolution of powers and resources to lower levels of government and adequate provisions for popular participation. Their rhetoric, which is frequently prone to macrolevel generalizations, pays little attention to how local democracy was being implemented on the ground. These authors also tend to neglect some crucial issues, such as the autonomy of urban popular movements, their links to other actors, and the internal workings of political alliances and coalitions. In particular, the issue of movement autonomy is not sufficiently addressed. This kind of autonomy can be tested severely when urban popular movements participate in political institutions permeated by traditional patterns of clientelism and co-optation. They also tend to gloss over the

1. The term "popular participation" is used here in the Latin American sense, denoting political participation by lower-class people, often by-passing established institutional channels. See the discussion in Chapter 1.

often conflictive relations between such movements and other actors, particularly political parties, as well as the bargaining and deal-making inherent in any political alliance.

Without going to the opposite extreme of denying the viability of local-level democracy altogether, I will attempt to address these shortcomings by taking an empirical case as its starting point. By examining the specific example of the Peruvian capital, Lima, in some depth, I hope to shed light on the concrete interactions between various local-level actors, institutions, and processes, paying particular attention to urban popular movements, local government, leftist political parties, and actors such as nongovernmental organizations (NGOs). In so doing, I hope to provide a base for meaningful generalizations, given the fact that the socioeconomic characteristics and the sociopolitical history of Lima share important similarities with urban areas elsewhere on the Latin American continent.

The first two chapters set out the theoretical framework for the study. In Chapter 1, I define urban popular movements as social movements and distinguish them from other forms of collective action, such as interest groups. I view urban popular movements as harboring a democratic potential contained in the collective identities of their participants, as well as in their social, cultural, and political practices. Under certain conditions, I argue, this democratic potential may serve to democratize other political actors and to render local political institutions more efficient and more democratic.

In Chapter 2, I situate urban popular movements in the real world of local politics, showing that any democratizing impact they may have on others depends on effective political decentralization and sufficient institutional openings for popular participation. Furthermore, to overcome their various weaknesses and to project their concerns into the political arena, urban popular movements cannot remain isolated but need to form alliances with other political actors, inevitably exposing themselves to co-optive pressures. Reviewing the various options available to urban popular movements, I argue that multiple alliances with a variety of other actors increase their bargaining power, maximizing their access to resources while at the same time preserving their autonomy.

In Chapter 3, I provide some essential historical background for the following empirical chapters, delineating the development of urban popular movements in Peru from their clientelist origins in the 1940s and 1950s to the conflictive relations with the reformist military government under General Juan Velasco Alvarado and the emergence of new collective identities and practices during and after the return to democratic rule in the 1980s.

Then in Chapter 4, I examine the new institutional relevance of local governments under the democratic regime, as well as the Peruvian left's sudden interest in local politics. Eager to renew its ties to the popular sector and to position itself in the newly created democratic institutions, the Left developed two competing perspectives on local government, a revolutionary one viewing local governments as "bridgeheads" inside the political system and a radical-democratic one focusing on the Left's capacity to govern. Subsequently, I look at five leftist-controlled district governments in Lima between 1981 and 1983 that largely followed the revolutionary approach. I contend that by doing so, they largely relegated urban popular movements to a role as passive bases of mass support and limited their role as agents of popular participation.

Following an ideological shift within the Peruvian left, the leftist-led city government of Metropolitan Lima between 1984 and 1986 became the most prominent example of the radical-democratic approach to local politics; I examined this in Chapter 5. Viewing local governments as vehicles for social reform and increased popular participation as a means to improve local services and to democratize the municipal administration from below led to new possibilities for popular participation in local politics. At the same time, organizational support from the municipal administration allowed urban popular movements to flourish, largely without infringements on their autonomy. However, despite a fairly positive record, the Left was defeated at the polls, leading to a resurgence of old ideological and strategic differences.

In Chapter 6, I examine the impact of these struggles at the local level, based on an in-depth case study of El Agustino, a low-income district of Lima. Urban popular movements were now confronted with not one, but two competing approaches, resembling the revolutionary and radical-democratic approaches mentioned earlier. I show that urban popular movements were careful not to take sides, accepting benefits and support from both camps but taking care not to compromise their autonomy. In fact, my findings show that by establishing multiple alliances with other actors, urban popular movements were successful in safeguarding their independence and in maximizing benefits available to them. At the same time, however, this strategy was mostly defensive, and the influence of urban popular movements on institutions and other political actors remained rather limited.

The principal conclusion emerging from the cases studied is that the democratic potential of urban popular movements is genuine, but that its realization is hampered by several obstacles, among them institutional, legal, and other barriers to popular participation in local politics, the structural and programmatic weaknesses of urban popular movements themselves, and politically motivated interference by other actors. Under these conditions, the best option for urban popular movements seems to be a strategy that relies on multiple alliances with several other actors, but it is clear that such a strategy is mainly defensive and that it requires a certain degree of organizational consolidation and fairly developed negotiating skills. The challenge therefore remains for other actors, and particularly the political left, to construct a political alternative capable of integrating urban popular movements in a nonmanipulative way, while addressing their impulses for democratizing political institutions and the political arena as a whole.

PART one

one

urban popular movements in latin america

identity, strategy, and autonomy

Latin American social movements, long a limited range of relatively homogenous entities representing workers, peasants, or students, have changed dramatically over the last three decades. The return to democratic rule and the economic crisis of the 1980s propelled new social actors to the scene, the so-called popular movements. Much less homogenous than their predecessors and often exhibiting a particularistic outlook reflecting their diverse social origins, these new social actors were nevertheless characterized by a wide array of novel collective identities and social practices.

Without doubt, the emergence and proliferation of these movements, particularly in urban areas, has been one of the hallmarks in the development of Latin American societies since the late 1970s. In one form or another, most large urban centers in Latin America witnessed an upsurge of urban squatters fighting for secure land titles, residents of low-income neighborhoods organizing to obtain improvements to the infrastructure of their settlements, groups of women running communal soup kitchens, and organizations of informal sector entrepreneurs, youth clubs, and human rights associations, all of which came to be known as "urban popular movements." Some observers were quick to hail these movements as harbingers of a new social order, capable of challenging clientelist and authoritarian traditions and infusing the fragile institutions of the new democratic regimes with new vigor. Others were less sanguine, pointing out that urban popular movements tended to be fragile and disorganized, easily co-opted, and incapable of forming strategic alliances to increase their own political clout. Consequently, they were unlikely to have any lasting impact on the direction of social and political change in Latin American societies.

In this chapter I build on these debates in order to highlight the current significance of urban popular movements, focusing on the key issues of identity, strategy, and autonomy.[1] I show that these movements play a pivotal role for social change: their emergence, as well as the collective identities and practices they represent, have transformed the face of urban civil society in Latin America for good. At the same time, it is much less clear to what extent these movements can influence political parties, political institutions, or the formulation of public policy. I contend that the realization of such a potential for political change is difficult, but nevertheless crucial for the future development of urban popular movements, which would otherwise risk becoming marginalized and losing any influence at the political level.

---

1. The fact that most debates on popular movements in Latin America revolve around these issues highlights the influence of theoretical developments from outside the region. While the identity paradigm associated with Western European new social movement theory has clearly been more influential in the Latin American context than the strategy paradigm connected with North American resource mobilization theory, neither of the two perspectives has become dominant. Instead, there exists a certain theoretical and methodological eclecticism, and most current studies make different, and usually limited, claims as to their own theoretical validity and empirical range (see, for example, Escobar and Alvarez 1992a; Eckstein 1989). Special focuses of attention are the links between popular movements and other actors, such political parties, political institutions, and NGOs (Kaufmann and Dilla 1997). For an overview of recent theorizing, see Haber 1996 and Roberts 1997, as well as Foweraker 1995.

Coming to Grips with Urban Popular Movements: Conceptual Clarifications

A useful first step in coming to grips with urban popular movements is to distinguish them from other forms of collective action, particularly interest groups. Urban popular movements are part of the larger universe of social movements, which are themselves characterized by a number of key features. Using Kuechler and Dalton's definition,[2] I conceive of social movements as

> a significant portion of the population developing and defining interests that are incompatible with the existing social and political order and pursuing these interests in uninstitutionalized ways, potentially invoking the use of physical force and/or coercion. In this sense of the term, a social movement is a collectivity of *people* united by a common belief (ideology) and a determination to challenge the existing order in pursuit of these beliefs outside institutionalized channels of interest intermediation. (Kuechler and Dalton 1990, 277–78; italics in original)

In other words, social movements are characterized by a potential for social and/or political change, a preference for using noninstitutional forms of action to achieve their goals, and a unifying bond in the form of a set of common beliefs that movement participants share. All three of these features merit a closer look.

The first defining characteristic of social movements, their potential for social and/or political change, can be seen as embodied in the interests and demands of their participants. These can reflect postmaterialist value orientations that are at odds with the societal consensus, as is the case with the new social movements of Western Europe, or they can express the desire of their participants to break out of their political, economic, social, or cultural marginalization, which is more typical in Latin America.[3] What is important in either case is the fact that these demands go beyond the grievances of specific social groups, in the sense that satisfying them would require profound changes to the existing social and political framework. Social movements are therefore challengers (Lo 1992; Schwartz and Shuva

---

2. Kuechler and Dalton themselves build on Foss and Larkin (see Foss and Larkin 1986, 2).
3. Foweraker recalls that "the initial enthusiasm for 'new social movements' in Latin America" has subsided and that the concept is now only rarely applied to the Latin American context (Foweraker 1995, 24–25). But see Escobar and Alvarez 1992a.

1992) representing societal outsiders; by contrast, interest or pressure groups often represent more powerful social and political actors that have a stake precisely in the *continuity* of the existing social and political order.

A few words are in order on the *kind* of social and political change that social movements can bring about. Traditionally, most social science theorizing has situated social and political change at the level of regime or system transformation. Dependency and modernization theories, for example, conceive of such changes as moves from one regime type or development model to another, usually following a struggle between two clearly identifiable adversaries, such as the workers' movement versus the bourgeoisie, or traditionalists versus modernizers. Social movement theories have long been framed in much the same way. For example, Manuel Castells (Castells 1977, 1978, 1983), whose work builds on Alain Touraine and has been very influential in the Latin American context, has proposed reserving the term "urban social movements" for those urban movements that are able to have an impact on the overall system of "urban structure" or "urban meaning."[4]

The problem with approaches such as these is that they tend to downplay the significance of social and political change taking place at a level below outright regime or system transformation, which is precisely the kind of change that urban popular movements are involved in. Consequently, I emphasize here the significant *incremental* changes that can be realized by addressing the nature of social and political practices themselves. I direct my attention away from the takeover of state power as the master switch for change and toward everyday social and political struggles. While the aspirations of the individual social movements involved in these struggles are often relatively modest and their potential for change is not always realized, a multitude of such movements could nevertheless have significant clout (Escobar and Alvarez 1992b, 3; Bennett 1992, 242). Taken together, these movements may well be able to effect more far-reaching changes at the grassroots level, notably by challenging the dominant political culture (Alvarez, Dagnino, and Escobar 1998), and thereby have an impact on other actors or on political institutions.

The second key characteristic of social movements, their tendency to rely on noninstitutionalized forms of action, is directly related to the one just mentioned. As challengers representing the demands of societal outsiders,

---

4. Alain Touraine, for his part, reserves the term "social movement" for those movements that are involved in the transformation of society as such, or what he calls the struggle to redefine "historicity" (Touraine 1984, 141–64).

social movements are faced with a rather narrow choice of strategies to pursue their goals.[5] In particular, their access to institutionalized forms of interest mediation is limited; and as a consequence, social movements often have to resort to noninstitutionalized forms of action in order to voice their demands, staging demonstrations, rallies, strikes, and the like. Depending on the response they receive from other actors and especially the state, as well as situational and a variety of other factors, these actions may or may not include violent forms of protest. By contrast, interest or pressure groups typically have access to institutionalized channels of interest mediation and will rely on them to pursue their goals; alternatively, they can exploit informal links to powerful elites and political decision makers.

While relying chiefly on noninstitutionalized forms of action, social movements will also develop more or less clearly defined organizational structures in the course of their lifetimes. There are inevitable tensions between these two poles, which are as present in urban popular movements as they are in social movements in general. Noninstitutionalized forms of action have the clear advantage of making social movements more open and accessible, facilitating participation and fostering direct face-to-face interaction between movement participants. As a result, social movements can acquire astonishing force and vitality, particularly when mobilizing around specific demands. At the same time, however, such mass mobilizations tend to be highly cyclical. After short bursts of intense activity—sometimes referred to as periods of "madness," or, more positively, as states of public hope or public happiness (Lummis 1996, 40–43, 154–58)—they

---

5. The notion of strategy lies at the heart of the resource mobilization approach (McAdam, McCarthy, and Zald 1988; McCarthy and Zald 1977; Jenkins 1983) developed in North America in response to earlier collective behavior theories (Gurr 1970; Smelser 1962; Turner and Killian 1972). While these latter theories regarded the behavior of social movements as largely irrational and driven by emotional impulses such as frustration and anger, the resource mobilization school has shown that social movements are quite capable of defining goals and pursuing strategies in a rational manner.

The strategy notion is useful in the Latin American context, given that popular movements typically interact with the state, political parties, and others and therefore have to behave strategically, even though the assumption of "normal politics" and the heavy emphasis put on activities such as fundraising campaigns, lobbying, playing the media, etc., seem inapplicable to political systems characterized by highly unequal power relations. Resource mobilization theory has also been hampered by its inability to overcome the free-rider problem (Olson 1965), that is, to explain why individuals participate in social movements in the first place. Authors such as Calhoun (1991), Ferree (1992), and Oxhorn (1995) have attributed this difficulty to an individualist or "thin" notion of rationality, arguing that there are contextual, collective forms of rationality apart from the largely fictitious model of individual cost-benefit analysis.

often lose steam before their objectives have been reached. An exclusive reliance on noninstitutionalized forms of action would therefore render social movements unstable and ineffective, while a minimum of organizational coherence can assure continuity and improve their chances of success. Obviously, though, greater organizational coherence entails its own dangers, making social movements less accessible and increasing the distance between leaders and the rank and file. Taken to the extreme, these tendencies can turn social movements into lifeless creatures tightly controlled by ossified bureaucratic leaderships.[6]

Social movements also need a minimum of organizational coherence if they want to negotiate or strike alliances with others. This can greatly enhance the effectiveness of mass protests and other noninstitutional forms of action; however, by exposing social movements to the outside, it also poses a potential challenge to their autonomy.[7] In the Latin American context, for example, popular movements have typically turned to the state with their demands, and their success has depended to a large degree on their skills in bargaining with the political authorities. Under previous authoritarian regimes, this often took the form of a clientelist relationship, in which popular movements and especially their leaders established links with well-placed politicians or public officials, essentially receiving favors in exchange for political support or simply quiescence. After the return to democratic rule, the emphasis shifted to the level of political institutions, particularly local government. At least potentially, local elections and new possibilities for direct popular participation made popular movements less dependent on political patronage and increased their influence on local policymaking. However, by exposing popular movements to the clientelist structures that continued to dominate the local scene, the new institutional arrangements also highlighted their persistent vulnerability to co-optation.

And third, social movements are characterized by the fact that their participants share a set of common beliefs, or what has more appropriately been called a collective identity.[8] Acting as a unifying bond, a collective

---

6. Robert Michels labeled this the "iron law of oligarchy" in his famous study on political parties in modern democracies (Michels 1957). Piven and Cloward claim that such tendencies are typical for labor unions and working-class parties and therefore advocate disruptive mass action as the only weapon poor people have (Piven and Cloward 1979).

7. For Cohen and Arato, social movements have "a dual face and a dual organizational logic" (Cohen and Arato 1995, 514): they are rooted in civil society but at the same time try to influence economic structures and state policy.

8. The identity notion is associated with the new social movement approach developed in Western Europe (Touraine 1984, 1985; Melucci 1985, 1988, 1989; Brand 1985; Brand,

identity lends internal cohesion to a social movement and gives its participants a sense of purpose. Even more importantly, it serves as a frame of reference for the definition and interpretation of shared interests or grievances, whose mere existence would otherwise not result in collective action. As a crucial intervening variable, a collective identity can be a powerful stimulus for people to unite with others around common goals. Its presence—or lack thereof—therefore goes a long way in explaining why social movements appear in some cases and not in others, and why some stakes become issues and others do not (Scott 1991).

The formation of collective identities presupposes the existence of social networks that to some extent predate the emergence of actual social movements. The importance of these networks is no longer contested in the social movement literature, and much attention has been devoted to their role in the "framing" of shared interests and common grievances.[9] The fact that collective identities emerge in a social context implies that they are never stable and immutable; on the contrary, they are constantly reshaped in the course of collective action. In the sense that collective identities represent an interpretation of a given situation by a group of people, they are always open to challenges from competing interpretations. Obviously, these pressures increase with

---

Büsser, and Rucht 1986; Hirsch and Roth 1986; Dalton and Kuechler 1990; Offe 1987). New social movements are seen as reactions to major structural changes in developed Western societies, particularly the environmental crisis resulting from an obsession with economic growth and material wealth, as well as the proclivity of the modern welfare state to steadily encroach on the private realm or "life world" (Habermas 1987). Opposing these tendencies, new social movements seek to create spaces for face-to-face interaction where autonomous subjects and identities can be formed. The identity notion is a useful tool to analytically capture processes of social change taking place at the level of civil society in Latin America, as well as to understand the dynamic behind the ongoing development of popular movements. At the same time, new social movement theory largely ignores the existing links between social movements and other actors and has little to say about these links or about the strategies these movements employ in order to reach their goals.

9. Despite their different points of departure, both new social movement and resource mobilization theory now agree that mobilization into social movements is the result of microlevel group processes. For new social movement theory, these processes take place within social networks allowing people to devise a common interpretation of their shared grievances and concerns (Melucci 1988), while resource mobilization theory points to "micro-mobilization contexts" and other group processes that are variously called frame alignment, consensus mobilization, and the like (see Klandermans 1991 and McAdam, McCarthy, and Zald 1988). Obviously, these notions have a lot in common with that of a contextual rationality proposed by Ferree and others (see note 5). The partial convergence of hitherto diametrically opposed theoretical perspectives has intensified calls for a fusion of the two paradigms (see Cohen 1985; Salman 1990; Escobar and Alvarez 1992b; Klandermans 1991; and McAdam, McCarthy, and Zald 1996).

exposure to the outside, and other actors, particularly the state or political parties in the Latin American context, will try to influence the formation of collective identities within social movements. As a result, collective identities are often fragile and heterogeneous, but at the same time, their formation is never entirely predictable and can never be fully controlled.

While part of the larger universe of social movements, urban popular movements in Latin America differ from other social movements in several important ways, particularly in their respective social bases and the processes leading to the formation of collective identities, as well as in the processes related to the construction of common goals and strategies.

These differences are particularly striking when urban popular movements are compared to older social movements. Whereas older social movements drew on relatively clearly defined constituencies—workers or peasants, for example—urban popular movements have their roots in the urban popular sector, which has rightly been described as a "heterogeneous social collective" (Moisés 1982, 26).[10] Referring to that part of the population which lives in urban shantytowns or low-income neighborhoods, this category is obviously broad and at the same time fairly loose, encompassing groups with distinct social, economic, ethnic, and other characteristics. In occupational terms, for example, the urban popular sector comprises, not only those workers regularly employed in the formal economy, but also the un- and underemployed, the growing numbers of informal workers and small entrepreneurs, as well as that part of the working population which is largely excluded not only from the formal but also from the informal sphere.

In spite of being slightly unwieldy, the notion of the popular sector is useful in the context of the highly segmented and unequal societies of Latin America. Defined as that part of the population, usually the majority, which is disadvantaged in its life chances and consumption possibilities in comparison with the middle and upper classes, it reflects a fairly accurate picture of the empirical reality in these countries. Using the popular sector notion also has the distinct advantage of avoiding a fundamental problem sometimes associated with other concepts, that of reductionism. Concepts such as the urban poor, the informal sector, the working class, and so on, tend to highlight only one defining characteristic, such as poverty, participation in the informal economy, or the condition of being a worker. They

10. Related terms used in the literature are *lo popular* or the popular classes. See Mainwaring 1987; Portes 1985; Galín, Carrión, and Castillo 1986; Palma 1988; Oxhorn 1995; and Adrianzén and Ballón 1992. The term "popular sector" is used here in an analytical fashion and is not meant to deny the existence of links between different "sectors" of society.

therefore fail to capture the full diversity of the popular sector and of the movements emanating from it, especially in the urban realm, and should only be applied to certain groups within it. Not only that, these concepts can also obscure the fact that different popular movements may actually have certain interests and demands in common, which could provide the basis for collective action on a larger scale.

The identification of such common interests and demands is one of the greatest challenges that urban popular movements face, a challenge that relates back to the formation of collective identities. Again, a comparison with older social movements is instructive. In the case of these movements, collective identities are generally thought to be rooted in socioeconomic structures: the position of the individual in the production process forms the basis for the formation of class interests, which in turn give rise to the development of class consciousness and the emergence of social movements. Structuralist Marxists have conceived of this link as an almost mechanical connection, insisting on the primary influence of socioeconomic structures (Althusser 1965; Althusser et al. 1965). Other authors have put more emphasis on the role of social struggle in the formation of collective identities. For E. P. Thompson, for instance, "class formations . . . arise at the intersection of determination and self-activity" (Thompson 1978, 298). Ira Katznelson, taking Thompson's analysis a step further, has argued that economic structure has to be complemented by shared ways of life and collective dispositions in order to lead to collective action (Katznelson 1986, 13–22). Despite these differences, however, all these authors agree that socioeconomic structures and class interests are related and that they are fundamental for the emergence of collective identities and of social movements.

By contrast, in urban popular movements the link between social class and the formation of collective identities is tenuous at best. Class-based social movements are rooted in the sphere of production and react to the specific contradictions and conflicts characterizing it. Urban popular movements, on the other hand, emerge from the sphere of reproduction and respond to a different set of conflicts and contradictions, mostly focusing on urban living conditions. Emanating from the urban popular sector, they comprise elements of several social classes and groups and consequently do not represent the interest of any one class in particular. Urban popular movements cannot be defined conclusively along class lines,[11] and their collective

---

11. Provided one conceives of social classes in the same way as the authors just mentioned, all of whom follow Marx in regarding the position of individuals in the production process as fundamental for the formation of class interest and of classes themselves. Obviously, however, this is but one of several competing definitions of class. Building on Katznelson, Oxhorn for

identities are not based on shared class characteristics. Rather, these collective identities emerge *directly* from the social struggles that urban popular movements are involved in, or more precisely speaking, they emerge around the *demands* that give rise to these struggles. Under certain conditions, these demands can provide a common rallying point for individuals and groups with otherwise diverse interests, and they can serve to unite a wide variety of seemingly diverse movements.

For example, the first urban popular movements in Latin America surfaced in the context of demands for adequate housing by urban squatters, who had been arriving in the cities from the countryside in successive waves of migration since the 1940s. The speed and the magnitude of these migrations, a pronounced lack of resources on the part of the settlers, and outright opposition by the state and the established elites to the illegal land occupations left the new settlements in a precarious state. These settlements were not only in a legal limbo; the living conditions in them were deficient in many ways: they lacked paved roads, sidewalks, public transportation, safe water supply, sewers, electricity, and the like. Since these issues were obviously relevant for most residents of the newly established popular settlements, they consequently lay at the heart of most early urban popular movements.

More recently, concerns for better housing, more secure land titles, and improved urban services have been overshadowed by demands related to material survival, mainly as a result of the persistent and severe economic crisis of the 1980s. In this context, so-called survival movements emerged, such as soup kitchens or health groups, which were mostly led by women and aimed at securing elementary levels of nutrition and public health. In addition, a variety of other urban popular movements appeared, such as those centered around small-scale economic activities and the creation of employment possibilities in the urban informal sector. While the concerns and demands of all these movements obviously differ, they overlap in the sense that they are related to the living conditions in urban popular neighborhoods (Mainwaring 1987, 132). Urban popular movements, then, are centered around a variety of

---

instance proposes a break with the Marxist tradition, arguing that "economic structure, particularly sudden and/or dramatic changes in that structure, ways of life, shared dispositions and collective action should be seen as mutually interdependent with important feedback between all four levels so that none is theoretically prior to the others" (Oxhorn 1991, 12). Oxhorn's "political" view of class bears clear resemblances to post-Marxist approaches such as Laclau and Mouffe's (1985, 1987). See also Portes 1985, in which Portes proposes another way of redefining the concept of class, referring especially to those sectors of the population which are excluded from the capitalist production process.

demands, but their common territorial reference point can serve as a basis for a shared, territorially based "popular identity" (Moisés 1982, 26).

The strategies that urban popular movements pursue to reach their goals put them squarely in the political realm, another difference between them and other social movements. Whereas the workers' or the peasant movements, for example, operate chiefly in the economic sphere (Moisés 1982, 26–27; Foweraker 1990, 5) and interact primarily with management or landowners, urban popular movements address most of their demands directly at the state.[12] Given the nature of these demands, this is no accident. The state, be it in the form of local government or of central government agencies, is responsible for the administration of most urban services and thereby for the quality of living conditions in urban shantytowns and popular districts. Furthermore, the state is generally held accountable for extreme poverty and its consequences, especially in times of severe economic crises when many low-income families barely have enough resources to survive. Significantly, demands for concrete material benefits are increasingly framed in terms of citizenship rights, which are inherently political.

The fact that most urban popular movements rely on allies to help them reach their goals further underlines their political character. By seeking support from well-placed politicians or bureaucrats, joining forces with political parties or labor unions, or even receiving programmatic and organizational assistance from NGOs, they tend to become part of the broader political struggles that these actors are involved in. As a result, they may very well be instrumentalized for ends other than their own. However, they may also stand a better chance of projecting their critique of traditional social and political practices from the grassroots to the political arena, thereby influencing other actors themselves.

Obviously, the two issues of identity and strategy just discussed are intimately related to a third one, that of autonomy. Urban popular movements clearly have to possess a minimum of autonomy; otherwise, they will not be able to define interests and identities that are different from those of other actors, nor will they be in a position to devise strategies independently. Rather, they will quickly be co-opted and absorbed by the state, by political parties, or by other actors that will use them as welcome tools to further their own agendas. In all likelihood, such co-optation would strip urban popular movements of their potential for social and political change.

---

12. Many of these movements also rely on self-help, although rarely exclusively. See the discussion at the end of Chapter 2.

However, it would be a mistake to think that urban popular movements need to be *completely* autonomous to avoid co-optation and to preserve their potential for social and political change. For one thing, complete autonomy is probably unattainable. As I just mentioned, urban popular movements typically make demands on the state, which implies a certain degree of interaction even if they eschew direct contacts with state institutions and instead voice their demands via protests and mass mobilizations. Moreover, urban popular movements often rely on allies in order to achieve their objectives.

Even if it were possible, complete autonomy from others would in all likelihood render urban popular movements sterile and ineffective. Totally autonomous urban popular movements would not only be sheltered from co-optation, they would also be cut off from the positive input that other actors can provide, such as new ideas, experiences from other struggles, organizational assistance, and so on. As a consequence, the development of collective identities within these movements would probably remain stunted and their organizational structures would not evolve beyond an initial stage, which, ironically, might even increase the possibility of co-optation. Conversely, and perhaps more importantly, these movements would not be able to project their own potential for social and political change into other spheres, and they would therefore forgo the possibility of influencing other actors.

What is at stake, therefore, is not complete autonomy from others, but a sufficient degree of *relative* autonomy. The relations between urban popular movements and other actors do not function as a one-way street: urban popular movements are not inevitably co-opted and absorbed by the state or political parties, nor are they likely to overturn the political system from the grassroots single-handedly.[13] More often, these relations resemble a "play of mirrors" (R. Cardoso 1992, 292), in the sense that all actors involved in social and political struggles tend to exert some kind of influence on others, while their own identities and strategies are likewise shaped

---

13. As Judith Adler Hellman has pointed out, researchers who espouse such a dichotomous view often juxtapose their own ideal of a completely autonomous social movement with existing movements that they see as having been co-opted, deploring the fact that so often "something pure and wonderful (a popularly based, grass-roots movement) is replaced by something less desirable" (Hellman 1992, 56). These researchers generally blur the crucial distinction between co-optation in the true sense of the word and other forms of relations between social movements and other actors, such as "adherence to a charismatic, populist figure based on personal loyalty, and the kind of political learning and growth of consciousness that may occur when a neighborhood group articulating narrow, limited goals is drawn into a broader struggle" (Hellman 1992, 56).

by these interactions. Thus it is less important that urban popular movements be able to fend off any kind of interference from the outside; and more important that they remain capable of defending their interests in alliances with others and of influencing the outcomes of negotiations. In other words, the question is not how urban popular movements can remain completely autonomous, but rather, how they can retain a sufficient *margin* of autonomy to maintain their potential for social and political change and to maximize their influence on others, while at the same time safeguarding their identities and their ability to devise independent strategies.

Whether or not urban popular movements are able to attain this margin of autonomy depends to a large extent on the contexts in which they operate, or more precisely speaking, on the political opportunity structures they face (McAdam 1996). Often criticized for its vagueness (Gamson and Meyer 1996), this notion is nevertheless useful in that it captures the principal dimensions of the political environment surrounding the activities of social movements, namely, the relative closure or openness of the institutionalized political system, the stability of elite alignments undergirding it, the presence or absence of elite allies, and the state's capacity and propensity for repression (McAdam 1996, 27).[14] Obviously, these factors are significant both for the formation of collective identities and for the choice of strategies by social movements. Potential allies, such as political parties or NGOs, can play a central role in how urban popular movements identify and interpret common grievances, by offering advice, training, and even complete frames of reference. Conversely, urban popular movements may be able to impose their own interpretation on a given situation, thereby "framing" the political opportunity structure and possibly influencing other actors themselves.

Political opportunities also affect which strategies a social movement chooses and which "action repertoires" it develops, and can be decisive for their success or failure. For example, during and after the transitions to democracy in Latin America, urban popular movements benefited from a decrease in state repression to break out of their relative isolation and take part in mass mobilizations against the authoritarian regimes. Under democratic rule, they increasingly claimed a role in the institutional process, making use of a more open institutional system and the creation of new channels and mechanisms for popular participation, particularly at the local

14. The "notion" of a political opportunity structure is, therefore, by definition made up of various political opportunities and obstacles.

level. Changing elite arrangements made this easier: the crisis of the developmentalist state and the radical reduction of the state apparatus all over Latin America meant that urban popular movements were no longer confronted with single hegemonic actors. At the same time, other elite actors such as political parties reclaimed their places at the heart of the political system, while new ones were created from scratch. At least potentially, this gave urban popular movements greater possibilities to strike alliances with a variety of other actors and to exploit fissures between various elites groups, reducing the temptation to enter into clientelist relations in order to reach their goals. On the other hand, the exposure to a multitude of other actors, often with superior resources and negotiating skills, obviously meant that the risk of co-optation increased as well.

The Resurgence of Civil Society and Return to Democratic Rule: The New Significance of Urban Popular Movements

Urban popular movements in Latin America attracted renewed scholarly interest following the wave of democratic transitions that swept through the region in the late 1970s and early 1980s. Often instrumental in the popular protest movements to unseat the authoritarian regimes of the day (O'Donnell and Schmitter 1986), these movements frequently displayed an array of new social and cultural practices that ran counter to established clientelist and authoritarian patterns of political behavior (see Eckstein 1989; Escobar and Alvarez 1992a). The vigor of these movements, which threw a stark light on ongoing processes of social recomposition and organization taking place at the base level, motivated many observers to see in them the hallmark of a resurgence of civil society, as well as a crucial resource for the democratization of the political system from below (Pease et al. 1981).

The idea that popular movements could help democratize formerly authoritarian societies received a further boost when it became clear that the institutions of the new democratic regimes were still extremely fragile and that democratic consolidation was by no means assured. In the face of these difficulties, it was hoped that somehow it would be possible to tap into the democratic potential of a newly invigorated civil society by linking popular movements to the political system, thereby helping to stabilize the precariously weak institutions of the new democratic regimes. As I discuss in more detail later, local governments seemed to be ideal vehicles for such a political project, given their proximity to the population and their perceived bridging function between the state and civil society.

The new enthusiasm for urban popular movements and their perceived potential for social and political change contrasted markedly with how prior approaches had depicted the social and political reality of low-income urban neighborhoods in Latin American. Marginality theory (DESAL 1968, 1969; Germani 1980; Nun 1969; Quijano 1974; F. Cardoso 1971),[15] for example, portrays the inhabitants of urban shantytowns as divorced from the rest of society, socially fragmented and anomic, as well as politically volatile. Unable to organize on their own, they are (supposedly) easy prey for totalitarian demagogues or, alternatively, a potential mass basis for a socialist revolution. However, the underlying dualist assumptions of marginality theory are hard to sustain, since they obscure the multitude of existing links between the "marginals," the political system, and the rest of society. Furthermore, in contrast to its dire predictions, the so-called marginals often proved to be fairly optimistic, organized, and politically rather conservative (Perlman 1976).

Accepting that shantytown dwellers are capable of organizing and defending their interests collectively, a number of studies undertaken by U.S. political scientists in the 1960s and 1970s (for example, Leeds 1969; Cornelius 1974; Collier 1976; Powell 1976; Goldrich, Pratt, and Schuller 1976; Leeds and Leeds 1978; Stepan 1978; and Dietz 1980), instead focused on how urban squatter movements related to the state, particularly in the context of authoritarian regimes controlled or backed up by the military. According to these studies, authoritarian rulers usually found these movements to be easily co-opted and controlled, given their dependence on state resources, as well as their willingness to exchange material benefits for political support. By accepting some of the squatters' principal demands for better housing, urban services, and the like, authoritarian regimes often succeeded in heading off potential sources of conflict, while at the same time strengthening their own bases of popular support.

For example, in his study of settlement policies in Peru, David Collier (Collier 1976) depicts squatter movements and the elites controlling the state apparatus as two sides of the same coin. Both are seen as the result of processes of modernization and social mobilization that brought about the emergence of new economic and political groups and elites. Settlement policy in this scheme is no more than an instrument for the elites to co-opt the

15. See Kay 1989 and Perlman 1976 for useful overviews of the debates on marginality theory. Perlman's emphasis lies on the modernization variant, while Kay concentrates more on later Marxist approaches and their critics.

lower classes and to diffuse potential social and political conflicts. The dominant elite group, Collier argues, "has shaped settlement policy to fit its overall strategy of rural and urban development and its particular conception of the appropriate form of mass political participation and of the appropriate role of the state in society" (Collier 1976, 16). Accordingly, different dominant elites produce different settlement policies; yet the co-optation and manipulation of squatter movements remains a constant.

Henry Dietz's monograph on the urban poor in Lima under the reformist military regime of General Velasco comes to similar conclusions, even if Dietz sees the urban poor "not only as vitally affected by the nature and structure of power at the nation-state level but also as capable of influencing policy" (Dietz 1980, 5). While the policies of the Velasco regime toward the urban poor were clearly designed to provide channels for organized, controlled participation in support of the regime, Dietz points out that they also helped in the creation of demands and consequently became a source of conflict when the state fell short of satisfying them. Nevertheless, squatter movements and particularly their leaders are seen as far from radical and careful not to overstep institutional boundaries (Dietz 1980, 124–26). According to Dietz, this is because they are rational actors who believe in the possibility of incremental change via the institutions and know that moderate demands are more likely to be met than extreme ones (Dietz 1980, 166–68).

Manuel Castells (Castells 1983, 173–212) echoes many of the views first expressed by Collier, Dietz, and others. Castells's principal argument is that the "dependency of squatter settlements upon state policies and the heteronomy of the squatter movement vis-à-vis the political system" is rooted in "the vulnerability of [the squatters'] status as urban dwellers. Without the state's tolerance, or without some effective political support, they would not even have the right to their physical presence in the city" (Castells 1983, 211). In the case of Lima, Castells builds mainly on David Collier's earlier study, going so far as to describe squatter movements as "a manipulated mob, changing from one political ideology to another in exchange for the delivery (or promise) of land, housing, and services" (Castells 1983, 193).

Unlike the approaches just discussed, urban social movement theory regards such movements as part of the political opposition to authoritarian regimes, and not of the corporatist consensus backing them. Originally developed in the Western European context (see Borja 1975; Lojkine 1977; and Castells 1977, 1978, 1983),[16] urban social movement theory was later

---

16. For an excellent review of Manuel Castells's thought, see Lowe 1986. For critiques of the urban social movement school, see Saunders 1981 and Pickvance 1976.

adapted to fit Latin American reality (see Evers, Müller-Plantenberg, and Spessart 1979 and Moisés 1982). Essentially, urban social movement theory holds that protest movements erupt in cities as the result of crises of collective consumption, or in other words, of growing deficiencies in the provision of public services, such as housing, transport facilities, education, and so forth. Given that the state is at the same time responsible for these services and either unwilling to or incapable of providing them, it becomes the logical target for these protests.

By advocating the integration of urban protest movements into the broad-based, progressive alliances that were favored by large parts of the political left in the 1970s, urban social movement theory effectively contributed to the gradual erosion of the classical vanguard-masses model of orthodox Marxism-Leninism. At the same time, owing to its roots in structuralist Marxism,[17] it never completely broke with the idea that these alliances should be oriented and led by the workers' party. In practice, this stance lent legitimacy to a political reality in which formally broad-based and nonhierarchical political alliances could be completely dominated by one or several leftist political parties. Popular movements that were part of such alliances risked being co-opted and absorbed, which not only cost them their autonomy but made them dependent on the political fortunes of their respective partners.

In his later work, in which he began to distance himself from his structuralist origins, Manuel Castells (Castells 1983, 199–209) provides an example of how the Chilean left in the late 1960s effectively "created" squatter movements in Santiago de Chile by organizing land invasions and by establishing squatter settlements around the Chilean capital. After the 1970 election victory of the Unidad Popular alliance, the various leftist parties consolidated their hold on the respective settlements they controlled and used them as mobilization platforms for their own political initiatives. As a result, "the participation of the *campamentos* in the political process very closely followed the political line dominating in each settlement" (Castells 1983, 201), often replicating the divisions within the Chilean left itself. When intraleftist

17. Manuel Castells's early work in particular owes a lot to the Marxist structuralism that was developed by Althusser and Balibar (Althusser et al. 1965) and later refined by Poulantzas (see Poulantzas 1971). Following its basic line of argument, Castells acknowledges that protest movements arising from urban contradictions can contribute to social and political change, but only if they are incorporated into broader class struggles led by the workers' movement. For Castells, this is precisely what separates urban *social* movements from other urban movements whose protests remain largely inconsequential. Class struggles are seen as predominant over other social struggles, given their location at the level of primary contradictions between labor and capital, which are considered as determinant "in the last instance."

divisions came to a head after October 1972, "each sector of the *pobladores* aligned with its corresponding political faction, and the squatters' movement disappeared as an identifiable entity" (Castells 1983, 208).

Various attempts were made to address these shortcomings from within urban social movement theory itself, by insisting on the nonhierarchical nature of progressive political alliances (Evers, Müller-Plantenberg, and Spessart 1979) or by arguing that the struggle between popular movements and the state had primacy over that between labor and capital (Moisés 1982). Before long, however, urban social movement theory became the victim of a more deep-seated critique of traditional Marxism and its insistence on the centrality of class struggle. Disillusioned with the ideological rigidity of the old model and the failure of the working class to live up to its role as the motive force for change, political activists and researchers alike began to look for "new historical subjects."[18] In Western Europe, these developments coincided with the rise of the so-called new social movements, which favored the emergence of new theoretical approaches that collectively became known as new social movement theory. In Latin America, the popular protest movements that surfaced in the context of the anti-authoritarian struggle, with their new social practices and collective identities, seemed to have similar characteristics.

Initially, Western European new social movement theory was applied more or less directly to the Latin American context (see Kärner 1983, Mainwaring and Viola 1984, Slater 1985, and Fals Borda 1986). Popular movements were seen as the expressions of a new, autonomous social fabric that was being constructed at the grassroots, which would eventually lead to the emergence of a more democratic political culture and new power structures existing parallel to those of the political system. However, it soon became clear that Western Europe, with its focus on culture and postmaterial values, was very different from Latin America, which continued to be dominated by material concerns such as housing, health, nutrition, and so forth. Whereas in Western Europe, the new social movements could afford to retreat from the political system, popular movements in Latin America were compelled to interact with the state, political parties, and others because of the nature of their demands. Consequently, their activities could not be seen in isolation, but only in relation to other actors.

Subsequent approaches did not employ new social movement theory as such, but instead used some of its key concepts, particularly that of identity.

18. It would go too far at this point to describe these intellectual developments in more detail. See, for example, Gorz 1980 and Laclau and Mouffe 1985, 1987.

For example, a number of Peruvian social scientists (Arnillas 1986; Ballón 1986a; T. Tovar 1986a, 1986b; Degregori, Blondet, and Lynch 1986) examined the formation of three successive types of collective identities in the context of the development of urban popular movements in Peru since the 1950s: the *poblador* (settler) identity, the *vecino* (neighbor) identity, and the *ciudadano* (citizen) identity.[19]

According to these authors, the *poblador* identity reflected the precarious situation of the rural migrants of the 1950s and 1960s, whose urban settlements were largely the result of land invasions. Economically, legally, and politically powerless, the settlers founded neighborhood associations in order to secure their settlements and to obtain urban services. In turn, they were willing to pledge their political support to the regime of the day. Typically, leaders were selected on the basis of their skills to negotiate with the authorities and to establish clientelist relations with civil servants or politicians strategically placed in the state bureaucracy. Clientelism—the exchange of benefits for pledges of political support—was frequently encouraged by the authorities and was also expressed in the often personalist and undemocratic structures of early neighborhood associations.

The *poblador* identity was succeeded in the early 1970s by the *vecino* identity (T. Tovar 1986a, 144). Following the relative stabilization of many settlements, maintaining clientelist links to the authorities became less important, and urban popular movements could afford to be more militant and to keep a greater distance from the state. This increased militancy, which was initially helped along by the policies of the reformist military regime under General Velasco but which later fueled the opposition to military rule, eroded the dominance of the traditional neighborhood associations and their leaders. In addition, new concerns prompted the emergence of a multitude of new movements that placed a novel emphasis on autonomy from others and democratic internal structures. Taken together, these "new democratic and social practices" or "new ways of doing politics" were seen as the beginnings of a "new social order" and as a direct challenge to the traditional authoritarian and clientelist patterns permeating the existing political system (Arnillas 1986, 36; T. Tovar 1986b, 101).

After the return to democratic rule, the growing importance of institutional politics and the opening up of "new democratic spaces," particularly the democratization of local governments, paved the way for the emergence of a *ciudadano* identity. Material benefits, which the *poblador* considered

---

19. The social and political processes that form the backdrop for the formation of collective identities during this period are described in more detail in Chapter 3.

favors to be bartered for from a patron and which the *vecino* had come to demand from the state, the *ciudadano* now increasingly perceived as rights. In addition, there was now increasing pressure for greater participation in the institutional decision-making process, particularly at the local level. The participation of urban popular movements in leftist-controlled local governments, transforming them into "bridgeheads" that would allow the "new ways of doing politics" to infuse the political system as a whole, was seen as a step in that direction. At the same time, it became clear that granting political citizenship rights alone would not be enough to overcome the discrimination that prevented some groups, particularly women and indigenous people, from exercising them. To address the causes of this discrimination would necessitate a considerable redefinition and enlargement of the notion of citizenship itself.[20]

The *poblador, vecino,* and *ciudadano* identities were considered significant because of their potential to cut across the demands and concerns of many different urban popular movements and to serve as rallying points for the urban popular sector as a whole.[21] More specific collective identities, particularly those associated with gender, likewise met with great interest and were sometimes considered even more significant (Barrig 1989; Jaquette 1989a, 1989b; Jelin 1990; Vargas 1990). The emergence of specific women's identities and women's movements was facilitated by the growing involvement of women in the workforce during the economic crisis of the 1980s, as well as their increased contacts with other women and outside advisers because of their involvement in soup kitchens and other "survival movements." Albeit limited to a minority and subject to multiple obstacles, these changes were nonetheless significant. In the private realm, many

20. These debates are of course far from over. Recent contributions (Foweraker 1995, chap. 5; Jelin 1996) have shown that the development of citizenship rights does not necessarily follow the sequence established by Marshall for the case of England, where political rights followed civil rights and were themselves succeeded by social rights (Marshall 1992). In Latin America, social rights at least for certain groups have preceded political or even civil rights, frequently under authoritarian or corporatist auspices. More importantly, such rights can and have been reversed and can therefore never be taken for granted. Bottomore (1992) has pointed out that the equality principle inherent in the notion of citizenship continues to militate against existing inequalities, which are no longer conceived exclusively in terms of class, but also of gender, ethnicity, the North-South gap, and other characteristics. Obviously, this is particularly evident in the Latin American case. Jelin (1996) recalls that the construction of citizenship involves, not only the fight for certain rights, but also the construction of social actors capable of exercising them in a responsible manner.

21. According to the so-called *indigenista* school (Matos Mar 1988; see also Franco 1991), a widely shared ethnic identity could perform a similar role.

women began to question traditional gender roles that confined them to the house, often having to overcome the resistance of their husbands, who did not want to accept the growing independence and assertiveness of their wives. In the public sphere, women began to break down gender barriers that prevented them from running for public offices previously reserved for men, first in neighborhood associations, then in political institutions like local governments. Thus women's movements contributed to social and political change by redefining the identities of movement participants and by changing the relations between these movements and other actors, as well as political institutions.

The identity approaches just discussed cast a stark light on the multitude of new social actors, collective identities, and social and political practices that emerged in many Latin American countries during and after the transitions to democratic rule. At the same time, as noted by subsequent critics (for example, Mainwaring 1987, 1989; R. Cardoso 1983, 1992), these approaches clearly overestimated the strength and cohesiveness of the new movements, and particularly their capacity to have an impact on other actors, political institutions, and the formulation of public policy. For one thing, the new collective identities were in fact much less representative, less concentrated, and less robust than earlier thought. Typically emerging in the context of protest movements or mass mobilizations around specific demands, they were subjected to their ebb and flow and therefore rarely stable. While some of these mass movements acquired astonishing force and vigor, they often tended to dissipate as quickly as they appeared, and the formation of collective identities remained restricted to a core group of movement leaders assuring a minimum of continuity. Moreover, instead of one single overarching "popular identity," there generally existed a multitude of different collective identities all rooted in particular demands and concerns. These different collective identities did not necessarily coalesce; in fact, they could be contradictory, since individual popular movements tended to compete with one another for limited resources.

Perhaps the greatest obstacle to the formation and consolidation of new collective identities lay in the fact that older identities and practices did not simply disappear. On the contrary, individualist and clientelist strategies in particular remained deeply entrenched, reflecting the power of tradition, the influence of other actors, or simply the fact that these strategies could appear more conducive to attaining certain goals. Even in normal circumstances, collective action has certain drawbacks—it takes time and effort on the part of participants, it may offend powerful elite actors, it may provoke state repression, and its success can never be assured. Therefore, individualist or self-help strategies such as working longer hours, engaging in informal economic activities, and investing in one's education or that of one's children may seem safer roads to individual advancement. Clientelist strategies may likewise appear more promising: individual problems such as finding a job for one's daughter or son may be tackled with the help of a powerful patron, while the needs of urban popular settlements can often be looked after by state agencies or special government programs that will provide roads, sidewalks, or other urban services in exchange for pledges of political support.[22] In a context of severe economic crisis marked by widespread under- or unemployment, as was typical for the 1980s, the lure of these alternative strategies can become hard to resist. Faced with the stark choice of either participating in a popular movement or finding work in the informal sector to meet the basic needs of their families, many urban poor simply had no time for political organizing. As a result, participation in urban popular movements declined, despite the parallel rise of survival movements that explicitly addressed the effects of the economic crisis. In addition, as I will explain in more detail in Chapter 3, popular movements often had to compete with state-run public works programs such as PAIT in Peru, which offered small salaries to participants willing to express their support for the governing APRA party.

The corrosive effects all this had on popular movements were compounded by the fact that their new collective identities and budding democratic practices were often ambiguous themselves. Laced with fragments of other practices and competing identities, urban popular movements were not spared their share of problems with autocratic, unaccountable leaders, embezzlement of funds, nepotism, and the like, that were so characteristic of the political system and the "old" political parties. As a result, the democratizing potential of urban popular movements often remained unrealized. Unable to single-handedly transform the political system from the grassroots, as some of the identity theorists had hoped, they were often in dire need of organizational and political assistance themselves. This not only highlighted their reliance on allies, it also brought the old problem of autonomy and co-optation back to the fore.

22. Examples include the National Solidarity Program (PRONASOL) implemented by the Salinas de Gortari administration in Mexico to head off the strong challenge mounted by Cuauhtémoc Cardenas in the presidential elections of 1988 (Piester 1997), or the PAIT program set up by the APRA government in Peru (Graham 1991). Of course, none of this means that people will always opt for individualist or clientelist strategies and let others shoulder the risks of collective action. As shown above, the free-rider argument may explain why some people do not participate in social movements, but not why others do.

What conclusions can be drawn from these debates? Notwithstanding the caveats just mentioned, the collective identities of contemporary urban popular movements appear to be stronger now than they were previously. Drawing on past experiences under authoritarian rule, as well as their involvement with the political institutions of the new democratic regimes, more urban popular movements are resisting the temptation to enter into clientelist relationships in the hope of reaching their goals, refusing to let themselves be co-opted in exchange for the promise of material benefits. At the same time, these movements have put more emphasis on the democratization of their own structures, allowing for the participation of previously excluded groups, particularly women, and undermining the position of autocratic leaders whose legitimacy stemmed largely from their ability to establish links to powerful patrons. Put differently, many urban popular movements have gone beyond simple demand-making and have begun to question the *contexts* in which their demands are made. In so doing, these movements have challenged the authoritarian and clientelist traditions that are a fundamental trait of the political cultures of most Latin American societies.

At the same time, it remains to be seen whether this potential for social and political change will largely remain dormant, as it seems to be at present, or whether it can be brought to bear on other political actors, political institutions, and the formulation of public policy. Several aspects of this question are worth considering here. As I have explained, urban popular movements typically rally around fairly specific concerns and are often poorly structured; they therefore need allies to integrate their concerns into more universal political programs and project them into the political arena. Other actors likewise have an interest in making alliances with urban popular movements: political parties and individual politicians need popular support; state agencies and public institutions may want to increase the effectiveness of public policy; and NGOs need to prove to international donors that they have strong links to potential beneficiaries. What is important in the context of this study is the fact that the breakdown of authoritarian rule, the return to democratic politics, and the concomitant demise of the developmentalist state in the late 1970s and early 1980s fundamentally altered the context in which the relations between urban popular movements and other actors were played out.

In particular, the relations between urban popular movements and the state underwent drastic changes during and after the transition to democracy because of a decrease in state repression and the radical downsizing of the state apparatus in the course of neoliberal adjustment programs. In Peru, for example, the demise of a military regime that had long tried to co-opt the popular sectors into its reformist political project led to a retreat of central state agencies from lower-class neighborhoods and a reduced state role in policy fields such as urban development and social policy. Coinciding with the end of the street mobilizations against the authoritarian regime and the resurgence of institutional politics at the central level, this led to a vacuum at the grassroots that was only slowly filled by other actors, such as NGOs, the Church, or leftist political parties. Largely shut out of the political process, it is no surprise that many urban popular movements allied themselves with the political opposition against the central government. In countries such as Brazil, by contrast, the end of a far more repressive military regime not only meant that urban popular movements now had greater freedom to express their concerns and to strike alliances with other actors. Because the authoritarian regime had been able to retain a much greater degree of control over the transition process, which had enabled reformist elements in the state bureaucracy to come to the fore (R. Cardoso 1992), state involvement at the local level actually *increased* during and after the transition phase, with some state officials actively seeking to consult popular movements over the design and execution of public policy. Urban popular movements were not adverse to these offers, despite the fact that they simultaneously entertained relations with a variety of other actors, most notably the opposition Workers' Party (PT) with its deep roots in the popular sector.

In both cases, popular movements were no longer confronted with only one dominant interlocutor, the state, but now faced a variety of actors, such as regional and local governments, central government agencies, and political parties, as well as nongovernmental actors such as NGOs and the Church. Depending on these actors' interests and the resources they could offer, this could actually produce a situation in which co-optive pressures on urban popular movements were greater than before. However, depending on their own resources and negotiating skills, urban popular movements could also turn this situation to their advantage by exploiting frictions between these other actors and thus enlarging their own political breathing space. To be sure, the need to interact with more than one interlocutor was undoubtedly more complicated and time-consuming than having to deal only with the central state bureaucracy, and not all urban popular movements were up to this task. When successful, however, they were not only be able to obtain increased resources from different sides, but more importantly, they could avoid becoming dependent on one specific actor by striking multiple alliances. In this way, urban popular movements were able to take part in what Chalmers, Martin, and Piester (1997) have called the building of "associative networks" at the local level.

Aside from its impact on the relations between urban popular movements and other actors, the return to democratic rule also led to a different institutional context for political participation, particularly at the local level. Following the return to democratic rule, the powers and responsibilities of local governments were set to increase significantly because of political decentralization. In many municipalities, democratic elections to chose mayors and local councillors were held for the first time in many years. In addition, some local governments, often those controlled by the political left, established new mechanisms for direct popular participation, such as popular assemblies to consult the population or joint committees to manage municipal programs. These mechanisms were bound to alter significantly the way urban popular movements related to political institutions, by offering them an opportunity to participate directly in local decision making and thereby have a more sustained impact on public policymaking at the local level. Arguably, the participation of urban popular movements in local political institutions would also act as a counterweight to ingrained clientelist and authoritarian practices, as well as exert a democratizing influence on other actors, such as political parties. Taken together, these changes added up to a rather favorable political opportunity structure for the realization of such a project.

two

decentralization and the participation of urban popular movements in local government

The return to democracy in the late 1970s and early 1980s produced a political and institutional environment that was substantially different from the one urban popular movements had faced during previous years. Benefiting from a marked decline in political repression, urban popular movements had greater freedom to pursue their goals in the political arena, while the slimming down of the central state

An earlier version of this chapter was published under the title "New democratic spaces at the grassroots? Popular participation in Latin American local governments" in *Development and Change* 28, no. 4 (October 1997): 750–73.

apparatus and the greater prominence of such actors as political parties and NGOs provided them with a wider choice of potential allies. Most importantly though, political decentralization and the reinvigoration of local governments created new institutional openings for popular participation at the local level. Bolstered by relatively stronger collective identities and more experienced in their dealings with other actors since participating in the mass movements against military rule, urban popular movements appeared well positioned to make use of these openings, and even to have a democratizing impact on political institutions and other political actors.

The idea that political decentralization and increased popular participation at the grassroots could make local political institutions more accountable and efficient, as well as exert a democratizing influence on other political actors, is of course not entirely new. Similar ideas have been expressed in the literature on decentralization and local government in the third world for quite some time (see Conyers 1983, 1984, and 1986 and Mawhood 1987), and they have long been popular with the international development establishment (see Carroll 1992, Peterson 1997, and UNDP 1993). The intellectual roots of these ideas are deep: they can be traced back to the democratic city-states of Greek antiquity (Dahl 1989; Dahl and Tufte 1973) or more recently, to nineteenth-century liberal democratic thought, especially de Tocqueville's musings on citizen participation in the towns of New England (de Tocqueville 1945). In the Latin American context, however, they are still relatively new, which at least in part can be attributed to the long-standing obscurity of local governments in the region, together with an overwhelming presence of strong centralist states and a relative weakness of civil society.[1]

Following the transitions to democracy, this situation was rapidly beginning to change. Long confined to a relatively small circle of left-leaning academics and politicians sympathetic to popular movements, political decentralization and popular participation soon entered the political mainstream and became central planks in the programs, or at least the discourse, of most governments in the region. Fed by a variety of factors (see Boisier 1991, Nohlen 1991, and Lowder 1992), such as the economic crisis of the 1980s and the critical state of public finances, the demise of the developmentalist state and the obvious inefficiency of most central bureaucracies, and the crisis of the modernization and dependency paradigms and the rise

1. An indication for the novelty of these issues is the fact that most of the relevant literature is relatively recent. See, for example, Fox 1994 and Nickson 1995 on local government or Morris 1992 and Nohlen 1991 on political decentralization.

of neoliberalism, as well as the persistent calls for more democracy from local and regional movements, the ideological and strategic motivations behind the sudden popularity of these ideas were quite diverse, and their realization was to serve very different goals.

In the eyes of economic neoliberals or political conservatives, for example, the economic crisis of the 1980s and the often catastrophic state of public finances was a welcome opportunity for a radical downsizing of the developmentalist state and its paring down to a series of core functions. In addition to stripping the state of its previous role as one of the principal economic actors, neoliberals often advocated the privatization of public services, notably at the level of local government. By contrast, citizen participation in local affairs was accorded a relatively low priority, and collective actors such as popular movements hardly figured at all. Seen from this angle, decentralization could also be used to shield the central state apparatus from potential social or political conflicts by devolving unwanted responsibilities to regional or local governments, which were often without the corresponding resources to meet them.[2]

Mainstream modernizers, on the other hand, favored decentralization as a way to reform a central state apparatus seen as bloated and inefficient. By devolving powers and resources to lower levels of government, it was hoped that public institutions would become more effective and accountable and that service delivery would greatly improve. At the same time, decentralization could help to attain other goals, such as regional development or greater control over outlying border areas through an increased state presence. Popular participation in this scheme was basically seen as a means to an end: by consulting citizens on the quality of public services, the planning and execution of public works, and the like, it was thought that needs would be identified more clearly and problems in service delivery spotted with greater precision. In addition, citizen participation often played a crucial role at the implementation stage, for example, in the form of unpaid labor during the realization of public works programs.[3] This "pragmatic" view of decentralization was often espoused by international organizations,

---

2. According to Peterson (1997), this is a thing of the past. Peterson states that in countries such as Brazil or Colombia, the transfer of resources actually preceded the transfer of responsibilities to local and regional governments, with the predictable result that these responsibilities often remained ill-defined and resources were not used efficiently.

3. A similarly limited view of popular participation at the microlevel, but without any pretext at institutional reform, lies at the heart of many populist-style poverty relief programs that remain tightly controlled by the central government, such as those implemented under President Fujimori in Peru.

on the assumption that it was essentially a technocratic tool that could be used in different political settings.[4]

The political left, finally, saw decentralization first and foremost as a means to increase the political participation of the lower classes, or in other words, as an instrument for popular empowerment. Consequently, it not only advocated the devolution of resources and responsibilities from the central to lower levels of government, as did mainstream modernizers, but it also supported demands by regional and local movements to create new and more extensive channels for popular participation. In this "political" perspective, decentralization would perform a double role: it would not only make regional and local governments more effective and accountable and improve overall service delivery, but it would also make them more democratic, by opening them up to the scrutiny and active participation of civil society. Interestingly, though, the Left embraced political decentralization only when its chances for taking power nationally had grown fairly remote. At least in part, this shift was motivated by strategic considerations: the Left obviously hoped that by building on its existing strengths in many localities and regions and by constructing strategic alliances with regional and local movements, it would be able to mount a credible challenge at the national level later on. Other political challengers can and have used the same strategy, while political incumbents can employ similar tactics to build or strengthen power bases away from the center.[5]

Obviously, then, decentralization meant different things to different people, and the reasons for opposing or supporting a given policy often had more to do with the underlying strategic motivations of the actors involved

---

4. A case in point is the significant reorganization and deconcentration of service delivery responsibilities started by the Chilean military regime and later pursued by the civilian government under President Patricio Aylwin (Nickson 1995, 132–33). Interestingly, though, what began as a process of administrative deconcentration designed to strengthen overall social and political control subsequently became an instrument to democratize and revitalize the rigid system of local administration inherited from the military regime. The Chilean case therefore illuminates the political character of any decentralization process, a point to which I will return below. See also note 6.

5. Dietz and Shidlo, in their edited volume *Urban Elections in Democratic Latin America* (Dietz and Shidlo 1998), provide numerous examples of how political challengers use local politics to build support and to prepare themselves for nationwide contests. The regionalization process in Peru in the 1980s shows how central governments can manipulate decentralization policies in order to build local support bases. "The whole decentralization process was highly politicized, and [President] Garcia's strategy was 'successful' in that regional governments came to be controlled by APRA after the 1989 and 1990 regional elections. The Peruvian case shows how far decentralization can be used for personalistic or partisan interests in a fragile democracy" (Kim 1992, 249). See also Gonzales 1989 and Méndez 1990.

than with its stated goals. While not necessarily incompatible, these strategic motivations reflect the different political interests of these actors and will inevitably color the stance they take. Independently of the beneficial effects that decentralization may have on the accessibility and functioning of political institutions, it is inherently political: by altering the distribution of power between different political actors, it is likely to undermine the position of some while furthering that of others, and it may even help new political actors to emerge. For these reasons, it is not surprising that decentralization schemes have often remained stunted[6] or blocked by significant obstacles, such as resistance by powerful local elites fearing the loss of their privileges,[7] an entrenched tradition of bureaucratic centralism,[8] or reluctance on the part of those in power to tolerate the rise of political challengers. The fact that these obstacles are often underestimated goes some way in explaining why decentralization schemes have often fallen short of their intended objectives, in particular with regard to wider goals such as achieving greater social justice and economic equity, as well as furthering democratic change.

From the perspective of popular and other social movements, the obvious question was of course how political decentralization could further their own interests. In one sense, the answer seemed rather straightforward.

6. For example, many decentralization schemes entail nothing beyond administrative *deconcentration*, that is, the shifting around of responsibilities within the central bureaucracy, as opposed to *devolution*, a genuine transfer of responsibilities to lower levels of government. Deconcentration typically means that administrative responsibilities and/or decision-making powers are shifted from the highest level of the central government to other, lower levels of the same bureaucracy located elsewhere. The degree to which real powers to make and implement decisions are transferred can vary, but in any case, overall control of the process remains with the highest level of the central administration. In a related fashion, which is particularly important in the Latin American context, administrative responsibilities and/or decision-making powers can be transferred to semi-autonomous or parastatal agencies (Harris 1983). In this case, one would speak of *delegation*.

7. If badly conceived, political decentralization may actually have the opposite effect: by curtailing the powers of higher levels of government it may strengthen the position of local elites, making it close to impossible to implement nationwide standards or policies. Possibilities for popular participation in such a scenario would likely be further reduced instead of enlarged.

8. As Willis, Garman, and Haggard (1999) have shown, even formally highly decentralized systems such as Mexico's can remain highly centralized when measured in terms of control over spending powers. In cases such as this, "the basic challenge is to ensure that lower levels of government gain the political autonomy that will allow them to govern responsibly. Otherwise, 'decentralization' may reflect little more than an effort to maintain central control and limit political challenges emanating from lower levels of government" (Willis, Garman, and Haggard 1999, 48).

To the extent that decentralization was likely to give greater powers and resources to regional and local governments, it had obvious appeal to popular movements, given that their most pressing concerns were usually dealt with at that level. Furthermore, popular movements were bound to benefit from any increase in popular participation, which would give them greater clout with local and regional administrations and a more direct say in the identification of priorities, the use of resources, and even issues related to day-to-day management. However, becoming more directly involved in local and regional politics also carried obvious risks. In particular, alliances with other actors such as political parties or individual politicians were not without problems, since these were often prone to co-opt popular movements into their own agendas. The possibilities for doing so were endless: for example, popular movements could be made dependent on the resources a particular organization provided, or they could be enticed to establish clientelist links in order to satisfy some of their demands, thereby compromising their autonomy. Furthermore, if they chose to ally themselves too closely with any one actor, they were likely to lose out when that actor's political fortunes faded.

In sum, popular participation at the local level takes place in a very complex environment full of pitfalls. Consequently, popular movements that participate in local political institutions have to be very careful when choosing their courses of action, if they want to achieve their objectives and at the same time maintain their autonomy, not to speak of possibly exerting a democratizing influence on other actors. Seen against this background, the main purpose of this chapter will be to examine more closely the conditions under which decentralization processes and local governments can indeed be vehicles for democratic political change. In particular, it will ask to what extent decentralization policies can create or even widen political openings for greater political participation of the popular sectors at the local level, and under what conditions they are likely to serve the opposite purpose, namely, the integration and co-optation of the popular majorities into a political system that essentially remains unchanged.

Decentralization and Popular Participation at the Local Level

Before proceeding, it will be helpful to take a brief look at the notion of popular participation itself. Broadly speaking, two different usages of the term can be distinguished in the literature (see Fadda 1988, Midgley 1986, and Stiefel and Pearse 1982). One such usage sees popular participation primarily as a means to an end, that is, as a tool to increase the effectiveness and efficiency of development projects, public works programs, and the like. In this perspective, popular participation is typically accorded great importance at the implementation stage, but it plays little or no role in project design or evaluation. In another, quite different sense, popular participation is defined, not pragmatically in a means-end fashion, but as an end in itself. In Stiefel and Pearse's classic formulation, it can be viewed as "the organized efforts to increase control over resources and regulative institutions in given social situations, on the part of groups and movements of those hitherto excluded from such control" (Stiefel and Pearse 1982, 146). In other words, popular participation is interpreted politically, that is, as a central ingredient in the empowerment of the lower classes.

Generally, what distinguishes the two views is the degree of decision-making powers attributed to the agents of popular participation, such as local voluntary organizations or popular movements. Pragmatic means-end approaches often limit the extent of popular participation to consultations about popular needs and concerns, while reserving a prominent role for the mostly passive participation of the population in the execution of development projects or public works programs that are planned, designed, and later evaluated by others. Political approaches, on the other hand, typically go a step further by enlarging the sphere of popular participation to the stages of project planning and evaluation, and by insisting that popular participation has to encompass participation in decision-making processes at each one of these stages. The direct involvement of popular movements and other agents of popular participation in such decision-making processes is thought to have a democratic influence on other actors, particularly political institutions. By the same token, it is hoped that popular movements can also benefit from such involvement and strengthen their own integrity and organizational structures.

As mentioned before, these two views of popular participation correspond to equally diverse perspectives on political decentralization, without being mutually exclusive—the pragmatic and the political.

The Pragmatic Approach to Decentralization

The first perspective, which I will call the pragmatic approach to decentralization (Cheema and Rondinelli 1983; Rondinelli 1990; Rondinelli,

McCullough, and Johnson 1989; Rondinelli and Wilson 1987),[9] is concerned primarily with how decentralization can contribute to local and regional development, and more specifically, how it can improve the provision and maintenance of public services and infrastructure in developing countries (Rondinelli, McCullough, and Johnson 1989, 57). Essentially, decentralization is viewed here as a policy tool that can be used by the state, often aided in these efforts by international organizations. However, despite the fact that most protagonists of the pragmatic school effectively adopt a top-down perspective, they generally consider popular participation to be crucial for decentralization to achieve its ends. Local voluntary organizations need to play a role in order for decentralization programs to be successful. Apart from mobilizing local resources, these organizations are considered important intermediaries between the state and the local population, providing invaluable information about the target communities and allowing decision makers to better focus their policy measures. Therefore, state officials in charge of decentralization programs are well advised to enlist their support in order to better tailor these programs to the conditions at hand (Cheema 1983).

The pragmatic school does not completely disregard the political context in which decentralization takes place, but it places most of its emphasis on its "technical, spatial, and administrative aspects" (Rondinelli 1990, 496). This preoccupation with the practical aspects of decentralization reflects a fundamental belief on the part of the pragmatic school that it is flaws in the planning and execution of decentralization programs, and not the social, economic, cultural, or political environment in which these programs are set, which ultimately determine their success or failure. Consequently, any improvements made in this regard would greatly improve the effectiveness of these decentralization schemes.

The pragmatic school's emphasis on the design and implementation of decentralization programs is most clearly expressed in the ambitious attempt by Rondinelli and his colleagues to develop a "political-economy framework" of decentralization (Rondinelli, McCullough, and Johnson 1989). Essentially, what they are proposing is a "meta-approach" to decentralization in the sense of a universal model that can be used to design and implement decentralization programs and advise governments independently of the specific political, social, and economic context. Their framework, which draws on public choice theory as well as policy analysis while

---

9. Samoff has called the same approach the liberal-interventionist school (Samoff 1990, 515).

trying to overcome their respective shortcomings, purports to include all variables relevant for the design of policy interventions and instruments as well as for the evaluation of their successes or failures. Armed with such an "optimizing blueprint" (Fisette 1990, 33), the policymaker would have to do little more than fine-tune it to fit his or her needs, for instance, by determining the characteristics of the target community, selecting the proper policy instruments, and identifying possible obstacles to their implementation.

The many studies of decentralization undertaken from the pragmatic perspective, often under the auspices or with the support of international organizations,[10] have the undeniable merit of having accumulated a wealth of empirical evidence on the practical problems and obstacles that decentralization schemes can run up against. At the same time, as numerous critics have pointed out, the pragmatic approach disregards the impact of politics on decentralization by relegating politics to the status of an "environmental variable." Such a separation between a policy instrument which is approached from a technical perspective and thought to be politically neutral and the political and other "environmental variables" that impinge on it from the outside is unsound. Decentralization is *by definition* political, since it concerns the "territorial distribution of power" (Smith 1985, 1) and thereby affects the relative power of different social classes or groups. Consequently, all of the various possible outcomes of decentralization processes are also inherently political, be it the empowerment of the poor, the fortification of the central state apparatus via an improvement of its administrative efficiency and increased outreach to the regions, or the strengthening of entrenched local elites.[11]

The pragmatic school's narrow emphasis on the practical problems of program design and implementation and its failure to adequately account for the political context of decentralization processes has a profound impact on its treatment of the issue of popular participation. As already mentioned, popular participation has an important, but largely instrumental, role to play in the pragmatic approach: it facilitates decentralization schemes that are planned and executed from above. Conceived this way, popular participation can easily be limited and controlled, and it is therefore not unreasonable to assume,

---

10. See Conyers 1983 and 1984 for a bibliography of some of this material.

11. A mentioned before, to turn a blind eye on the political and other implications of decentralization policies would also make it impossible to understand why and how these policies are frequently used for purposes other than the ones stated, or in other words, why they so often "fail." Clearly, this cannot be attributed exclusively to flaws in their design and implementation (Smith 1985, chap. 10).

as the pragmatic school does, that there will be openings for decentralization and for popular participation under any type of regime, given the perceived benefits of these policies on administrative efficiency, political stability, and the like. For the same reasons, however, it is difficult to see how this kind of decentralization could "strengthen the administrative capacity, and eventually the political influence, of larger numbers of organizations in developing countries, . . . [which] may create the potential for wider participation in economic and political processes" (Rondinelli 1990, 496). In all likelihood, for this to happen policymakers would have to address the political implications of decentralization head-on, which the pragmatist school is reluctant to do.[12] Even if limited and controlled forms of decentralization and popular participation could produce incremental changes at the local level, the pragmatist school fails to provide the crucial link to the more fundamental socioeconomic and political changes that would be needed for the empowerment of the popular sectors.[13] The second approach to be examined, on the contrary, claims to provide just such a link.

The Political Approach to Decentralization

Whereas the pragmatic school tends to neglect the political implications of decentralization and to focus on the more immediate aspects of designing and implementing decentralization policies, what I call the political approach (Boisier 1987, 1991; Borja 1988a, 1988b, 1989a, 1989b; Castells and Borja 1988) puts the political aspects of decentralization at the center of its analysis. Essentially, the political school sees in decentralization a vehicle for political reform, or more precisely, a means to democratize a state apparatus that has been the principal roadblock on the way to full

---

12. This may not be surprising, given that many of its protagonists are closely affiliated with international aid organizations and may therefore be hesitant to express views that could be construed as interventions in the internal affairs of recipient countries. However, I would not go as far as Slater (1989, 1990), who accuses Rondinelli and others of willfully conspiring with undemocratic regimes and international capital by developing an "official discourse" of decentralization designed to weaken the resistance of third world nation-states to capitalist penetration and dependency and to cement existing social injustices. Slater provides no real proof for his accusations, and I see no reason to doubt Rondinelli's claims to reformist aspirations (Rondinelli 1990, 496, 499). On the other hand, it is hard to see how these aspirations could be realized within Rondinelli's own framework.

13. In some form or other, the same problem crops up in much of the literature on decentralization and popular participation. See, for example, Esman and Uphoff 1984, 28, and Illy, Kaiser, and Schimitzek 1988, 3.

democracy. Despite the relatively recent return to representative democracy in most Latin American countries, the political school argues, the state continues to be heavily centralized, permeated by antidemocratic traditions, and controlled by the political elites. Under such conditions, representative democracy risks remaining formal and meaningless, since the state apparatus is likely to be used to perpetuate existing power relations as well as social, economic, and regional inequalities. By decentralizing the state apparatus and by opening up new channels for popular participation inside the political system, the political school hopes to infuse it with the democratic potential represented by local and regional movements operating at the level of civil society and thereby create the conditions, not only for more equality between the regions, but also for the empowerment of the hitherto excluded popular masses.

There are two ways in which decentralization would achieve these goals (Borja 1988a, 47–48). First, the decentralization of the state apparatus would open the way for a thoroughgoing administrative reform, by which powers as well as resources would be devolved from the central to lower levels of government. As a result, the dependence of regional and local governments on the central government would greatly decrease, and they would be in a position to identify and meet most of their development needs autonomously. Not only would this help redress existing regional disparities, but it would also lead to greater administrative efficiency, since lower levels of government are considered more apt at identifying existing problems and needs than higher ones and better capable of administering resources efficiently in addressing them. Furthermore, given their relative proximity to the population, regional and especially local governments are seen by the political school as potentially more accountable and responsive to its needs.

Second, decentralization would create new avenues for direct popular participation at the base level, supplementing the opportunities for electoral participation provided by representative democracy. The establishment of such new channels for popular participation, which can range from simple consultative mechanisms to elaborate schemes of joint control and decision making, would have important implications. On the one hand, new openings for popular participation would serve as a means for the inclusion of the popular masses into the political system, providing a "practice ground for democracy," and thereby furthering political stability. On the other hand, new participatory mechanisms would allow for more direct input from popular and other social movements (Borja 1989b, 72). Given the democratic and participatory character of these movements, their participation in local institutions would exert a democratizing influence on the administration, helping to counter existing antidemocratic tendencies such as authoritarianism, clientelism, and corruption.[14] Local and regional governments play a crucial role in this regard, since they constitute a sort of meeting place between the state and civil society. Opening up spaces for the demands for democracy, participation, and regional equality emanating from civil society, while at the same time providing new institutional channels to accommodate these demands, local and regional governments are seen as the place where a potential "new social contract" (Boisier 1987, 134) between the state and civil society can be negotiated.

Obviously, decentralization thus conceived is an ambitious undertaking which simultaneously challenges existing power relations, as well as the established distribution of economic and social resources. By putting the political character of decentralization at the center of its analysis, the political school undoubtedly constitutes a significant advance over the pragmatic approach. It also goes beyond the pragmatic view in putting greater emphasis on the political obstacles that decentralization schemes can run up against, frequently leaving them stunted and deformed (Borja 1988a, 48–49), even if it can never convincingly explain how these obstacles can actually be overcome. At the same time, however, the political school has rightly been criticized for its tendency to idealize local communities, which are often characterized by very real differences relating to social class and political power (de Mattos 1989a, 124–25), as well as for not going far enough in its treatment of the political context of decentralization. For de Mattos, who sums up the general thrust of these critiques, the political approach runs the risk of falling victim to the same institutional fetishism as the pragmatic school, since it, too, overlooks the fact that political-administrative reforms cannot by themselves change the socioeconomic and political power relations of the societies in which they are implanted (de Mattos 1989b, 29).

---

14. From a theoretical perspective, the political school consists of an interesting, if at times uneasy, mix of ideas borrowed from nineteenth-century liberal thought on democracy and local government (Smith 1985, chap. 2), as well as from more recent theories of social and popular movements. While it shares some of liberalism's concerns with political integration and stability (Borja 1989b, 72; Castells and Borja 1988, 41), the political school parts ways with liberal thought in assigning a much greater role to collective action, even welcoming the relative disorder and unpredictability of political life that this implies (Borja 1988b, 43). At the same time, the tension between political stability and social and political change is never fully resolved in the political approach, a point to which I will return.

The critics offer two related ways of dealing with these problems. On the one hand, they contend, the political content of decentralization needs to be made much more explicit, by further distancing it from the idea of a purely administrative reform and by linking it more directly to an increase in the participation of popular movements and the empowerment of the popular classes (Slater 1989, 522). Additionally, and more importantly, the idea of decentralization as well as the local and regional movements supporting it would have to be integrated into a broader political project designed to promote the interests of the lower classes as well as to propose a comprehensive political alternative to neoliberal and other conservative projects (Coraggio 1989, 520–21). In more concrete terms, what the critics mean is that the Left would lead the struggle for political decentralization and that local and regional movements would form an alliance with leftist political parties and possibly other members of the leftist block, such as trade unions. The notion of decentralization as well as the social forces advocating it would thus be incorporated into a political project of the Left, a project which is often referred to as popular democracy or *autogobierno popular.*

A coalition between locally and regionally based popular movements and the political left is not without appeal, for several reasons. First, the idea of integrating popular movements into a leftist-led political alliance highlights the particular importance of political parties as a link between the political system and popular and other social movements operating at the level of civil society. As was explained in the previous chapter, popular movements often emerge as reactions to immediate and fairly particularistic concerns and therefore lack continuity as well as organizational and programmatic coherence. As a consequence, many of them have been unable to attain a higher degree of cooperation with one another or to identify a set of core objectives that a majority of popular movements would share. Political parties, on the contrary, usually have less difficulty in devising and implementing political strategies and can therefore project the concerns of urban popular movements into the political arena and represent them there.

Second, if decentralization is indeed a political undertaking that challenges the established distribution of power and resources as well as the control of the central state apparatus by entrenched elites, it would be hard to see how it could succeed without political support at higher levels. Local and regional movements alone clearly do not have sufficient clout, and an alliance with the Left—or with other political parties—therefore becomes a necessity. In fact, even if it might lead to even stronger opposition, such an alliance might very well be the only way to prevent the political and economic elites from blocking decentralization schemes outright or from exploiting these schemes for other than their intended goals.

Finally, the political left in fact appears to be the most likely ally of popular movements. There are some clear affinities between their respective goals—greater democratization of public life, stronger emphasis in policymaking on the needs of the poor and economically disadvantaged, and administrative reform and devolution of powers away from the center—and by joining forces, they would not only strengthen the Left as a political force, but also give greater clout to calls for increased popular participation from below. Strengthened by the political support popular movements can provide, the Left could indeed be in a position to create or enlarge the institutional space needed for implementing far-reaching decentralist reforms, as well as overcoming the political resistance to them. Furthermore, given the ideological transformation of the Latin American left in the 1980s (see Castañeda 1993 and Carr and Ellner 1993), it may indeed prove willing and able to create new mechanisms for popular participation and to tolerate or even encourage a stronger and more independent role of popular movements than in the past.

At the same time, the idea of an alliance between popular movements and the Left as presented by the critics leaves a crucial problem unaddressed, namely, that of how the principal decisions concerning the ideological and political orientation of the alliance would be made. Just as in any other political alliance, leftist political parties and locally or regionally based popular movements would have to find ways of resolving conflicts and of negotiating and reconciling potentially divergent interests, and it would be highly unrealistic to assume that such a potential for conflict did not exist. This, however, is precisely what some of the critics seem to do, possibly because of their own sympathies for the Left. Furthermore, given the aforementioned discrepancies in terms of organizational resources, ideological and programmatic coherence, and so on, the Left would likely be the predominant partner in such an alliance. This not only raises the question of the extent to which locally and regionally based popular movements can put their own stamp on such a partnership, it also refers back to the problem of autonomy and co-optation.

If the historical record is any indication, the Left cannot always be expected to play the role of a benevolent partner and to respect the autonomy of its allies. For example, as was explained in the preceding chapter, during the 1970s the Left was prone to dominate the popular fronts that it formed with urban popular movements and other allies, backed by a vanguard ideology derived from orthodox Marxist-Leninism (Castells 1983, 199–209). While there is reason to believe that this attitude has begun to change and that the Left is now more pluralist than before, even in a more optimistic scenario, the Left would probably remain in a position to determine how decentralization and popular participation was to fit into its overall political project. In other words, even if the organizational autonomy and integrity of popular movements are respected—which depends to a considerable extent on the strength of the movements' identities and on their negotiating skills, but in the last instance on the willingness of the political left to do so—this would mean that popular movements would be presented with a certain model of popular participation, complete with advantages and drawbacks, which they could either take or leave.

It is interesting to note that this flaw in the critics' reasoning crops up in the political approach to decentralization itself, albeit not in relation to the Left. Several authors belonging to this approach make the observation that local and regional movements alone are too weak to overcome the resistance against decentralization and popular participation, and that they therefore have to be propped up by benevolent allies. Sergio Boisier, for example, argues that successful decentralization "implies the need to 'construct' the region in social terms" (Boisier 1987, 143), by which he means, not only the creation of structures of regional self-government, but also the development of social actors capable of self-administration and of developing a regional identity. For Boisier, the construction of such social actors, or at least the task of bringing them closer together, presents a "challenge to politicians and social scientists" (Boisier 1987, 135). Jordi Borja, for his part, insists that sympathetic state bureaucrats play a crucial facilitating role in the implementation of decentralization policies and the creation of new spaces for popular participation. In fact, while both issues have been put on the agenda by social movements operating at the level of civil society, they can only come to fruition if they are backed up by the "political will" (Borja 1988a, 50) of a "democratic, honest, and efficient" administration (Borja 1988b, 26). The problem with such an argument is of course its inherent voluntarism: the political will of state bureaucrats, social scientists, or politicians can change, and neither Boisier nor Borja can explain why and when these allies would choose to respect and encourage the autonomy of popular movements instead of trying to control and dominate them. Borja himself at one point expresses a willingness to do just that: popular participation, he argues, should be restricted to consultation, information, and cooperation in the local administration, but it should not be extended to decision making, which is the prerogative of elected representatives (Castells and Borja 1988, 47).

An Inventory of Possible Courses of Action for Urban Popular Movements

A first and general conclusion that can be drawn from the foregoing discussion is that neither of the two approaches to political decentralization provides a satisfactory answer to the basic question asked in the introduction to this chapter. In other words, neither the pragmatic nor the political approach to decentralization can sufficiently explain whether or not, and under what conditions, political decentralization can in fact create or widen openings for popular participation at the local level and thereby contribute to the democratization of political institutions.

Of course, this is not to say that these approaches have no contribution to make. The pragmatic school has the undeniable merit of highlighting the multiple ways in which political decentralization can render political institutions, public works programs, or development aid projects more efficient and effective. Likewise, based on a large body of empirical research, this school points to the various practical difficulties decentralization programs can run up against and proposes ways to their solution. At the same time, however, the pragmatic school does not adequately address the political context in which these programs take place, and it remains unable to explain how it affects their success or failure.

The political approach, in turn, has its strength in proposing ways in which decentralization could make political institutions, not only more effective and efficient, but also more responsive to popular concerns and thereby more democratic. Making the political context of decentralization the centerpiece of its analysis, this school not only highlights the crucial role popular movements would have to play in this process, it also points to other actors as their indispensable allies. However, this strength of the political school also conceals its most important weakness. As we saw, the political approach can never fully account for the often conflictive relations between popular movements and their various allies, and it therefore tends to downplay the risks such alliances bear for the autonomy of these movements. Once co-opted and absorbed into the political project of their respective allies, popular movements lose much of their potential for democratic political change.

What options does all this leave for urban popular movements? On the face of it, those of them that want to become involved in local politics still seem to be wading into a minefield in which their participation risks being either blocked or instrumentalized for other ends, and in which they themselves are likely to be co-opted by stronger allies and thereby lose their autonomy. Put differently, they are still faced with the old dilemma of autonomy or co-optation. At the same time, the return to democratic rule and the increasing popularity of political decentralization in the region clearly changed the institutional and political environment in which popular movements operate, giving them greater room to maneuver and an enlarged range of strategic options to chose from. Other than resorting to violence or deliberately opting for a clientelist strategy,[15] four such basic options seem to be available to urban popular movements, none of which are mutually exclusive.

First, although total independence and the construction of an autonomous social project from the grassroots are (most likely) unworkable,[16] popular movements can still decide against institutional participation and alliances with others and try instead to pressure state institutions from the outside. In most cases, this would take the form of marches and other mass mobilizations, although at least in theory, it could also take the form of public relations campaigns and other ways of influencing public opinion. Contacts with other actors would be restricted, with the possible exception of links to other popular movements and efforts to devise joint campaigns and strategies.

As its main advantage over institutional participation, such a strategy would facilitate the defense of movement autonomy, precisely because contacts with others and therefore opportunities for co-optation are minimized. For the same reasons, however, the success of such a strategy is likely to be limited, either because popular movements alone are too weak to extract substantial concessions from the state, or because they can be repressed

---

15. These two options fall outside the scope of the present discussion and will therefore not be pursued further. Political violence, by definition, takes place outside the realm of institutional politics. A clientelist strategy, on the other hand, implies that popular movements forsake their autonomy and pledge their support to powerful patrons in exchange for certain material benefits. As a result, the participation of these movements in local politics would be unlikely to have a democratizing influence on local political institutions or on other political actors operating at the local level, which is the main focus of the present discussion. At the same time, popular movements could of course consider that trading their autonomy for concrete material benefits is in their best interest and therefore opt for a clientelist strategy deliberately.

16. This option used to have a certain theoretical appeal, especially to social scientists, but it has since been pointed out that most urban popular movements find it indispensable to establish some kind of links to the state apparatus and to other actors. This is due mainly to the nature of their demands, which generally center around the improvement of urban living conditions (Mainwaring 1987; R. Cardoso 1992). See also Chapter 1.

fairly easily if their protests threaten to get out of hand. In his discussion of the movement of the *posesonarios* (squatters) in Monterrey, Mexico, Manuel Castells (Castells 1983, 196–99) shows how the relative isolation of a popular movement can limit its overall success, despite an impressive degree of internal organization, a proven ability to exploit contradictions within the ruling elites, and the existence of certain strategic links to other groups such as student militants. In short, a strategy that puts too much emphasis on popular mobilizations from outside the political system and neglects the relations between popular movements and others will most likely lead to the marginalization of the respective popular movements themselves. By the same token, such a strategy will impede the ability of these movements to have a democratizing influence on local political institutions or on other political actors.

As a second option, urban popular movements can try to penetrate political parties and/or state institutions in order to wield influence from within. If successful, such a strategy will enable at least some representatives of popular movements to rise to leadership positions within the political system, which may give them access to resources and even offer them a chance of achieving institutional changes. In Chapter 4, I examine such a case in more detail, based on the example of five low-income districts in Lima where many of the new mayors and district councillors that took office after the municipal elections of 1981 had been active at the neighborhood level before. However, aside from the fact that political parties and state institutions are often impenetrable for lower-class people and that individuals often wield limited influence, there are other problems associated with this approach.

At a general level, popular movement leaders that become involved in state institutions or political parties run the risk of losing touch with their bases and often find it difficult to juggle the different, and sometimes competing, loyalties to their movement, political party, and public office. In some cases, these leaders may be easily co-opted and thereby facilitate the integration of their respective movements into existing clientelist structures. In the case of the Argentinean city of Salta (Herzer and Pirez 1991, 85), for example, neighborhood associations that were closely associated with political parties played an essential role in helping individual candidates to be elected to the municipal council. As a result, the respective associations could obtain certain benefits from the state via the municipal authorities, not least because of the existence of strong personal relations. At the same time, however, they were reduced to dependent beneficiaries, and the political parties or individual councillors with whom they were associated were able to retain close control of the flow of the benefits in question. In a sense, therefore, it could be said that the close association between neighborhood movements and political parties produced inroads into the popular sector for the latter, and not the other way around. Consequently, an approach that aims to influence the policies of state institutions or of political parties by strategically placing local popular movement leaders inside them certainly has its limits.

To overcome these limitations, urban popular movements can decide to form broader-based alliances with other actors, particularly with the political left. As opposed to the previous approach, such alliances would revolve less around certain individual leaders and instead put more emphasis on the specific roles played by the respective partners. In more explicit terms, the principal role of the Left in such an alliance, and especially that of leftist-led local governments, would be to create and enlarge institutional opportunities for popular participation at the local level, aside from lending greater weight to popular demands in the political arena. Urban popular movements, in turn, would support the Left politically and would use the new opportunities for popular participation to become involved in the planning and execution of municipal policies. This could include the management of specific municipal programs in fields such as housing, infrastructure, public health, and nutrition, or even the participation in municipal decision making as such, via mechanisms such as joint committees. Relatively successful examples of such alliances between the Left and urban popular movements can be found in the case of Brazilian local governments (see Assies 1993, Nylen 1997, and Abers 2000). Others are the Frente Amplio government of Montevideo (see Winn 1995, and Winn and Ferro-Clérico 1997) and the IU administration of Metropolitan Lima in the years 1984 to 1986. I examine the latter case in greater detail in Chapter 5.

Despite its obvious advantages for both sides, this third course of action also bears some significant risks, particularly for urban popular movements. Aside from the fact that the Left in the past has tried to co-opt and control popular movements and to turn them into more or less dependent political support bases, an exclusive focus on one preferred ally can also prove risky in other ways. A particular danger lies in the fact that openings for popular participation at the local level tend to be tenuous and often depend more on support from political incumbents than on concrete institutional guarantees. As a consequence, such openings often vanish when their backers are removed from office. In the case of Metropolitan Lima, this is precisely what happened when Izquierda Unida lost the 1986 municipal elections to APRA, which abruptly terminated the participatory policies of its predecessor.

As a way to circumvent these dangers, urban popular movements could opt for a fourth course of action, namely, they could decide to form coalitions, not with just one preferred ally, but with several *simultaneously*. This could make them less vulnerable to co-optation, and it could provide some shelter from possible changes in the political fortunes of their respective allies. Moreover, such a strategy could enable urban popular movements to exploit the specific strengths that different actors have to offer. As shown above, political parties, for example, can integrate popular movements and their concerns into broader political projects and give them access to the political system. State institutions, like local governments or central government agencies, can provide resources, whereas NGOs have particular strengths in capacity building, linking strategies, and lobbying.

Obviously, not all of these actors have a true interest in the promotion of popular movements and their concerns, and they clearly have their own agendas. Therefore, the success of such a strategy depends on the ability of urban popular movements to resist external co-optive pressures, which requires fairly developed negotiating skills. While this may exceed the capacities of many of these movements, some of them seem to have consolidated to a point where they can handle such pressures and even take advantage of the potentially conflicting interests of their various allies. For instance, as I explain in more detail in Chapter 6, some urban popular movements in El Agustino, a low-income neighborhood in Lima, have demonstrated an astonishing ability to form coalitions with like-minded movements, and they have proved quite adept at defending their interests in their dealings with local government, political parties, and NGOs.

This last strategy seems to be the most promising of the four. The forging of multiple alliances with a variety of other actors appears to be the best way to safeguard the relative autonomy of popular movements operating at the local level and of maximizing the resources available to them; this strategy may also provide greater opportunities for popular participation in an often unfavorable environment. Obviously, the success of such a strategy depends to a considerable extent on the skill with which a popular movement can bargain and negotiate with others. At the same time, these movements will need to demonstrate they have not lost their greatest strength: if they want to be successful at preserving their own integrity and autonomy and also have an influence on other actors and the institutional environment they are operating in, they will have to strengthen their collective identities and practices, and they will have to demonstrate a greater ability to join ranks and to unite around some commonly shared concerns.

PART TWO

Part I furnished a theoretical framework for analyzing the participation of urban popular movements in local government. The main elements of this framework can briefly be recapitulated as follows. In Chapter 1, I argued that urban popular movements harbor a democratic potential, which is contained in the collective identities of their participants, as well as in their social, cultural, and political practices. The significance of this democratic potential derives from the fact that under certain conditions, it may serve as a resource to democratize other political actors, particularly political parties, and to render local political institutions more democratic and more efficient. At the same time, as I explained in Chapter 2, the realization of this democratic potential is conditional on effective political decentralization and the creation or enlargement of institutional openings for popular participation at the local level. Furthermore, in order to overcome their various limitations, urban popular movements have to form alliances with other political actors, such as political parties. Such alliances are indispensable to projecting the democratic potential of urban popular movements into the political arena;

however, they also expose these movements to co-optive pressures from various sides. I argued that multiple alliances with a variety of other actors could help counteract these pressures, making urban popular movements less dependent on any one actor in particular, while at the same time protecting their autonomy as well as their innovative character.

In the following chapters, I apply this theoretical framework to an empirical case study of popular participation at various levels of local government in Lima, Peru, in the period from 1980 to the early 1990s. More specifically, I focus on the relations between urban popular movements and the political left, their most likely ally in the political arena, as well as other actors operating at the local level, such as local governments and NGOs. The Peruvian case is of particular interest for a number of reasons. To begin with, Peru is a country with one of the richest tradition of popular movement activity in Latin America. After a long period of relative obscurity, popular movements entered the political scene in full force in the early 1970s, establishing themselves as social and, albeit to a lesser degree, political actors in their own right. Initially helped along by the reformist policies of the authoritarian Velasco regime and subsequently part of a leftist-led alliance against military rule, popular movements later stepped out of the shadows of other actors. More recently, popular movements were crucial in organizing the struggle for material survival of a popular sector that was hardest-hit by the economic crisis of the 1980s and early 1990s, and they were one of the few organized responses of civil society against the terrorist and authoritarian project of Sendero Luminoso (the Shining Path).

Second, the democratic regime in Peru continues to be one of the least consolidated in all of Latin America.[1] Even before the partial suspension of democratic rights and freedoms following Alberto Fujimori's *autogolpe* of April 1992 and the subsequent adoption of a new constitution that attributed a disproportionate weight to the executive vis-à-vis the legislative and judicial branches of government, the weakness of Peruvian political institutions was evident. Because of a variety of factors, such as the persistence of authoritarian and clientelist traditions, widespread corruption, and bureaucratic inefficiency, as well as the persistent attacks on democratic institutions by both Sendero Luminoso and the military operating in the emergency zones, Peruvian democracy was under constant pressure from various angles since the

---

1. There is some debate over whether the Peruvian political system could still be considered democratic after Alberto Fujimori's "self-coup" in 1992 and the following drastic changes to the institutional fabric. See, for example, Cameron and Mauceri 1997a. To say the least, it appeared much less so than before. I will return to this issue in the conclusion.

return to civilian rule. In addition, with the partial exception of APRA, political parties in Peru were weakly structured and lacked stable popular support bases. Unable to aggregate interests or serve as intermediaries between civil society and the state, they were often little more than campaign vehicles for the political aspirations of their leaders. Against this background, the idea of a possible role of popular movements in the democratization of political institutions and political parties takes on added significance.

Finally, despite some obvious limitations, political decentralization in Peru went further than in most other Latin American countries. While it is true that decentralization policies were initially motivated by the exhaustion of state-centered development models, as well as the financial crisis of the central state and its need to divest itself of some of its responsibilities, these policies also increased the stature of local and regional governments and created new openings for popular participation. To a certain degree, powers as well as resources were devolved from the central to lower levels of government. At the same time, new opportunities for direct popular participation were created at the local level that were generally more extensive than in other Latin American countries. Popular movements, particularly urban ones, were quick to move into these "new political spaces" at the grassroots while actively pushing for their further entrenchment and enlargement. These efforts were strongly supported by a political left that since the 1970s had considered popular movements to be one of its major allies.

Within the Peruvian context as a whole, Lima occupies a special place and therefore deserves special attention. Lima dwarfs all other Peruvian cities in demographic terms, concentrating about one third of the Peruvian population within its limits, and it is the undisputed political and economic center of the country. Not surprisingly then, in the period studied, urban popular movements in the capital were more developed, diverse, and vocal than elsewhere. Consequently, they were more likely to develop the new collective identities and social and political practices that were mentioned previously.[2] Furthermore, a long history of political struggles, which had often centered on Lima as the national capital, had produced strong links between urban popular movements and leftist political parties. These links date back to the early 1970s, when an emerging New Left branched out from its rather narrow roots in intellectual circles, and to some extent in the

2. Of course, this is not to say that experiences with popular participation in the provinces were irrelevant. For a discussion of the case of Ilo, see Díaz Palacios 1990; for other municipalities, see Iturregui and Zavaleta 1988.

working class and trade unions, to reach out to the population of urban shantytowns as a new popular base and as an ally in the anti-authoritarian struggle. In later years, leftist local governments in Lima championed some of the most extensive experiences with popular participation in Latin America in the 1980s, often stretching legal and institutional provisions to the limit in order to allow for more input from urban popular movements.

The relations between urban popular movements and the political left in Lima can be roughly divided into three distinct phases. During the first phase in the early 1980s, the Peruvian left was still heavily influenced by a revolutionary vanguard ideology that regarded local governments chiefly as "bridgeheads" inside the capitalist system. Popular movements were considered valuable partners in political mass movements and coalitions, and some of their members rose to leadership positions in a number of municipal councils following the 1981 municipal elections. By and large, however, these movements were assigned a subordinate role as a political mass reservoir to be instructed and led by the vanguard party of the Left itself.

Toward the mid-1980s, moderates gained strength within the Peruvian left, advocating an institutional strategy as the road to political power. Reaching their apogee when Izquierda Unida gained control of Metropolitan Lima in 1984, they favored a more independent role for urban popular movements, seeing their "new ways of doing politics" as a source of inspiration for the Left itself. Local governments were regarded as a means to increase the political participation of the previously excluded popular masses, with the aim of reforming and thoroughly democratizing the political system from the grassroots.

Finally, toward the late 1980s, a string of electoral losses reactivated the latent tensions between those who held more moderate and those who held more radical views, which ultimately led to the breakup of the Peruvian left and its subsequent decline. As a result, urban popular movements often found themselves confronted by different and sometimes competing leftist factions which were increasingly willing to resort to co-optive and manipulative tactics in order to win their support. These tactics were sometimes successful, especially when the popular movement being targeted had been weakened by internal squabbles or declining participation rates. But many popular movements maintained their independence, either by withdrawing into themselves or by intensifying their contacts with other actors in order to improve their own bargaining power. As a consequence of this, the previous two-way alliances between urban popular movements and the Left lost some of their significance and were partially replaced by an increasingly complicated network of multiple alliances that include a growing number of other actors.

The political strategies and projects advanced by the Peruvian left are key to understanding how it structured its relations with popular movements, drawing on their new social and cultural practices and striking political alliances on an even footing—or, by contrast, co-opting and controlling them, thereby relegating them to a role of largely passive support bases. The concrete forms and mechanisms of popular participation that actually emerged can also be related back to these strategies and projects. Did popular participation mean to take part in actual decision making, or was it restricted to consultation by a municipal government more interested in drumming up support for its policies than listening to its constituents? Was popular participation institutionalized and thereby made independent of the support of a particular political party or municipal government? And finally, did popular participation have an impact on the institutional make-up and the political practices of local governments and political parties operating at the local level, or did it make urban popular movements more vulnerable to co-optation by compromising their integrity and autonomy?

three

urban popular movements, political parties, and the state in peru

Urban popular movements in Peru truly came into their own only after 1968, but their emergence can be traced as far back as the early 1940s. It was intimately related to the onset of mass migrations from the Andean highlands to the cities on the coast and in the interior of the country, following the long-term decline of Andean agriculture. The arrival of ever-increasing numbers of migrants from the *sierra* was viewed with abhorrence by the urban-based political and economic elites, but despite repeated attempts to halt or even to reverse what José Matos Mar has called the *desborde popular* (Matos 1988), it eventually proved to be unstoppable. Nevertheless, given the reluctance of the elites to accommodate the migrants in the cities and the resulting absence of concerted state policies to integrate them economically, socially, and politically, they risked remaining permanently marginalized.

One of the most pressing problems facing the newly arrived migrants was undoubtedly the lack of affordable housing, which prompted many of them to squat on unused land on the city fringes. In this context, the first neighborhood movements were formed, initially serving to organize illegal land occupations and subsequently helping to defend the new settlements against eviction at the hands of state security forces or private militias set up by the legal owners of the land. If the new settlements could weather this early onslaught, the neighborhood movements would then begin the lengthy process of lobbying politicians and bureaucrats for legal title to the occupied land and to secure the provision of urban services, such as roads, piped water, and electricity.

Most of the early neighborhood movements were hierarchically structured and, despite the outward militancy displayed by some of them, generally clientelist in character. Their leaders often lacked democratic credentials and drew their legitimacy in the eyes of the rank and file from their ability to establish links with powerful patrons, such as politicians and strategically placed state bureaucrats. In exchange for protection from eviction and certain material benefits, neighborhood movement leaders generally did not hesitate to forsake the autonomy of their movements and pledge their support to the political leaders of the day. Conversely, these leaders, starting with military dictator Manuel Odría in the late 1940s, soon realized that establishing clientelist relations with urban squatters was preferable to outright repression, since doing so allowed them to control and neutralize potential sources of conflict within the growing urban popular sector, as well as to create political support bases. In February 1961, squatter settlements acquired a certain degree of legal recognition beyond such purely clientelist links via the enactment of Ley No. 13517. The new law granted land titles to the inhabitants of existing popular settlements and even provided a certain level of state support, with the explicit purpose of preventing illegal land occupations in the future (Collier 1976, 84–87).

The military coup d'état of 1968 and the following reformist military regime significantly altered this panorama, ushering in a period of unprecedented popular movement activity that ultimately led to the transformation of urban popular movements into social and political actors in their own right.

The reformist military regime under General Juan Velasco Alvarado, which was Peru's first and only experience with institutionalized military rule, differed substantially from previous military dictatorships in the country itself, as well as other, more repressive military regimes in the Southern Cone.[1] While sharing a fear of revolution with these regimes, its ideological and programmatic orientation derived from a particular interpretation of the doctrine of national security, which was seen as being inextricably linked with national development (North 1983). Consequently, while they could hardly be accused of communist leanings, the new military rulers were opposed to the strong presence of mostly U.S. multinational companies in the country, most of whom concentrated their activities around the mining sector and the extraction of other raw materials such as petroleum, and the alliance between these companies and the traditional oligarchies, which had their principal bases in the large, export-oriented agricultural estates on the coast.

In order to implement its reformist agenda, the new military regime needed to curtail the might wielded by foreign capital and, even more importantly, to break the back of the traditional oligarchies, which up to that point had held a stranglehold on political and economic power, often with the help of repressive military dictatorships. For this purpose, the new regime embarked on a series of large-scale nationalizations within days of the military coup, the most spectacular being the expropriation of the International Petroleum Company, and enacted a number of fundamental structural reforms that affected almost all spheres of society and dramatically increased the relative weight of the state. Among these reforms, the agrarian reform of 1969 stands out as one of the most sweeping land reforms ever to be carried out in Latin America, leading to the expropriation of the large agricultural estates on the coast and in the Andean highlands and transforming many of them into agricultural cooperatives. The industrial reform of 1970, for its part, gave workers a share of the profits realized by their companies and mandated their representation on the board of directors, thus opening the door to joint decision making between workers and owners. Other reforms implemented during this period included the reform of the public administration and the creation of new public enterprises in 1969, the reform of the banking sector in 1970, and the reform of the educational system in 1971.

    1. The literature on the reformist military regime in Peru is immense. See, for example, Lowenthal 1975, McClintock and Lowenthal 1983, Stepan 1978, and Pease 1977 and 1979. With respect to the previous oligarchic regime, some of the best analyses are still Astiz 1969, Bourricaud 1970, and Cotler 1978.

The structural reforms and the nationalization of foreign multinationals carried out during the early phases of the new military regime were initially very popular and left the principal actors of the previous regime, particularly the "old" political parties AP and APRA, discredited and largely devoid of public support. However, heightened aspirations for rapid social and economic improvements that were fueled by the reformist language used by the new military leaders, together with a renewed impetus for activism flowing from the initial reform measures, quickly led to an upsurge of social protests for which the military government was entirely unprepared. Several violent labor conflicts in the coastal sugar cooperatives and numerous strikes in the mines of the Andean highlands, as well as the Pamplona land invasion in Lima in 1973, prompted the military government to rethink its relations with the population, specifically with its organized sectors.

The military government had at least two crucial reasons for doing so. On the one hand, it was vital for the long-term stability of the military regime to prevent future social outbursts, if only to keep traditional political actors, particularly political parties, from regaining their previous role as links between the political system and the population. In the eyes of the military leaders, this would lead to a return of the old "divisive" forms of political participation that were common under the previous regime, thereby undermining the military's stated objective of achieving national security through national development. On the other hand, the social upheavals had made it starkly obvious that the military government itself lacked institutionalized links with the population, which severely limited its ability to deal with popular demands without resorting to outright repression. Consequently, if the military rulers wanted to be able to prevent social unrest in the future, they needed to establish more stable and direct channels of communication, particularly with the organized population. Not only would such mechanisms improve the regime's social and political control of the country, but more importantly, they would incorporate the popular masses politically and thereby help create popular support bases for the regime and its program.

The military government's main instrument in the implementation of this strategy, which Alfred Stepan has termed inclusionary corporatism (Stepan 1978), was the Sistema Nacional de Apoyo a la Movilización Social (SINAMOS), or National System for the Support of Social Mobilization (Collier 1976, 106–16; Guerra 1983; Stepan 1978, 158–89; Woy 1978). The stated objective of SINAMOS, which was created under the provisions of D.L. No. 18896 in June 1971, was to assist in the training (*capacitación*), orientation, and organization of the population, with the ultimate goal of creating "organizations of social interest" that would facilitate the communication and the dialogue with the military government (Guerra 1983, 682). The mobilization and organization of the population through SINAMOS was explicitly seen as an alternative to the traditional party system, which explains why the military government had previously decided against establishing a political party of its own.

As the main institutional link between the population and the military regime, SINAMOS absorbed a variety of other state organisms and became involved in numerous policy areas, such as agrarian reform and the development of the cooperatives movement. However, despite its far-flung activities, SINAMOS acquired specific importance as the principal intermediary between the military government and the inhabitants of urban shantytowns, particularly those surrounding the capital.[2] For this purpose, SINAMOS united several previous government programs addressed at urban popular settlements under one roof. Among other things, SINAMOS continued the efforts begun by the Organismo Nacional de Desarrollo de Pueblos Jóvenes (ONDEPJOV), encouraging the organization of shantytown dwellers down to the *manzana* or block level of their settlements and promoting self-help activities in the construction of homes and other areas of urban development, often in cooperation with the private sector. At the same time, however, SINAMOS differed markedly from its predecessor in that it took a much more political stance in favor of the military regime, actively drumming up support among the settlers, for instance, by organizing huge political demonstrations. Through their constant presence in the settlements and their intimate knowledge of neighborhood organizations and their leaders, SINAMOS *promotores* also provided the military heads of the agency with an invaluable source of information and a means of political control.

While it is debatable whether the establishment of SINAMOS made the military regime as a whole more amenable and responsive to popular demands, there can be no doubt that the agency's activities in urban shantytowns fostered the participation of shantytown dwellers in decision-making processes at least at the local level. Likewise, thanks to the support

---

2. After the Pamplona land invasion, SINAMOS assumed a particularly active role in the new settlement of Villa El Salvador. President Velasco and his wife took a personal interest in the development of the settlement, which became a showcase project for the military regime to demonstrate its support for the urban popular sector (Collier 1976, 104–6, 111–12; Dietz 1980, 27, 151–52).

provided by SINAMOS, neighborhood movements proliferated and were often able to democratize and consolidate their organizational structures. One of the principal protagonists of this view is Teresa Tovar, who argues that the reforms carried out by the Velasco government encouraged the creation and invigoration of popular movements by creating conditions that favored their organizational consolidation (T. Tovar 1985, 72–75; 1982c, 70).[3] Any further expansion of popular participation, however, despite being advocated by many SINAMOS activists, met with opposition from the agency's military leaders, most of whom viewed any form of popular mobilization with suspicion. The tension between the majority of SINAMOS *promotores* and their military superiors mirrored a more deep-seated rift within the military regime itself, pitting different tendencies against one another (see Pease 1977, North 1983, and McClintock 1983). A progressive group of officers around General Juan Velasco Alvarado, and particularly the president's chief civilian advisers (C. Delgado 1975; Franco 1979, 1983), favored an increase in popular participation up to the point of establishing what was called in the Organic Law of SINAMOS, D.L. No. 19352, a "fully participatory social democracy." In other words, at least in theory, this group was in favor of a gradual transfer of economic and political power from the state to economic cooperatives and other popular organizations. The majority of the military leadership, however, independently of their affiliation with a particular ideological tendency within the regime, remained diametrically opposed to this view, regarding any such increase of popular participation as tantamount to growing political instability and therefore as a threat to national security.

The divisions within the military regime became more intense toward the mid-1970s, when a rapidly deteriorating trade balance and dramatically higher levels of public debt announced the beginnings of an economic crisis. Aside from simple mismanagement, the economic difficulties were due

---

3. Tovar's view that the organizational consolidation of popular movements laid the groundwork for the emergence of a critical consciousness and the transformation of the popular classes into historical subjects, was borne out by historical events, notably the participation of urban popular movements in the opposition movement against the military regime at the end of the 1970s. Previously, Etienne Henry had concluded from his account of the Velasco period between 1968 and 1975 that the regime had been largely successful in "imposing a social and urban order that was contrary to the interests of the settlers" (Henry 1978, 183). According to this view, urban popular movements did not evolve beyond basic demand making—they essentially remained *movimientos reivindicativos*—and failed to link up with the more universal struggles being waged at the same time by the workers' movement. Thus, for Henry, there was no urban social movement in Manuel Castells's sense of the term.

both to the policies of the regime and to external factors.[4] On the one hand, while the military regime had significantly increased the role of the state in the economy and had made massive new investments in a variety of state-sponsored projects, its policies had not produced a corresponding increase in state revenue. Furthermore, the terms of trade for Peru's main raw material exports were deteriorating, and the state's capacity to bring new projects up to full capacity proved to be limited, resulting in a worsening trade balance and further decreasing state revenue. In particular, the new petroleum reserves in the Amazon basin proved to be much smaller than anticipated and failed to generate the expected level of income. Finally, on 25 August 1975, forces under the command of General Francisco Morales Bermúdez deposed President Velasco in a bloodless coup, and in 1976 the new government adopted more orthodox economic policies and accepted an IMF-inspired adjustment package.

General Velasco's ouster had been preceded by a continuous erosion of the progressive faction's position within the military regime since around 1972.[5] Simultaneously, public support for the regime as a whole had been tapering off, which was evidenced by an increasing number of work stoppages between 1973 and 1975 and particularly the Lima riots of February 1975, following a strike of the Guardia Civil, when no political force came out in favor of the regime. Aside from the economic difficulties just mentioned, this loss of public support can be explained by the failure of the military government to satisfy the heightened expectations for social and economic change, which to a large extent it had created by its own pronouncements. Put more bluntly, the practice of the military regime had not been able to keep pace with its progressive, but often lyrical and imprecise rhetoric, and the population had become disillusioned with the regime's many unkept promises. SINAMOS in particular had antagonized many settlers by focusing increasingly on its role as a generator of public support for the regime and as a vehicle for political control, instead of lending them practical support. The latent conflicts between the agency and the *pobladores* came to a head when SINAMOS refused to support new settlements that had been formed after October 1972—the military government,

---

4. For a discussion of the economic policies of the military regime, see FitzGerald 1983 and Schydlowsky and Wicht 1983.

5. According to Cynthia McClintock, the fact that General Velasco moved away from the progressive group and closer to the rightist "La Misión" in 1974 and 1975 explains the alienation of the progressives and their decision to support Morales in the 1975 coup (McClintock 1983, 281).

just like its predecessors, tried to stem the flow of new land occupations—and furious settlers set fire to the SINAMOS headquarters responsible for their area of Lima (Collier 1976, 123).

The mounting resistance to SINAMOS among shantytown dwellers, which was especially pronounced in, but by no means restricted to, the regime's showcase settlement of Villa El Salvador,[6] bore clear evidence for the failure of the regime's model of inclusionary corporatism. Moreover, the increasing resistance of the *pobladores* to state co-optation, their insistence on the autonomy of their organizations, and their refusal to be taken in by flowery rhetoric and empty promises marked a major ideological shift and the emergence of a novel *vecino* identity (which I described in Chapter 1). While SINAMOS had played a major role in mobilizing the settlers and had given a decisive push to the democratization of many neighborhood organizations, it was no longer able to control the mobilizational potential it had helped to create.

The shift to orthodox economic policies under the Morales government, which ushered in the second phase of military rule, did little to quell the popular opposition against the regime. On the contrary, the adoption of a harsh economic stabilization package in July 1976, which nevertheless failed to resolve the economic crisis and instead led to a deep recession, wide-spread unemployment, a severe drop in wages and salaries, a decline in public services, and higher prices for many consumer goods caused by the reduction of public expenditures and state subsidies, fanned the flames of public unrest and led to renewed strikes and to rallies against the regime. The new military government was unable to contain these protests, despite the declaration of a state of emergency and the adoption of much more repressive tactics than under Velasco (although they never approached the level of repression customary in the Southern Cone countries at the same time).

Within about a year, what had begun as a series of relatively isolated and unconnected strikes and demonstrations centered around specific issues, such as salary cuts, job losses, or price hikes for construction materials and basic public services in urban shantytowns, evolved into a coordinated political mass movement encompassing labor unions, neighborhood organizations, and regional movements or *frentes de defensa*, which had sprung

6. On 23 April 1975, around 20,000 settlers from Villa El Salvador staged a march to the Governmental Palace in downtown Lima demanding solutions to problems related to the provision of safe water, urban transportation, and so on. The marchers were stopped by security forces and only 3,000 reached the Plaza de Armas (Valdeavellano 1981, 22).

up in many provinces of the coast and the interior over the previous years (T. Tovar 1986a; Valdeavellano 1981). Under the leadership of the labor unions and strongly influenced by the New Left, which had also won followers among the leadership of many neighborhood movements, the popular opposition against the regime underwent a process of rapid politicization and radicalization, increasingly combining issue-based protests with a challenge to military rule as such. The extent of popular mobilization against the regime and the impressive capacity of the antiregime movement to act in a coordinated fashion became most starkly visible during a series of militant general strikes between July 1977 and May 1978, which largely paralyzed the country (T. Tovar 1982a, 21–26; Valdeavellano 1981, 25–31). Neighborhood movements played an integral part in the planning and coordination of these strikes, participating in the strike leadership, the Comando Unitario de Lucha, through the Comité de Coordinación y Lucha Barrial (CCLUB), as well as by setting up street blockades and confronting state security forces. Together with the worsening economic crisis and growing divisions within the military, which were exacerbated by divergent demands placed on the regime by different social groups and began to threaten the institutional unity of the armed forces themselves, the popular uprisings against the regime were instrumental in forcing the Morales government to embark on a controlled transition to democracy.

With the beginning of the return to institutional democratic rule,[7] the street mobilizations against the military regime began to run out of steam, and the locus of political activity shifted to the Constituent Assembly founded after the elections of June 1978. At the same time, the traditional political parties, particularly APRA and the PPC—former president Fernando Belaúnde Terry's Acción Popular party had decided to boycott the Constituent Assembly—reassumed their place at the center of the political system. It was in the sessions of the Constituent Assembly and in backroom deals involving military leaders and the representatives of the main political parties, particularly General Morales himself and APRA leader Agustín Haya de la Torre, that the precise conditions for the return to democratic rule were hammered out. The outcome of this astounding cooperation, which overcame the deep mutual enmity between the armed forces and

---

7. The transition phase began on 28 July 1977 with General Morales's announcement of a timetable for the return of the armed forces to the barracks, and it ended with the general elections in May 1980. For more details on the transition process, see Cotler 1986 and Pease 1979.

APRA that dated back to the Trujillo uprising in 1932, was reflected in the Constitution of 1979.

The political parties of the Left, for their part, were largely marginalized in the Constituent Assembly, despite their surprisingly good showing in the 1978 elections, in which they captured nearly one-third of the popular vote. Shut out of the negotiations between the military and other party leaders and constantly outvoted by the majority of APRA and the PPC, the Left took little part in shaping the Constitution of 1979 and increasingly resorted to using the Assembly merely as a sounding board for popular demands. At a more basic level, the Left was highly ambivalent toward representative democracy as such, without, however, being able to present a coherent political alternative (Nieto 1983). After it had become clear that the popular mobilizations of 1977 and 1978 would not immediately result in a transition to socialism, as some had hoped, the Left became increasingly embroiled in internal ideological struggles, deeply alienating its supporters within the popular sector. Subsequently, when the Left was unable to present a unified list for the first general elections after the return to democratic rule in May 1980, the popular sector proved that it was no captive constituency and threw its support behind Belaúnde's Acción Popular.

Aside from the relative decline of the Left, the popular protest movement against the military regime was further debilitated by the dismantling of some of the labor legislation passed during the Velasco era by the Morales government, which severely affected the powerful labor unions (Parodi 1986, 48–51). The dismissal of about 5,000 union leaders after the general strike of July 1977 dealt a severe blow to the union movement, and the labor federations' subsequent inability to halt the rapid erosion of wages and salaries in the late 1970s proved to be highly disillusioning for a membership that had grown accustomed to growing union power and easily achieved wage and salary increases during the Velasco years. Consequently, labor militancy leveled off substantially toward the end of the decade, foreshadowing the even further decline of the workers' movement in the 1980s, and the unions were less and less able to provide the same kind of leadership and direction to the antimilitary protest movement as before.

Neighborhood movements, on the other hand, experienced a new dynamism toward the end of the 1970s, largely as a response to the enactment of D.L. No. 22612 by the military government on 25 July 1979. The essence of the new law, which profoundly altered the status of urban popular settlements, was contained in its first two articles. On the one hand, D.L. No. 22612 considerably facilitated the distribution of land titles to urban squatters, thereby accelerating the legalization of previously illegal popular settlements. At the same time, however, the new law decreed that the newly legalized settlements would be subject to the same laws and regulations governing all other residential areas, thereby eliminating the special status that the *pueblos jóvenes* had enjoyed since the Velasco era. Among other things, what this meant was that the inhabitants of urban shantytowns were no longer exempt from paying municipal taxes, but would be treated in much the same way as the residents of well-to-do areas, despite the huge differences between their respective neighborhoods. Furthermore, shantytown dwellers could no longer count on receiving support from state agencies such as SINAMOS or ONDEPJOV to consolidate and develop their settlements, especially with regard to the provision of urban services such as roads, piped water, and electricity. Finally, and maybe most importantly, the new law broke with the declared goal of both SINAMOS and ONDEPJOV to promote the organizational development of popular settlements. Under the terms of D.L. No. 22612, existing neighborhood organizations were no longer considered legitimate interlocutors of the state and its agencies, once the distribution of land titles was completed.

In a sense, the enactment of D.L. No. 22612 shortly after the dissolution of SINAMOS in 1978 can be seen as one of the clearest indications that the military government intended to dissociate itself from the reforms of the Velasco era. Undoubtedly, the new law implied that the regime was burning its last bridges to the urban popular sector, and that the central state was extricating itself from the responsibilities that the Velasco government had previously assumed with regard to the consolidation and urban development of the *pueblos jóvenes*.[8] Not surprisingly, D.L. No. 22612 spawned a new wave of urban popular mobilizations against the regime. While earlier protests by neighborhood movements had often been relatively spontaneous and unorganized, with the exception of the general strikes of 1977 and 1978, these later mobilizations were characterized by a significantly higher level of coordination between different movements. From 1979 to 1980, numerous federations and *frentes* sprang up all over the country, uniting neighborhood movements at the level of districts, departments, or *conos* in

---

8. Strictly speaking, the municipalities had been responsible for the urban shantytowns or *pueblos jóvenes* that fell within their jurisdiction since the enactment of D.L. No. 22250 in July 1978 (Zolezzi and Sánchez 1979). D.L. No. 22612 merely continued this process by stripping urban shantytowns of their special status as *pueblos jóvenes*. Incidentally, the fact that the municipalities were assigned responsibilities without at the same time being given the appropriate resources, foreshadowed a practice typical of later decentralization policies.

the case of Lima (T. Tovar 1982b, 25–33; Henry 1981; 1982, 142–43).[9] In November 1979, the centralization process led to the foundation of the Federación de Pueblos Jóvenes y Urbanizaciones Populares (FEDEPJUP) in Lima, and in July 1980, culminated in the establishment of the nationwide Confederación General de Pueblos Jóvenes (CGPP). During the same period, neighborhood movements became more actively involved in the ongoing anticentralist struggles waged by local and regional movements in the provinces (see Ballón and Filomeno 1981 and Henríquez 1986).

In sum, the 1970s witnessed the emergence of popular movements, and of urban popular movements in particular, as social and political actors in their own right, marking a sharp break with the dependence of these movements on populist politicians and other powerful patrons in previous years. Most notably, after 1975, neighborhood movements in urban shantytowns shook off the co-optation by the Velasco government, which had unsuccessfully tried to combine a stronger commitment to the urban development of the *pueblos jóvenes* and the promotion of their social organization with the mobilization of support for the military regime and tighter political controls. The increasing autonomy of neighborhood movements from the state and their potential to mobilize and organize growing numbers of people were demonstrated during their participation in the general strikes of 1977 and 1978, as well as by the centralization processes toward the end of the decade. Neighborhood movements also proved that they were capable of moving from relatively isolated and specific demands to more global and political ones, and that they could form alliances with other actors, particularly leftist political parties, unions, and local and regional movements.

Urban Popular Movements in the 1980s: Proliferation and Relative Decline

In the period immediately following the transition to democracy in 1980, the political influence of urban popular movements began to wane. Given the vigor of the antimilitary protest movement of the late 1970s and the relative strength of urban popular movements at the end of the decade, this may seem somewhat paradoxical, especially if one considers that the return

---

9. It should be pointed out that this process was propelled by the politicized leadership of certain neighborhood movements, while the mass base of these and other movements was largely left untouched. In Teresa Tovar's terms, which are typical for the language used during the period, the centralization process was restricted to the "most enlightened sectors" of "the" neighborhood movement (T. Tovar 1982b, 29).

to democratic rule implied a decline of political repression and greater opportunities for legal political activity, not to mention the significant electoral weight of the popular sector.[10] Nevertheless, as Guillermo O'Donnell and Philippe Schmitter have pointed out, it is by no means uncommon for popular movements to lose political ground in the course of transition processes, since the return to democratic rule usually goes along with a decline of political mass mobilizations and a new focus on institutional politics (O'Donnell and Schmitter 1986). In the Peruvian case, as I explained previously, the popular opposition movement against the regime lost much of its force following the 1978 elections to the Constituent Assembly. Conversely, the traditional political parties reassumed their place at the heart of the political system and came to dominate the negotiations with the military over the conditions for the retreat of the armed forces to the barracks. Urban popular movements, on the other hand, found themselves shut out of this process. Their political influence was further minimized because the disintegration of the antiregime movement was followed by the decline of the labor unions and by the fragmentation of the political left, which could have served as a link to the new democratic institutions.

At least initially, the severing of their links with the central policymaking process proved to be something of a boon for urban popular movements, in the sense that they benefited from a political vacuum at the local level. With central government agencies largely absent since the dissolution of SINAMOS in 1978, the traditional political parties vying with one another for control over the newly democratized political institutions, and the political left mired in internal ideological disputes over how to react to the return to democratic rule, they were more or less left alone, and attempts to manipulate or co-opt them were relatively feeble and infrequent. Concentrating again on more immediate concerns related to the living conditions in low-income urban neighborhoods, urban popular movements thrived in the early 1980s, and a plethora of new movements emerged. Considerably broadening the rather narrow focus of the established neighborhood organizations on infrastructural improvements and the provision of urban services, these movements addressed a wide range of other issues, such as nutrition, public health, education, small-scale economic activities, and the preservation of Andean culture.[11] Not only that, there was a much stronger

10. The Constitution of 1979 had extended the suffrage to illiterates for the first time in Peruvian history, which considerably increased the electoral weight of the popular sector.
11. Luis Chirinos provides a "typology" of these organizations (Chirinos 1984). See also T. Tovar 1986a, 146–47.

emphasis put on democratic forms of organization, the political and institutional autonomy of the individual movements, and the stronger participation of those groups that had previously been excluded. This was particularly relevant with respect to women, who came to play a much larger role after having been marginalized in the often male-dominated neighborhood movements of the previous decade. As I explained in Chapter 1, this flourishing of urban popular movements in the post-transition phase and the proliferation of what was often called "new social practices" or "new forms of doing politics" (Ballón 1986b, 1986c; Pease et al. 1981; Pease 1983a) prompted many observers to proclaim the emergence of a "new social fabric" at the grassroots.

Aside from the return to institutional politics in the 1980s, a profound shift in economic policy under the new government led by Acción Popular's Fernando Belaúnde had an equally important impact on urban popular movements. The economic policies that were implemented by the Belaúnde government, together with even higher public spending than before, plunged the country into the worst economic crisis it had ever experienced (Stein and Monge 1988, 21–86; Reid 1985, 81–105). As a consequence of lower tariff barriers and the opening up of the economy to foreign competition, domestic industry took a severe beating, resulting in job losses on a large scale, decreasing wages and salaries, and the rapid expansion of the informal economy. At the same time, the level of public debt was rising steadily, mainly to finance a huge state-sponsored infrastructural building program. Since export returns were falling again and tax revenues were also declining, public spending was increasingly financed by external borrowing or simply by printing money, thereby fueling inflation.

Following a combination of external shocks and natural disasters, this economic strategy quickly became unsustainable. The crash of world market prices for Peru's principal raw material exports at the beginning of the 1980s, a particularly strong *El Niño* current in 1983, which hurt the fisheries and caused flooding that wiped out most of the cotton crop, as well as rising interest rates, brought on an acute crisis in the external balance of payments and made the country unable to service its foreign debt. In 1982, the government turned to the IMF for assistance and subsequently implemented a harsh austerity program, consisting of cuts in public spending and state subsidies, a devaluation of the sol, higher interest rates, and a reduction in the money supply. These measures did little to improve the overall economic situation; on the contrary, they threw the country deeper into recession and led to a further deterioration in the living standards of the lower classes.

The impact of the economic crisis on the living conditions of the popular classes was truly devastating. By 1984, the gains of the Velasco period had been wiped out, and real per-capita incomes had fallen back to the level of the early 1960s. Wages for blue-collar workers in the formal sector stood at about 40 percent of their 1973 peak, while salaries for white-collar workers had decreased to a mere third of their 1973 level (Reid 1985, 94). Still, formal sector workers at least had access to collective bargaining mechanisms and were protected by what remained of the labor legislation of the Velasco years. The approximately two-thirds of the workforce that were under- or unemployed, on the other hand, most of whom worked in a variety of odd jobs in the informal sector (Carbonetto, Hoyle, and Tueros 1988), enjoyed no protection whatsoever, and whole families often had to work exceedingly long hours just to ensure their bare survival. As a result of radically reduced wages and salaries and widespread under- and unemployment, poverty and extreme poverty were rampant, and large parts of the population were becoming increasingly destitute, especially in urban shantytowns and in the rural areas of the central Andes. At the same time, health standards were becoming critically low, which was evidenced by a rapid rise in infant mortality and infant malnutrition rates, among other indicators (Reid 1985, 97–98; Haak 1987, 58–59; T. Tovar 1986a, 158).

In response to the rapidly deteriorating living conditions of the popular sector, a growing number of so-called survival movements sprang up in the popular settlements around Lima, as well as in other large urban centers. The overwhelming majority of these movements were made up of women, who were prompted into action by the concern that their spouses' decreasing salaries were no longer sufficient to feed their families. Many of these women saw the answer to the problem of material survival in the establishment of communal soup kitchens or *comedores populares,* which enabled them to pool what little resources they had in order to buy larger quantities of food more cheaply in the market and to save on other expenses, such as cooking fuel. At the same time, the sharing of cooking and child-rearing duties with others made it possible for them to leave the house and to take on paid employment, usually in the informal sector, in order to supplement the family income.

During the early 1980s, the number of *comedores populares* multiplied; by January 1986, almost eight hundred communal soup kitchens existed in Lima alone (Allou 1989, 74). Most *comedores populares* were run by their members and were democratically structured and politically autonomous, even if they received organizational assistance and food donations from the outside, for example, from the Catholic charity Caritas, various other NGOs, or through the FOVIDA program administered by the municipal government of Lima. The same can be said about the Vaso de Leche (glass of milk) committees in Lima, which were set up by the municipal government in cooperation with existing women's groups after Izquierda Unida's victory in the 1983 municipal elections. The Vaso de Leche committees, which numbered about 7,500 in late 1985 (Allou 1989, 74), provided a daily glass of milk for children up to a certain age, as well as for pregnant women. While the municipal government assured the delivery of the (powdered) milk to the popular districts of the capital, the day-to-day management of the program was largely left to the Vaso de Leche committees themselves.

Apart from their growth in sheer numbers, it soon became clear that survival movements were replacing neighborhood movements as the most dynamic element within urban popular movements as a whole. There were several reasons for this. For one thing, material survival was a more pressing concern in a time of severe economic crisis than the distribution of land titles and the improvement of urban services, which had traditionally been the domain of neighborhood movements. Furthermore, the traditional demands of neighborhood movements were becoming less urgent, since a considerable number of land titles had already been distributed by the early 1980s, and many popular settlements were becoming increasingly consolidated. Finally, the militancy of neighborhood movements declined somewhat because many of their activists had become involved in local politics, some of them joining leftist-dominated local governments after the first democratic municipal elections in 1980. In a sense, local governments were taking over the role of neighborhood movements in coordinating popular protests and channeling popular demands to the central government.

The explosive growth of survival movements had a number of important consequences; most notably, it profoundly affected the gender relations within urban popular movements and led to the empowerment of women.[12] Despite the fact that many women had initially been motivated to participate in survival movements by their concerns for the material well-being of their families, many of them were later able to move beyond this rather traditional interpretation of their gender role and to shake off some of the limitations it entailed. At a very basic level, to participate in survival movements for many

12. There exists a huge amount of literature on the women's movement in Peru and in Latin American in general. See, for example, Barrig 1986; Vargas 1990, 1992; Jelin 1990; and Jaquette 1989b.

women meant quite simply that they could leave their homes and become more independent from their husbands, who often viewed their wives' new activities with suspicion. Furthermore, many women, particularly those involved in the leadership of the respective committees, gained invaluable organizational experience, as they practiced how to address public meetings and recruit new members and learned how to stand up for themselves when negotiating with state officials, representatives of NGOs, and others. For many women, these experiences served as an important boost to their self-confidence, which enabled at least some of them to penetrate neighborhood organizations, where they had traditionally been marginalized, to make inroads into political parties, or even to enter local politics. Carmen Barnet and Amanda Collazos, both members of an all-female *directiva* of a neighborhood organization in the Lima district of El Agustino, recalled in a personal interview with the author:

> It was a trajectory that cost us dearly. . . . Typically, in a neighborhood organization, the functional [women's] organizations are always marginalized. . . . About ten years ago, the functional organizations also entered into the life of the settlement. . . . When we took over [the leadership of the neighborhood organization] we did so for the first time as the result of a democratic vote. . . . It cost us dearly. A whole year we fought to be recognized as equals. . . . Still, when we talk to engineers, architects, or technicians about public works . . . they ask us, are you really *dirigentes?*[13]

In terms of their organizational capacities, the development of survival movements was equally impressive, especially in Lima, where they were stronger and more dynamic than elsewhere in Peru. Both the *comedores populares* and the Vaso de Leche committees established multitiered organizational structures, ranging from the grassroots to the district and metropolitan levels, which consisted of democratically elected coordinating committees, the so-called *coordinadoras*. Survival movements also refined their programmatic capacities. Branching out from their initial focus on survival issues and the distribution of emergency relief funds, which had motivated some to qualify them as "assistentialist," that is, dependent on the state or donor agencies, they proved that they could develop concrete policy proposals, particularly in the fields of nutrition and public health.

13. All translations in this chapter are mine.

In some cases, survival movements even spun off small businesses, such as bakeries, which made them less dependent on food donations and created employment possibilities for their members.

As a result, many lower-class women began to regard material survival no longer as the subject of demands that were addressed at the state, much less as a favor that could be granted or refused. On the contrary, they began to see material survival as a right that should be guaranteed as such, along with other guarantees for basic social and economic living standards. In addition, the programmatic evolution of women's movements and their shift away from simple demand making was symptomatic for similar developments within other popular movements, indicating a stronger push for democratic participation and greater influence on institutional decision-making processes. In sum, the astonishing development, particularly of survival movements, as well as women's movements in a more general sense, can be regarded as the clearest sign that a *ciudadano* identity had emerged among urban popular movements.

While these were impressive achievements, it needs to be pointed out that urban popular movements in Peru in the 1980s were also plagued by some serious weaknesses and shortcomings. To begin with, despite the fact that some urban popular movements, particularly the survival movements just mentioned, displayed an impressive dynamism, relatively high levels of participation, and substantive programmatic development, participation in urban popular movements as a whole remained rather sporadic and was often linked to specific and relatively narrow demands. At the same time, the organizational development of most urban popular movements lagged behind that of the more successful examples. Not surprisingly in these conditions, the centralization of urban popular movements likewise made little progress. Apart from some noteworthy exceptions, such as the various federations of neighborhood movements at the beginning of the decade, the *comedores populares* and the Vaso de Leche committees in Lima later on, and specific communities such as Villa El Salvador in the south of Lima, urban popular movements as a whole remained relatively fractured and fragmented. Several attempts to lend greater unity to urban popular movements met with limited success, such as the *Encuentro Metropolitano de Organizaciones Vecinales,* which was organized in September 1986 by the municipality of Metropolitan Lima (González 1986; Carbajo 1986; Frías 1986), or the Asamblea Nacional Popular (ANP) in November 1987, in which survival movements and neighborhood movements participated, but whose agenda was largely set by unions and various leftist parties (Centralización del movimiento popular 1987; Zolezzi 1988). As a consequence of their failure to unite and to arrive at a common political agenda, the overall impact of urban popular movements on the political system and on other actors, particularly political parties, remained relatively limited.

The principal cause of the relative weakness of urban popular movements in the 1980s can be found in the economic crisis, which continued unabated for most of the decade, aside from a brief economic upturn at the beginning of Alan García's presidency. While the crisis in some sense spurred the growth and the dynamism of survival movements, its overall impact on the development of urban popular movements was decidedly negative. For one thing, the increased economic hardship that resulted from the crisis made urban popular movements and their members more dependent on material benefits that they could obtain from others, such as donations of food, medicine, or money, and therefore heightened the danger of political co-optation. For example, the APRA government had some success in drawing participants of urban popular movements into its PAIT program, offering them small salaries for their labor, while at the same time expecting them to take part in political rallies in support of APRA (Graham 1991, 105).

Furthermore, the economic crisis had a detrimental impact on the level of participation in urban popular movements, which relied on voluntary labor by their members to function. By pushing the standards of living of the urban poor down to a point where their bare survival was at stake, the crisis fostered the search for individualist solutions, or in other words, it made it more likely that individuals would abandon collective pursuits and put their own survival and that of their families before that of others. At a more practical level, the crisis pushed many individuals out of their jobs and forced them to work longer hours, usually in a variety of low-paying jobs in the informal sector, and to spend more time looking for work. Consequently, these individuals had less time to spend on collective activities, and the level of participation in urban popular movements therefore decreased.

One result of this decline in participation[14] was a growing rift between the leadership and the rank and file of many urban popular movements.

14. I know of no studies that provide reliable and comprehensive data on the level of participation in urban popular movements, which can of course be subject to great fluctuations. However, some figures can serve as an approximation. As was mentioned before, by 1987 there existed 7,458 Vaso de Leche committees in Lima, as well as 794 communal soup kitchens (Allou 1989, 74). Furthermore, 215 neighborhood organizations were recognized by the municipality of Metropolitan Lima, while another 57 were in the process of being recognized. While these numbers may appear relatively small, it can be assumed that most inhabitants of urban shantytowns have been members of some form of neighborhood organization, at least during the

Typically, leaders of urban popular movements were not only more politicized, but also economically somewhat better off than most of the membership and could therefore afford to spend more time on organizational activities (Ponce 1989). Consequently, their influence within the respective movements was often disproportionate, notwithstanding the existence of democratic structures and control mechanisms. When the participation of the rank and file began to level off, the leadership became even more powerful, often against the will of the leadership itself and despite the best efforts by many leaders to oppose this trend and to involve the membership more strongly in the activities of the movement.[15] Nevertheless, the increase of the relative weight of the leadership vis-à-vis the rank and file posed at least a potential threat to the democratic character of many urban popular movements.

Aside from the impact of the economic crisis, urban popular movements were further debilitated by the violent campaign waged against them by the Sendero Luminoso guerrilla movement.[16] In the case of Lima, this campaign became particularly intense between 1991 and 1992,[17] before leveling off after the capture of Sendero leader Abimael Guzmán and other members of the movement's inner circle in September 1992. Sendero Luminoso had previously undergone a critical strategic shift: after years of focusing on the central Andean highlands, its leadership had decided to carry the insurrection from the countryside to the urban areas and particularly to the capital.[18] The guerrilla movement was confident that it had reached the stage of

---

period when their settlements were founded. With respect to associations of migrants from other departments, Carlessi puts their number at 6,000 (Carlessi 1989, 15). Pásara and Zarzar, on the other hand, quote from a 1990 survey by the Lima polling firm Apoyo, in which three out of four respondents from the two lower socioeconomic categories declared that they did *not* belong to any type of institution or association (Pásara and Zarzar 1991, 193).

15. Barrig (1990) has shown the consequences of such a development for the Vaso de Leche committees in Lima. While many women leaders were empowered by their participation in the committees, for the rank and file, the Vaso de Leche program sometimes came to signify little more than a service provided by the state. Seen from this angle, the leadership acted as some sort of intermediary between the program recipients and state institutions, and the characterization of the program as "assistentialist" is not entirely misplaced. See, however, the conclusion to this chapter.

16. The considerable literature on Sendero Luminoso includes Palmer 1992, which brings together contributions by a number of renowned "senderologists" such as Carlos Iván Degregori, Gustavo Gorriti, and Cynthia McClintock. For the period after Abimael Guzmán's capture by Peruvian security forces, see Burt and López 1994.

17. See McCormick 1992, Smith 1992, and Burt 1997. Journalistic accounts include Morales 1991, Cosecha roja 1991, and La batalla de Lima 1992.

18. This strategy was first announced by Abimael Guzmán in a lengthy interview with the newspaper *El Diario* in 1988 (Guzmán 1988, 17).

so-called strategic parity in its struggle and that it was strong enough to challenge the state security forces concentrated there on more or less equal terms.

Obviously, in order to follow through with its strategy of "encircling" the big cities, Sendero Luminoso needed to obtain a foothold in the urban shantytowns surrounding them, and if possible, to infiltrate and control the popular movements operating there. In the polarizing logic of Sendero Luminoso, which distinguished only between friend and foe, popular movements could play one of two roles. They could either submit to its supreme authority, in which case they would become valuable political support bases, or they could insist on their independence, in which case they deserved to be destroyed like all other political enemies. In line with this thinking, Sendero Luminoso adopted the same double strategy toward urban popular movements that it had used to win over peasant communities in rural areas, concentrating on ideological work and persuasion first and moving on to pressure tactics and more violent methods if propaganda and persuasion failed.

Sendero Luminoso's presence in Lima was nothing new: throughout the 1980s, the guerrilla movement had attempted to infiltrate urban popular movements in the capital by becoming involved in ongoing popular struggles, often via one of its legal front-line organizations such as Socorro Popular. This produced some remarkable successes, most notably in the districts of Ate-Vitarte, where Sendero Luminoso went so far as to stage its own land occupation on a plot adjacent to the strategic central highway linking Lima with the Andean highlands, and subsequently established its own popular settlement.[19] Short of such complete control, the more or less overt presence of Sendero Luminoso activists was felt in many other urban popular movements, often intimidating their members, who knew that opposing Sendero was dangerous and could result in reprisals.

In the early 1990s, Sendero Luminoso stepped up its activities and increasingly used terrorist tactics to subdue those urban popular movements it had not been able to penetrate before. Sendero Luminoso hit squads began to assassinate selected urban popular movement leaders, often in grotesque fashions, mowing them down with machine guns in front

19. The settlement was named after Felix Raucana, who was killed in a violent confrontation with security forces. Sendero Luminoso also made significant inroads in the settlement of Huaycán as well as in the district of San Juan de Lurigancho, particularly in a section called Canto Grande, and more recently in Villa El Salvador. See Morales 1991, McCormick 1992, Smith 1992, and Burt 1997 for further details.

of their families or supporters and blowing up their bodies with dynamite afterward.[20] Frequently, these assassinations were preceded by slander campaigns designed to discredit the victims in the eyes of the public by accusing them of mismanagement and corruption. Among Sendero Luminoso's favorite targets were women operating community soup kitchens and other leaders of survival movements, whom the guerrilla group accused of complicity with the system. In their jargon, survival movements served as a *colchón* (mattress) to cushion the impact of the crisis, thereby making the desperate living conditions of the popular masses somewhat more palatable and undermining their revolutionary potential. The most prominent victim of Sendero Luminoso's assassination campaign against urban popular movements was Maria Elena Moyano, who had risen through the ranks of the women's movement of Villa El Salvador to become vice-mayor of the district and a potential candidate of the Movimiento de Afirmación Socialista (MAS) for the Senate. Her brutal killing in February 1992 caused a public outcry all over Peru, as well as in many other countries around the world.

However, it would be a mistake to attribute the sustained presence and influence of Sendero Luminoso in Lima's popular neighborhoods exclusively to its terrorist tactics. By delivering certain material and symbolic goods, the movement also had some success in generating currents of sympathy and at least passive support among some sectors of the urban poor, including in districts like Villa El Salvador where Izquierda Unida and urban popular movements had traditionally been strong (Burt 1997; Pomar 1997). For example, Sendero Luminoso exploited the inability of the public authorities to guarantee security and public order in the *barriadas* by instituting its own form of "popular justice," meting out often drastic punishments to presumed thieves, drug addicts, and other offenders. Likewise, Sendero interfered in conflicts between often cash-strapped and understaffed municipal authorities and certain groups of settlers over issues such as legal land titles or the provision of water and electricity, arguing forcefully against compromise of any sort and urging the use of confrontational tactics. Finally, it played on the growing rift between the leadership and the rank and file of certain popular organizations, skillfully exploiting "assistentialist" attitudes among the population that equated these organizations with public institutions and saw them exclusively as providers of certain

---

20. According to Burt, "over 100 community leaders were killed in Lima's shantytowns between 1989 and 1992, including female leaders of the milk program and community soup kitchens" (Burt 1997, 286).

goods. In the face of declining resources and a worsening economic crisis, many of these organizations were no longer able to provide those goods, making it easier for Sendero Luminoso to blame their problems on corrupt and unaccountable leaders and single them out for summary punishment. The fact that corruption and embezzlement of funds were real problems in a growing number of popular organizations played into the hands of Sendero Luminoso and its creation of "truth by rumor." Whether or not individual leaders were in fact guilty of the offenses they were accused of did not matter much: in a climate of rampant public distrust in public authorities of any sort, many accepted these accusations at face value.

Undoubtedly, the attacks by Sendero Luminoso had a debilitating effect on urban popular movements in Lima; they weakened their organizational structures by forcing many leaders to go into hiding or to resign, and they caused widespread fear among their members, provoking a significant decline in the level of participation. At the same time, Sendero Luminoso was unable to generate much genuine political backing, except among some of the popular sector youth and the most destitute of recent migrants. Its ability to elicit more widespread sympathy and at least passive support by some remained tied to the delivery of certain goods, which suffered when it was forced to scale down its presence in Lima's shantytowns following the capture of its leader. Likewise, its terror campaign to debilitate urban popular movements was only partially successful, and only in those areas of the capital where it was particularly active. While the true influence Sendero Luminoso attained in the popular neighborhoods of Lima is of course difficult to assess, it is probably safe to say that the guerrilla group was never able to control more than a minority of urban popular movements, notwithstanding its sustained presence and the significant inroads it made in some cases. As in the case of many rural communities previously, it had severe difficulties in penetrating popular movements that were relatively consolidated and were strongly anchored in the population. Most urban popular movements in the capital seem to have refused to be turned into mere appendages of Sendero Luminoso or one of its various front-line organizations, despite the threats against their members and the murderous attacks on their leaders.

Conclusion: The Continuing Relevance of Urban Popular Movements

The present chapter has provided a historical sketch of the development of urban popular movements in Peru, examining their emergence in the late

1940s following the onset of mass migrations from the countryside to the urban areas, their insurgence onto the national political scene during the reformist military government of Juan Velasco Alvarado and the ensuing opposition movement against military rule, as well as their proliferation in the early 1980s and their subsequent relative decline, because of the double onslaught of the economic crisis and the violent attacks of the Sendero Luminoso guerrilla movement. It is instructive to take a brief look at some of the theoretical developments that accompanied these historical processes, in conjunction with some more general trends in the field of social movement theory that were examined in the first chapter.

Toward the end of the 1980s, students of urban popular movements in Peru began to distance themselves from their earlier enthusiasm, agreeing that these movements were weaker than they had thought earlier and less able to influence other actors and to induce social and political change.[21] In a clear parallel to the new social movements debate in Western Europe, urban popular movements were now often seen as harboring various conflicting logics (Ballón 1990, 1992; Tovar and Zapata 1990; T. Tovar 1991), or as a sort of last-ditch defense against the imminent danger of complete social disintegration (Rodrigo 1990). The work of Eduardo Ballón and Teresa Tovar, both of whom had championed the view that urban popular movements were the standard-bearers of a new political order, is indicative of this trend. Offering some important revisions to his earlier views, Ballón in his subsequent writings portrays urban popular movements as often self-centered, increasingly fragmented, and devoid of strong links to other popular movements or other actors, such as political parties. Instead of one dominant trend toward new social practices and new forms of doing politics, Ballón now sees urban popular movements as riddled with "tensions" (Ballón 1990, 46; 1992, 128), in the sense that demands for a new citizenship and clientelist and authoritarian forms of behavior, solidarity and individualism, and autonomy and co-optation often exist side by side.[22] Consequently, while it is still possible that urban popular movements can contribute to the construction of a new social and political order, their further decline might speed up overall social disintegration and decay.

21. The relative weakness of urban popular movements was further corroborated in a number of other studies. Grompone (1990), for example, argues that many associations formed by small entrepreneurs in the informal sector are extremely fragile, while Rodríguez (1989) points out the detrimental psychological consequences of extreme poverty.

22. Similarly, Susan Stokes discerns two different political cultures among the Peruvian lower classes, one of deference to authority and another one of contestation (Stokes 1995).

Teresa Tovar echoes Ballón's argument in the sense that she, too, stresses the diversity of urban popular movements, which for her is no more than an expression of social reality. For Tovar, the search for one single logic behind the practice of these movements has always been erroneous, since their diversity is the product of different ways of adapting to an adverse social, economic, and political environment. Not surprisingly in a situation of extreme crisis, these processes do not always result in what Susan Lobo has called "positive adaptation" (Lobo 1982); on the contrary, they often produce even greater individualization and social decomposition. At the same time, however, Tovar sees a potential for resistance against further social disintegration in the ongoing struggles for social mobility, better living conditions, and cultural affirmation (T. Tovar 1991, 31). Therefore, it would be false to focus only on the weaknesses of urban popular movements and to interpret them solely as a product of social disintegration and social anomie; rather, they should be read as an expression of the "common sense" of the popular masses in the Gramscian sense of the term, or of a developing alternative modernity.[23]

While both Ballón and Tovar acknowledged that urban popular movements were more diverse and ambiguous than they originally thought, Guillermo Rochabrún went beyond these self-criticisms by charging that the idea of a democratic potential of urban popular movements was little more than a "myth" in the first place (Rochabrún 1992). Rochabrún attributes the emergence of this myth to the need for a legitimizing ideology on the part of leftist intellectuals, who increasingly abandoned academic research in the early 1980s to become actively involved in politics and promotional work in the urban popular sector. The more these intellectuals committed themselves to building a political alternative, Rochabrún argues, the more their theorizing reflected their own political practices and preferences and not social reality; in other words, sociology degenerated into some sort of "high-level social work" (Rochabrún 1992, 104). Consequently, the imputed democratic character of urban popular movements and their assumed potential for social and political change may have little basis in fact. Quite possible, Rochabrún suggests, these movements are little more than a new form of self-help groups, in other words, they could be interpreted as an expression of some kind of neomutualism (Rochabrún 1989, 24). In order to arrive at more substantiated analyses of urban popular

---

23. The theme of an alternative modernity has been explored by various writers, among them Carlos Franco (1991).

movements, and of social movements in general, Rochabrún calls for a return to disinterested academic research that examines social movements in the context of an overarching analysis of the class structure of society (Rochabrún 1992, 110).

Maybe the fiercest assault on the old orthodoxy came from a group around Luis Pásara (Pásara et al. 1991; Pásara 1991). Unlike Guillermo Rochabrún, who shared at least some of the assumptions of the authors he criticized (Rochabrún 1988, 92), Luis Pásara and his coauthors attacked them head-on. Drawing on three empirical case studies of associations of small entrepreneurs in the informal sector, women's groups, and peasants' self-defense leagues, the so-called *rondas campesinas*, Pásara and his coauthors confirm many of the limits and weaknesses of popular movements that were mentioned by other authors, including Ballón and Tovar. Likewise, Pásara and his coauthors concur with Rochabrún's assessment that the capacity of popular movements for social and political change has often been overstated by the many observers inclined to substitute their own ideological biases for solid empirical research. Pásara and his coauthors part ways with Rochabrún and most other critics of the 1980s paradigm, however, when they assert that leftist intellectuals, not only idealized popular movements, but that for all intents and purposes, they *created* them. According to Pásara and his coauthors, leftist intellectuals needed popular movements, not only as a mass base for their own political projects, but quite simply as a clientele for the NGOs they controlled (Delpino and Pásara 1991). Since these NGOs had to demonstrate to mostly foreign donor agencies that they had links to organized groups within the popular sector which could effectively use the considerable funds that these donors provided, they often insisted that popular movements adopt certain organizational structures before they became eligible to receive any benefits.

Pásara and his coauthors paint a decidedly bleak picture of popular movements, which has some interesting parallels to the catastrophic visions of the marginality debate of the 1960s (Pásara 1991, 66–67; Pásara and Zarzar 1991, 197–203). In a context of profound social disintegration and social anomie,[24] they contend, popular movements emerge as loosely structured self-help groups designed to assure the survival of the family or other closely knit collectives. These groups establish more sophisticated organizational structures

24. The concept of anomie, which of course goes back to Durkheim's classical formulation, has also been applied to the Peruvian context by Neira 1987. See also the critiques of Neira's approach in Romero 1987, Lynch 1989, and T. Tovar 1991.

only when this is a precondition to obtain subsidies from others, as is often the case with resources provided by NGOs. As a consequence, popular movements are *necessarily* self-centered and particularistic, that is, they focus only on the needs of their participants, and they are dependent on others, since their whole raison d'être revolves around subsidies obtained from the outside. Given that these subsidies tend to decrease—the state is less and less able to generate any social policies and the resources managed by NGOs are on the decline as well—the tendency for pragmatic negotiations on the part of popular movements might soon be replaced by violent protests, which of course would militate against any sort of institutional stability. Therefore, instead of fostering the emergence of a new order of any kind, the practices of popular movements are in fact more likely to further accelerate social decay and to produce even more profound social anomie.

The principal flaw of this argument is that it is as ideological as the one that it tries to refute. To be sure, Pásara and his coauthors have a point when they insist on the various limitations and shortcomings of rural and urban popular movements, many of which were previously acknowledged by authors such as Ballón and Tovar. They are also right, as is Rochabrún, to caution against the idealization and reification of these movements and to be wary of a mythology of *lo popular* that has often proved to have little basis in fact. What they fail to recognize, however, is the fact that the practices of popular movements are also evidence for social and political change. It would be hard to deny the existence of new identities, new forms of struggle, and new social actors, even if these actors are often weak and undeveloped and their democratic practices and demands for democratic participation are often interspersed with authoritarian and clientelist forms of behavior. Consequently, to completely deny popular movements any potential for social and political change, as Pásara and his coauthors do by insisting on a virtually inexorable slide into social anomie, is not only defeatist, leaving no alternative other than a violent social upheaval or an authoritarian coup d'état. It also neglects the real diversity of social reality and therefore amounts to replacing one ideological interpretation with another; again, one might add, on the basis of a very limited empirical sample and not an exhaustive study of social reality, as the authors claim.

Rather than erect yet another myth, that of social anomie, after successfully debunking the previous ones of the proletariat and the people, we need to identify more clearly what Nicolás Lynch has called "las tendencias sanas del mundo popular" (Lynch 1989, 26) and to carefully distinguish them from the more destructive elements that also exist. In other words, the challenge consists in carefully weighing the considerable limitations of popular movements against their true potential for social and political change, and to examine if and how these movements could play a role in the democratization of other actors and the strengthening of political institutions.

four
the peruvian left and local government in the early 1980s

From the early 1980s on, political decentralization, the strengthening of local governments, and the creation and further enlargement of opportunities for popular participation at the local level have been central planks in the political platforms of the Peruvian left (Izquierda Unida 1983, 1985; Barrenechea 1989). On the face of it, this would hardly seem surprising. As we have seen in the foregoing, the Peruvian left, at least since the early 1970s, has always entertained links to popular movements operating at the grassroots level and supported their activities. In addition, the creation of "new political spaces" at the local level by the Constitution of 1979 and subsequent decentralization programs constituted a strong stimulus for all political parties, not just the Left, to become involved in local politics and to push for a further revaluation of local and regional governments.

However, there were also some more specific reasons that propelled the Peruvian left to take an interest in local politics. As I explained in Chapter 3, since the beginning of the transition to democratic rule, the Peruvian left had been virtually eclipsed on the national political scene by APRA and the parties of the Right and Center-Right, which came to dominate the newly created democratic institutions. Consequently, if the Left wanted to remain a major political player, it needed to secure a foothold in the institutional system for itself, which local governments seemed to provide. Local governments could also play an important part in the long-term political strategies of the Left to gain power at the national level, despite the seemingly mundane nature of local politics. In particular, local governments could provide the Left with an institutional link to popular movements operating at the grassroots, thereby facilitating the building or the consolidation of political support bases.

For all these reasons, the Peruvian left in the early 1980s turned its attention to local politics, but its various groupings and parties did so in different ways. Depending on these respective strategic and ideological outlooks, local politics came to play different roles, with profound implications for the political left and popular involvement.

Local Government Reform and the Political Situation of the Early 1980s

The political situation of the early 1980s provided strong incentives for the Peruvian left to turn its attention to the municipalities. As we have seen, following the return to institutional politics, the Left saw its grip on the national political process seriously loosened. This was due in large part to the decline of mass mobilizations during the transition period and the corresponding reassertion of the traditional political parties at the center of the political system. To make matters worse, the Left proved unable to translate the extensive popular support it had built during the mass struggles of the 1970s into electoral successes. In part because of internal divisions and ideological feuds, but also because of its inability to propose a credible political alternative to centrist and conservative political parties, the Left could not repeat its surprisingly strong showing in the elections for the Constituent Assembly in 1978 and lost a considerable part of its share of the popular vote, as well as a large number of its seats, in the presidential and congressional elections of May 1980.[1] Largely shut out of the policy-making process at the national level and deprived of its traditional means of influencing politics via mass mobilizations, the Left had every reason to fear a rapid erosion of its popular support base. For one thing, radical trade unions, which were dominated by the Left and had been the mainstay of the 1970s mass movement, were losing clout because of the persistent economic crisis and the increasing prevalence of the informal sector. Even more importantly, the results of the elections of May 1980 had exposed a growing rift between leftist parties, which were often dominated by middle-class intellectuals, and their supporters in the popular sector. While many leftists reacted to the electoral defeat by withdrawing into their respective organizations, intensifying ideological debates over often arcane subjects, and thereby amplifying existing divisions within and among leftist parties, their popular supporters were increasingly unwilling to tolerate such sectarianism and factionalism. As some leftist activists began to realize (Nieto 1983), the internecine feuds over matters of ideology and "correct" revolutionary strategy were harmful, not only because they conflicted with a strong desire for unity at the base, which they saw expressed in the decline of the divided Left's share of the popular vote in the 1980 elections. The fixation on such abstract and increasingly irrelevant matters also prevented the Left from proposing viable solutions for the very concrete and ever more pressing needs of the popular masses.

In sum, if it wanted to remain a political force to be reckoned with and halt the slide into sectarianism and political irrelevance, the Peruvian left at the beginning of the 1980s faced a twofold challenge. On the one hand, it urgently needed to shore up its mass support base by reinvigorating its links with the various popular movements operating at the level of civil society. At the same time, despite its critical stance toward the new democratic regime and toward representative democracy in general, the Left had little choice but to try to somehow break the institutional dominance of the

---

1. While the center-right Acción Popular party won a considerable share of the popular vote in the electoral contests of 1980, the popular sector mostly tended to vote for the Left or APRA in the following years (Dietz 1985, 1989, 1991; Cameron 1991). From the early 1990s on, the position of the traditional political parties, including the Left, was undermined by the rise of Alberto Fujimori and other political independents, such as Ricardo Belmont, in the late 1980s and early 1990s (Roncagliolo 1989/1990; Degregori and Grompone 1991).

traditional political parties. Becoming involved in local politics offered a chance to achieve both ends simultaneously.

While obviously not on a par with national level political institutions in terms of power and prestige, local governments had made substantial gains in their institutional stature since the implementation of the 1979 Constitution and were therefore a political sphere of considerable, and possibly growing, significance. For one thing, the new constitution mandated the democratic election of municipal councillors and mayors, who previously had been appointed by the central government. This was a momentous change, given that municipal elections had last been held in 1919, with the exception of a brief period between 1963 and 1968 during Belaúnde's first presidency.[2] The return to democratic elections at the local level, together with new possibilities for direct citizen participation in local affairs, enabled the population to exert some influence on the running of their municipality and thereby enhanced the democratic legitimacy of local governments. By the same token, the municipalities became politically more significant, which furthered the involvement of political parties in local politics and increased the level of partisan competition.

Aside from the return to democratic local elections, the new constitution recognized the economic and administrative autonomy of local governments from the central government and assigned them fairly extensive new powers and prerogatives, many of which were to be exercised in cooperation with other levels of government (Mejía 1990, 137–39; Castro-Pozo and Delgado 1989, 38–46). In particular, local governments were put in charge of the development of their constituencies in the broad sense of the term and were given new responsibilities in fields such as public education, public health, urban transport, public utilities, and urban planning, over and above their traditional responsibility for civil registration or the provision of local public services, such as garbage disposal, public hygiene, and so on. At least potentially, these legislative changes transformed local governments from dependent and purely administrative entities into political decision-making centers, even if their endowment with resources usually did not match their new responsibilities (de Althaus 1987).[3]

2. For a historical analysis of the development of municipal government in Peru, see Mejía 1990 and Castro-Pozo and Delgado 1989, 21–32.

3. At the level of the implementing legislation, these constitutional principles could be interpreted in a wider or more narrow sense, as evidenced by the Decreto Ley No. 051 of 1981 and the subsequent Ley Orgánica de Municipalidades, Ley No. 23852, of 1983 (Mejía 1990; 122–26; Delgado and Olivera 1983; Castro-Pozo and Delgado 1989, 38–45). In the first case, local governments were essentially seen as efficient providers of local services, or "service

The revaluation of local governments after the return to democratic rule has to be seen in the wider context of decentralist reforms contained in the Constitution of 1979. In fact, by enshrining political decentralization as an organizing principle of the Peruvian state in article no. 79, the new constitution not only strengthened the existing municipalities, but effectively created a whole new layer of government at the regional level.[4] In large part, this was due to the pressure brought to bear on the Constituent Assembly by local and regional movements opposed to the long-standing centralist bias of the Peruvian political system (Caravedo 1988, 210–16). The concerns of these movements were embraced not only by the parties of the Left, for reasons just explained, but to a certain extent also by President Belaúnde's Acción Popular party, which wanted to retain some of the political support it had received in the 1980 general elections (Wilson and Garzón 1985, 332).

In fact, political as well as economic decentralization had been an enduring preoccupation for most political forces in Peru, for at least three reasons. On the one hand, the leveling of the profound economic and social disparities between the different regions of the country, which had long been recognized as an impediment to national unity (Mariátegui 1971,

---

enterprises," centered around the mayor and the municipal bureaucracy with little or no input from councillors or the citizenry. The second law, on the contrary, opened the door to a more modern notion of democratic local *government* in the true sense of the word, allowing for the participation of municipal councillors in the running of local administrations, as well as making it easier for the citizenry to participate in the making of decisions at the local level. I will discuss these two legal norms in more detail below, as well as in the following chapter.

4. The unitary Peruvian state comprises twelve regions that are subdivided into twenty-five departments, including the constitutional province of Callao, which has the special status of an "honorary department." At the subdepartmental level, 189 provinces are in turn subdivided into 1,798 districts; both provinces and districts have municipal status (this two-tier local government system is unique in Latin America, see Nickson 1995, 237). At the subdistrict level there is a provision for the creation of administrative subunits called *municipalidades de centro poblado menor* or *agencias municipales* in rural or urban areas, respectively.

The system of regions was superimposed on the existing framework during the 1980s on the basis of constitutional provisions and subsequent laws, particularly the Basic Law of Regionalization, Ley No. 24650 (Gonzales de Olarte 1989; Méndez 1990; Slater 1991; Kim 1992). While the departments and the constitutional province of Callao are administered by a prefect appointed by the central government, the provinces, including the municipality of Metropolitan Lima, and the districts have been governed by democratically elected mayors and city councils since 1981. Attempts to establish a regional structure of government have long been marred by political controversy, especially after President Alberto Fujimori blocked the transfer of functions and powers to the regions following his *autogolpe* of April 1992 (Slater 1991, 39). The new Constitution of 1993 again allowed for the formation of regions, without, however, giving new momentum to the regionalization process.

153–81; Flores Galindo 1981), was a concern that many political forces shared.[5] Especially during the second half of the twentieth century, Lima had developed into the undisputed political and economic center of the country, concentrating about one-third of its population as well as attracting a disproportionate share of its financial resources, industry, and public services. The other regions, on the contrary, were politically subordinate to the capital and suffered from a relative lack of resources, which was reflected, for example, in slower economic growth or economic stagnation, fewer or nonexistent public services, lower per-capita incomes, and lower standards of living. Most national governments in the past, authoritarian as well as democratic, had tried without much success to redress these regional imbalances, largely by way of administrative deconcentration or delegation. These attempts had produced a variety of regional organisms with differing powers and resources, such as the departmental public works boards (JDOPs) founded in 1956, the regional development organizations (ORDES) created under the Morales Bermúdez government in the late 1970s, or the development corporations (CORDES), which were first established under Manuel Prado in the 1950s and 1960s and reinstalled under the second Belaúnde government as transitional organizations leading to regional governments (Caravedo 1988; Schmidt 1989, 17–36).

A second factor favoring political decentralization in the early 1980s was the emergence of a broad consensus opposing the concentration of political power in the hands of an increasingly unwieldy central state apparatus. The historical dominance of the central state had its roots in a long tradition of political centralism and the establishment of a development pattern based on raw material exports and dependent semi-industrialization (Gonzales de Olarte 1989). However, it was the experience with the previous military regime that had cast a particularly stark light on the limitations of a state-centered development model, making it more and more obvious that the state had neither the resources nor the managerial capacities to fulfill the host of new responsibilities that it had taken on. While the heavy involvement of the public sector in the economy and the resulting inefficiency and waste of resources was the object of particularly severe criticism, a downsizing of the central state apparatus was favored by more than just those

---

5. However, this should not be interpreted as a willingness to devolve *real* powers from the central to lower levels of government. As José Carlos Mariátegui has remarked quite fittingly, referring to the 1920s and the preceding period, "decentralization, no matter what form it has taken in the history of the republic, has always represented an absolutely centralist concept and design" (Mariátegui 1971, 166).

who espoused neoliberal economic theories. Many believed that a smaller central state and a devolution of powers to regional and local governments would improve overall administrative effectiveness and efficiency and thereby contribute to the building of a more modern state (Mejía 1990, 118). Even more importantly, a cash-strapped central administration had little choice but to delegate responsibilities—if not always scarce resources—to lower levels of government, hoping that it would thus be possible to deflect potential conflicts from the central level and thereby prevent a repetition of the social mobilizations of the late 1970s. In fact, as I mentioned in Chapter 3, the Morales government had provided an early example of such a strategy by transferring the responsibilities for urban shantytowns from the central state agency SINAMOS to the municipalities.

Finally, in a context of transition from authoritarian rule, political decentralization was also seen as a means to complement the democratization of a political system that had concentrated power at the central level for too long, while permitting little or no participation by its citizens. By devolving powers and responsibilities to lower levels of government, it was hoped that the regions and municipalities would be given a greater chance to defend their interests vis-à-vis the powerful central government, which was of course one of the key concerns of the local and regional movements mentioned before. At the same time, the return to democratic elections at the local and regional levels would allow for greater citizen participation in political decision-making processes, making local and regional governments more responsive to the concerns of the population. Taken a step further, political decentralization was seen by some as a means to introduce new forms of *direct* popular participation that would coexist with or even replace the existing representative political institutions. Such propositions, which were of course much more controversial than the previous two, were defended chiefly by parts of the political left as the embodiment of "real" democracy.

In sum, political decentralization in Peru was supported across the political spectrum following the return to democratic rule (Iguíñiz et al. 1986).[6]

---

6. Of course, such principled support is often tempered by the need to account for political necessities. In the Peruvian case, a strong centralist faction within Acción Popular came out against political decentralization after the party's victory in the 1980 general elections, because it feared that strong local governments would hinder the implementation of the neoliberal adjustment program required by international lenders. Another group of influential AP members was opposed to political decentralization because they saw their position as power brokers between the central government and the provinces threatened (Wilson and Garzón 1985, 332). Similarly, many political actors opposed the regionalization process in the

This constituted a window of opportunity for the Peruvian left. Local governments had become more relevant than before, and the Left was well positioned to make inroads at the local level. To do so was crucial, given that national power had eluded the Left in 1980 and that there was no chance of gaining it before the next general elections scheduled for 1985. However, at least as significant was the fact that the municipalities as the first level of government were the logical interlocutors for popular movements. Consequently, leftist-controlled local governments would be in a privileged position to identify popular sector demands and to rejuvenate existing alliances between leftist political parties and popular movements. In this context, local governments could fulfill two different functions: they could serve as an institutional means to address some of the needs of the popular sector; or if local resource scarcity made this impossible, they could be used as sounding boards that would amplify popular demands and redirect them at higher levels of government. In fact, these two options reflected some more fundamental political orientations within the Peruvian left itself.

Local Politics and the Political Strategies of the Peruvian Left

When it turned its attention to the municipalities, the Peruvian left did not lose sight of its long-term ambitions. On the contrary, its various factions incorporated local politics into their general political programs, with the ultimate goal of capturing power at the national level. While this principal goal was not in dispute, there was considerable disagreement over the best strategy to attain it, as well as over the underlying programs themselves. These ideological and strategic disagreements within the Peruvian left, which were closely related to similar divisions within the Latin American Left as a whole, resurfaced as fundamentally different views on the role of local governments and of popular participation.

Basically, what lay at the root of these divisions were different views on representative democracy and a critique of traditional conceptions of the role of the vanguard party of the Left. Fissures along these lines had been

---

mid- and late 1980s, on the grounds that they feared it would strengthen regional political support for the ruling APRA party. In sum, decentralization entails specific dilemmas, which is why it is more likely to be championed by political outsiders rather than insiders. For political incumbents, it is a risky business: its benefits are less tangible than conventional public goods and take more time to be realized; therefore, they are less likely to be attributed to the provider (Schmidt 1989, 40).

developing within the Latin American left since the 1970s; however, they became more accentuated in the following decade, when large parts of the Latin American left abandoned orthodox Marxist-Leninist positions in favor of at least a partial embrace of democracy.[7] This shift had important implications for the ideological and strategic outlook of the Latin American left. First and foremost, the revalorization of democracy as a good in and of itself and the espousal of the fundamental principles of representative democracy by the Left entailed a break with the tactical and instrumentalist stance that had dominated leftist thinking during the 1970s. By accepting the procedural rules of the democratic game, such as free elections and the alternation of different political forces in power, large parts of the Latin American left renounced revolutionary violence as a means to overthrow the democratic system and ceased to regard the democratic political process simply as an arena to accumulate forces for the struggle against the system.

Likewise, the acceptance of political pluralism and the recognition of the indeterminate character of the democratic political process facilitated the move away from economic determinism and other forms of teleological Marxism that had been prevalent before. Crucially, this entailed a redefinition of the role of leftist political parties and their relations to other actors within civil society. Without the idea of a predetermined course of history, there was no need any more for a vanguard party of the Left that by definition possessed the correct analysis for any given political situation and represented the single objectively progressive historical subject, namely, the proletariat. The debunking of the notion of the vanguard party, along with an almost exclusive focus on the state as the prime lever for political and economic change, also led to a reconsideration of the idea of political and economic change. Political and economic change was no longer thought possible solely via the seizure of the state apparatus by the armed proletariat and its party and the implementation of its revolutionary program, but via a long-term strategy of building political hegemony, or, in Gramsci's words, a war of position. Among other things, such a strategy involved the construction of alliances between one or several political parties of the Left, as well as other actors, particularly new and old social movements.[8]

    7. These developments have been analyzed in more detail elsewhere. See in particular, Lechner 1982, 1985, 1991; Cotler 1987; Munck 1989, 1990; Chilcote 1990; Petras 1988; Weffort 1989; and the 1988 special issue of *Latin American Perspectives*, "Democratization and Class Struggle." Barros 1986, Ellner 1989, Carr and Ellner 1993, Castañeda 1993, and Rénique 1995 provide useful overviews.
    8. Parallels to similar "post-Marxist" positions within the Western European left, such as those expressed by Laclau and Mouffe (1985), are not accidental. Gramscian thought was

It would be difficult to overestimate the significance of the Latin American left's espousal of democracy, but it was not universal. Traditional leftist positions remained fairly strong in some cases and continued to command sizable mass followings within and outside the organized left. Particularly in a country such as Peru, traditional criticisms leveled against representative democracy continued to ring truer than elsewhere.[9] Not only had democracy proved to be incapable of addressing the more deep-seated socioeconomic causes of poverty and inequality and could therefore be dismissed as merely "formal," a condition that was shared by almost all other Latin American countries. In addition, democracy in Peru had also failed to produce at least a minimum of *procedural* fairness, openness, and impartiality. In fact, given the extent of human rights violations committed by the Peruvian army in its fight against Sendero Luminoso, as well as rampant institutional chaos and inefficiency, one could indeed doubt whether democracy would ever be able to keep its procedural promises.

A further complicating factor in the Peruvian case was the presence of several armed guerrilla groups, such as the MRTA and Sendero Luminoso. The activities, especially of Sendero Luminoso, not only showed that violent opposition to the system was still viable, but its relative success in attracting mass support, first among the Andean peasantry and later among recent urban migrants and the impoverished youth of urban shantytowns, provided a constant challenge to the strategy of the "institutional" left to achieve change from within the system. As a result of this challenge from the extreme left, the democratic commitment of some of the more radical factions of the Peruvian left, which rightly feared losing some of their mass support to the armed opposition, remained tenuous and the option of revolutionary violence was never completely renounced.

In the light of these tensions and contradictions, it is not surprising that a wide variety of ideological viewpoints and strategic orientations developed within the Peruvian left.[10] In the present context, two of these merit

---

popularized in Latin America by leftists returning from exile in Western Europe, where the work of Antonio Gramsci had experienced a renaissance. For a more profound analysis of the theories and especially the concepts developed by Gramsci, see Sassoon 1987 and Kebir 1991.

9. Such criticisms have been voiced, for example, by Amin (1991), Nef (1986, 1988), and Herman and Petras (1985).

10. Using Barros's terminology (Barros 1986), the Peruvian left can loosely be subdivided into revolutionary, radical-democratic, and reformist orientations (Letts 1981; Nieto 1983; L. Taylor 1990; Rojas Samanez 1991; Haworth 1993). The revolutionary orientation was initially composed of a multitude of parties and groups that had emerged from within the New Left of the 1970s, most of which later coalesced into three main parties, namely, the Partido

special attention, which I will call the revolutionary and the radical-democratic approaches. While obviously reflecting more general differences over the conception of political power and the prospects for democratic social reform, these approaches are significant in the present context because they were particularly influential in the formulation of leftist policies concerning local government and popular participation. They share a number of key elements: both start from the assumption that an alliance between the Left and urban popular movements should lie at the heart of leftist local politics, and both would encourage participants of these movements to take on leadership positions in the municipal bureaucracy, as well as within the political left itself. In theoretical terms, the two approaches can therefore be situated between the second and third option mentioned in the framework developed in Chapter 2, combining elements of both. They differ in how they conceive the relationship between the Left and urban popular movements. Whereas the revolutionary approach insists on a leading role for the former, the radical-democratic view regards popular movements and their "new ways of doing politics" as a critical factor for the rejuvenation of the Left itself.

In the following, I will give a brief outline of the two approaches, concentrating chiefly on the writings and public pronouncements of two of their main protagonists, namely, Javier Diez Canseco for the revolutionary

---

Unificado Mariateguista (PUM), the Unión Nacional de Izquierda Revolucionaria (UNIR), and the Frente Obrero Campesino Estudiantil y Popular (FOCEP). Among its leaders were PUM-leader Javier Diez Canseco, Jorge Hurtado of UNIR, and the ex-guerrilla Hugo Blanco, who had acquired a certain celebrity from his prior involvement in peasant struggles. The oldest political party on the Peruvian left, the Partido Comunista Peruano (PCP), maintained an alliance with the revolutionary faction for most of the 1980s, but its stance often wavered and it cannot be easily subsumed under any of the three labels. The radical-democratic orientation, on the other hand, derived most of its support from independents within Izquierda Unida, among them such prominent personalities as Henry Pease and Rolando Ames, both of whom had been influenced by Christian ideas. Toward the late 1980s, two smaller parties emerged from within this orientation, the Movimiento de Afirmación Socialista (MAS), which was founded in 1991, and the Partido Mariateguista Revolucionario (PMR), which split from the PUM in 1989. The reformist orientation, finally, consisted chiefly of the Partido Socialista Revolucionario (PSR), which had been founded by pro-Velasco generals in 1978, the Partido Comunista Revolucionario (PCR), and the Convergencia Socialista. Enrique Bernales, who for much of the 1980s played an important role in the Peruvian senate, and PCR-leader Manuel Dammert were some of the key figures within the reformist orientation. The reformist faction became starkly visible in the late 1980s, when it separated from Izquierda Unida to form a competing leftist alliance, Izquierda Socialista, taking with it the hitherto independent and former IU president, Alfonso Barrantes. This breakup precipitated the decline of the United Left alliance, which was further accelerated by President Alberto Fujimori's populist and anti-institutional politics following his "self-coup" in April 1992.

approach, and Henry Pease for the radical-democratic one. Javier Diez Canseco, a member of the Peruvian legislature since 1978, was a founding member of the Partido Unificado Mariateguista (PUM), which became one of the key components of the radical wing of Izquierda Unida in the 1980s. Unlike other leftist parties, the PUM was more deeply involved in grassroots organizing and had relatively strong roots among popular movements. At the same time, its revolutionary stance and vanguardist ideology repeatedly clashed with autonomous base-level organizations. Henry Pease, for his part, had been influenced by progressive Christian ideas and in the 1980s became a chief representative of the large independent block within the Peruvian left. As such, he developed into the most prolific proponent of the "new ways of doing politics" that he saw represented by popular movements. In the mid-1980s, he served as deputy mayor of Metropolitan Lima under Alfonso Barrantes, where he was instrumental in pushing new forms of popular participation in local politics. Following the breakup of Izquierda Unida, Pease joined the Unión para el Perú led by former UN Secretary General Javier Pérez de Cuellar.

The revolutionary approach, which dominated toward the beginning of the 1980s and experienced a resurgence as the decade grew to a close, was nurtured by a deep skepticism of democracy (Adrianzén 1990). The transition from authoritarian to electoral regimes was welcomed, but representative democracy was at the same time faulted for being unable to change the underlying class divisions that were seen as the root causes of widespread poverty, social injustice, and international dependency. Therefore, representative democracy from the revolutionary vantage point amounted to little more than a formal electoral game in which different factions of the ruling classes competed with one another for power. Since achieving fundamental socioeconomic and political change was considered impossible within the confines of this system, the revolutionary approach advocated its ultimate destruction and replacement by a system based on the self-government of the people (*autogobierno de masas*), that is, the establishment of direct democracy exercised via popular movements.

The replacement of the old system, or the *viejo estado* (Diez 1992, 82),[11] would be brought about by a broad popular alliance, comprising popular movements, as well as trade unions and leftist political parties. It could, but

11. This kind of jargon is reminiscent of Sendero Luminoso. The fact that Diez began using terms such as *viejo estado* or *colchón* (mattress), which for him described the role of the Left as a buffer between the social movement and the state, can be read as an attempt to regain lost ideological terrain.

would not necessarily have to take the form of a violent overthrow. At least in theory, this popular alliance would be completely democratic, since it would be governed by its members, who would exercise their decision-making power through the popular movements or other organizations they belonged to. However, while the revolutionary standpoint explicitly denounced the old vanguardism of the 1970s and advocated political pluralism within the Left as well as intraparty democracy (Diez 1987, 80–81), there was a definite tension in its view of the relations between leftist parties and popular movements. This tension was evidenced by the fact that while all decision-making power theoretically derived from the bases, it was deemed equally important that the political party or parties of the Left *led* the alliance. Quite frequently, the revolutionary approach emphasized that "the" popular movement had to be "constructed" and "fortified" by the political parties of the Left (Diez 1990, 32). Such a process of constructing and shaping popular movements could of course throw them open to political manipulation of all kinds and could turn them into more or less dependent support bases.

With respect to democratic political institutions, among them local governments, the revolutionary approach essentially adopted a tactical stance. These institutions were considered "trincheras al servicio del pueblo" (trenches in the service of the people) (Delgado Silva 1982a, 8); in other words, they were seen as political spaces inside the system which could and should be occupied by the Left to prepare for its ultimate transformation. Basically, this could take two forms. On the one hand, political institutions, such as local governments, could serve as tribunes in the sense that they would be used to denounce the inadequacy of the existing institutional system in dealing with the most pressing problems of the popular majorities. On the other hand, by participating in political institutions, popular movements could acquire the organizational experience needed to administer their own affairs. In this context, local alliances between popular movements and leftist-controlled local governments, while developing within the existing institutional framework, were considered embryonic forms of a future *autogobierno popular.*

The radical-democratic stance, which was prevalent toward the mid-1980s and later shared an uneasy coexistence with the revolutionary approach, concurred with the latter view that fundamental changes were needed to alter the situation of the popular majorities. However, it assumed that such changes were attainable *within* the context of representative democracy, even if the required reforms would be radical and cut to the bone of the existing political system.[12] In fact, the procedural guarantees and civil liberties on which representative democracy is based were seen as a precondition for such reforms. Therefore, the radical-democratic approach did not propose to replace, but to *supplement* representative democracy with various forms of direct democracy. In essence, this would enable popular movements, which were seen as the expression of democratic practices that have developed within civil society, to participate directly in the political system and thereby help democratize political parties and institutions. The revalorization of local governments, as well as political decentralization at all levels, were considered important elements in such reforms, producing a redistribution of power away from the central state and established political actors and opening up the political institutions to participation from below (Pease 1984).

Local governments fulfilled two specific functions in the radical-democratic project. First, instead of being used primarily as tribunes, they would serve as an institutional means to pragmatically address some of the basic needs of the popular sector, thereby demonstrating the capacity of the Left to govern (Pease 1991). Given existing class divisions and interinstitutional power differentials, this would almost certainly entail confrontations with higher levels of government and other political actors over the allocation of sufficient powers and resources. However, in contrast to the revolutionary approach, these conflicts would stay within the boundaries of representative democracy, even if leftist local governments should decide to resort to extra-institutional forms of struggle, such as marches or demonstrations. Second, exercising power at the local level would give the Left a chance to build its political support base, or to put it in Gramscian terms, to lay the foundations for political hegemony and to pave the way for an eventual takeover of political power at the national level. In contrast to the revolutionary view, this form of political hegemony was not to be understood simply as a euphemism for rallying "the" popular movement behind the party or parties of the Left. Rather, popular movements were viewed as equal partners in this endeavor. Crucially, they were credited with moving the Left away from the vanguardist ideologies of the 1970s and toward a reconceptualization of how to "do politics" (Pease 1983a, 36), a view which reflected a growing recognition for the autonomy of individual popular movements as well as for the often heterogeneous viewpoints they expressed.

12. Consequently, in an interview by the author, Henry Pease insisted on labeling his approach "revolutionary," despite his renunciation of revolutionary violence (Pease 1992).

Both perspectives, the revolutionary as well as the radical-democratic one, are crucial for an understanding of the Peruvian left's stance toward local government and popular participation in the 1980s and beyond. Obviously, the two perspectives were not always as clearly spelled out and distinguished from each other in political reality. Reflecting the complicated alignments and realignments within the Peruvian left, which produced numerous ideological and programmatic shifts, they frequently appeared muddled, informing the programmatic stance of a particular leftist party or the policies of a specific local government sometimes simultaneously, if not to the same degree. Obviously, ambiguities and contradictions could also result from tactical considerations, inducing political leaders to clothe relatively moderate goals in radical political language so as not to lose mass support, or to hide an uncompromisingly antisystem stance behind somewhat more conciliatory rhetoric in order to justify competing in elections over political spaces inside the system.

Nevertheless, the revolutionary view was clearly dominant in the early 1980s, and it informed the politics of the five district governments in Metropolitan Lima that the Left controlled during this period.

Leftist Local Governments in Lima, 1981–1983

The first municipal elections after the return to democratic rule, which took place in November 1980,[13] ended with a qualified success for the Peruvian left. Only six months after its crushing defeat in the general elections of May of the same year, the Left regained a considerable share of the popular vote, enabling it to win a number of mayoralties at the provincial and the district level all across the country, five of them in low-income or "popular" districts of Metropolitan Lima. The Left's defeat in the May 1980 elections, coming only two years after its surprisingly strong showing in the 1978 elections for the Constituent Assembly, was partially a result of its ambivalent stance toward representative democracy and the institutions of the new regime (Nieto 1983). Even more importantly, the Left's tendency to air its differences in public, engaging in often arcane disputes over ideology and strategy, alienated voters and cast a stark light on its internal divisions and contradictions. Conversely, when the Left closed ranks and managed to unite under the banner of Izquierda Unida some months later, this newfound unity

13. For a detailed analysis of the results of this election, see Tuesta 1983.

immediately met with success at the polls, proving that the Left still had significant popular support, especially at the local level.[14]

Another reason for the weakness of the Left in the May 1980 elections—which it shared with the remaining contenders—was of course the impressive showing of Fernando Belaúnde's Acción Popular (AP). AP had boycotted the Constituent Assembly elections in 1978 on the grounds that the military regime that had disposed the democratically elected AP government in 1968 was still in power, only to score a decisive victory two years later. In the municipal elections of November 1980, Acción Popular repeated this performance, winning the majority of constituencies and virtually sweeping Lima. At the same time, the Peruvian left made an electoral comeback of sorts, achieving two important objectives simultaneously. On the one hand, the Left consolidated its presence on the electoral scene as the second-strongest political force in terms of the popular vote, while at the same time opening the door to gaining a foothold in the institutional system. On the other hand, and maybe more importantly, the remarkable turnaround of its electoral fortunes just months after the formation of the electoral alliance Izquierda Unida, served as a stark reminder to the Peruvian left of the absolute necessity to maintain organizational, if not always programmatic, unity.

Nevertheless, when the five victorious mayoral candidates of Izquierda Unida assumed their offices in the low-income districts of Comas, Carabayllo, San Martín de Porres, El Agustino, and Ate-Vitarte, they took on no easy task. For the first time in its history, the Peruvian left, which had emerged from the antimilitary struggle of the 1970s profoundly skeptical of representative democracy and marked by a political style of confrontation and mass mobilization, found itself in a position to assume the role of government, to administer resources, and to exercise power, albeit on a very limited scale. While there had been little quarrel within the Peruvian left before the elections about the necessity of occupying such "political spaces," there was little consensus afterward on how to fill them. Not surprisingly, it proved difficult to reconcile a predominantly antisystem rhetoric and ideology, often centered around the construction of an autonomous *poder popular* outside the institutions of the democratic state, with the requirements of public office, that is, with the necessity of finding solutions for the basic needs of the population from within these very institutions.

14. Henry Dietz points out that throughout the 1980s, the urban poor were more likely to vote for the Left in local than in presidential races. The Left's success was also helped by different electoral rules facilitating victory in multiparty races (Dietz 1985; 1989).

From 1981 to 1983, the tension between these two poles gave rise to that particular outlook on local politics and popular participation I call the revolutionary approach.

Revolutionary Local Politics in Practice

From a theoretical point of view, the principal choices and dilemmas of the revolutionary approach were fairly obvious, and its main protagonists were acutely aware of them. In a frequently cited work, Luis Chirinos (Chirinos 1980) questioned the purportedly democratic character of the local government reforms contained in the Constitution of 1979 and subsequent legal norms. In reality, Chirinos contended, these reforms were designed to deflect the demands of the popular sectors from the central state to the municipalities, thereby creating "the illusion that the fundamental problems and contradictions of the capitalist system could be solved in the municipal realm."[15] At the same time, the Left needed to capture the municipalities in its struggle to win power, transforming them into bridgeheads inside the political system and using them as sounding boards to amplify popular demands and to challenge the central government. Others echoed Chirinos's views, often putting an even stronger emphasis on the role of local governments as a tool in the anticapitalist struggle (Calderón 1980a; Delgado Silva 1982a; Rojas Huaroto 1982).[16]

Popular participation played a key part in this strategy by strengthening the links between leftist-controlled municipalities and urban popular movements. Taking part in the local decision-making process and gaining experience in the management of local policies and programs, urban popular movements would gradually become equal partners of the municipal administration. Ultimately, public forums practicing direct democracy could effectively take the place of the institutions of representative democracy, thereby laying the groundwork for popular self-government or *autogobierno popular* (Távara 1983).

While the revolutionary approach was largely rooted in ideological and strategic considerations, the institutional and economic environment for local politics rendered such a confrontational strategy more plausible. First of all, the Ley Orgánica de Municipalidades, D.L. No. 051 of 1981, which

15. All translations in this chapter are mine.
16. Chirinos, Calderón, and Delgado always recognized the need for pragmatic reforms and later drew closer to social-democratic ideas.

had been inspired by a very narrow interpretation of the provisions of the Constitution of 1979, severely limited the autonomy of local governments and therefore did not go much beyond the authoritarian conception of local governments as dependencies of the central government. Essentially, D.L. No. 051 did not see the municipalities as either autonomous or as local *government* in the true senses of the words, but as dependent "service enterprises" at the base of a hierarchy headed by the central government (Delgado and Olivera 1983; Mejía 1990, 122–24). Consequently, D.L. No. 051 stressed managerial and bureaucratic aspects of local government, such as administrative reform and the effective management of urban services, over other issues, such as democratic institutional reform. City councillors, for example, were kept from interfering directly in the municipal administration, which was controlled by the mayor and his *director municipal,* a newly created position to oversee the administration. In the field of urban services, local governments were reduced to mere appendages of the central government agencies and as such made unable to fulfill their constitutional role as autonomous agents of development.

Apart from these legal constraints, local governments, especially at the district level, had virtually no independent resource base at the beginning of the 1980s and were therefore almost totally dependent on transfer payments from higher levels of government. While resources were severely limited to begin with, by the acute economic crisis of the early 1980s, the five leftist-controlled district governments found themselves in an even more difficult situation. Both the provincial government of Metropolitan Lima as well as the national government and its agencies were in the hands of Acción Popular, and there was little hope for municipalities governed by Izquierda Unida to increase their share of the resource pie through interinstitutional bargaining. Since D.L. No. 051 had only recently been passed by the AP national government and quick changes in the overall political panorama seemed improbable, given the institutional dominance of AP, this situation was unlikely to change. Consequently, it made sense to push for greater municipal autonomy as well as an increase in municipal resources by using extra-institutional means, even if only to ensure effective and efficient local government.[17]

17. Potentially, this would apply not only to leftist-led, but to all local governments. It is no surprise, therefore, that the AP-led provincial government of Lima under Eduardo Orrego pushed for a replacement of D.L. No. 051, which later resulted in the promulgation of the new Ley Orgánica, Ley No. 23852 by the national government. I will explain how this law affected the situation of local governments in the following chapter.

A further handicap for the practice of the five leftist-led district governments was the fact that D.L. No. 051 severely restricted the right to popular participation, which had previously been guaranteed by the Constitution of 1979. It did so in two ways: first, by failing to specify the concrete mechanisms through which the rights of initiative and of information would be exercised and, more importantly, by refusing to recognize existing popular movements as the legitimate agents of popular participation. Instead, D.L. No. 051 stipulated that any organized participation of the population had to be channeled through *juntas de vecinos* or *comités comunales* specifically created for this purpose. These new committees, whose basic role was to ensure that the population contributed their labor to municipal projects and to supervise the provision of services by the local government, were completely lacking in autonomy, since the municipal council determined their composition as well as their precise functions. In other words, these *comités* were to be means by which the municipal government would bypass existing popular organizations.

Faced with such significant constraints, it was not easy for the five leftist district governments to implement even parts of their strategy. Accepting the premise that local governments were part of the state and therefore subject to its laws (Távara 1983, 251), they nevertheless stretched existing legal norms and institutional provisions to the limit, notably to create more space for popular participation. Several instruments were used to achieve this end (Chirinos 1986, 6–11; 1991, 101–5; Rojas Julca 1989, 10–13). For example, the municipal governments held meetings that brought together the mayor, the district councillors, and popular organizations, the so-called *cabildos abiertos*. These reunions, which took place once or twice in each district during the period from 1981 to 1983, were principally intended as a means to inform and consult the population about the policies of the municipal government. To participate, popular organizations simply had to register with the municipal government prior to the event; no further restrictions were imposed on them.

The *asambleas populares,* or popular assemblies, fulfilled a similar function as the *cabildos abiertos,* with the important difference that they were open to the population at large. As a consequence, the role of popular organizations was somewhat diminished and the municipal authorities, especially the mayor, could exert greater control over the proceedings. Victor Abregú, a neighborhood leader in the district of El Agustino, recalled in an interview with the author:

> The *asambleas populares* . . . were meant to express the will of the community as a whole and at times to be above the authority even

of the mayor. . . . This idea led to problems in its implementation because . . . [the popular assemblies] became forums for political confrontation, as opposed to the development of programs and . . . participation in decision making by the municipal government. . . . Furthermore, they served to legitimize decisions made by the political group in power and for which they needed some social support. . . . This alienated the common popular leader . . . and left only the political leaders that appeared to be representatives of a certain zone because they lived there, whereas in reality they weren't, they were just "un vecino mas" [one more neighbor]. (Abregú 1992)

Another form of popular participation, and maybe the most far-reaching one of all, was the *comisiones mixtas*. These joint commissions were composed of representatives of the respective municipality as well as of popular movements, mostly neighborhood movements, again without imposing restrictions on their participation. The commissions, which had often grown out of the *cabildos abiertos* just discussed had the mandate to develop a common strategy as well as to coordinate the activities of the municipal government and the neighborhood organizations in their demands on the central government and its agencies for improvements in urban infrastructure and services. Typically, the *comisiones mixtas* would organize mass mobilizations and marches that were openly supported by the local district government, thereby putting pressure on central authorities, often with surprisingly positive results. In Comas and Carabayllo, for example, the *comisiones mixtas* generated enough pressure to make SEDAPAL, an agency of the central government, accept bids for the execution of works designed to improve the provision of the two districts with piped water and sewers, as well as to assign sufficient resources. In San Martín de Porres, a *comisión mixta* had some success in speeding up the process of granting land titles to residents of this district (Chirinos 1991, 102–3).

More significant than their relative success in having their demands heard, the *comisiones mixtas* helped to alter the hitherto dominant relation between local governments and the population. On the one hand, by investing long-standing popular demands, which previously had been expressed chiefly outside the political system, with the authority and prestige of the institution of local government, these demands obviously gained force and respectability. Moreover, by recognizing the existing popular organizations as the legitimate representatives of the population and its demands and by refraining from applying the provisions of D.L. No. 051 concerning the *juntas de vecinos* and the *comités comunales,* the district governments elevated the stature of these organizations; in other words, they strengthened the agents of popular participation. This new attitude on the part of the local authorities allowed for a greater degree of cooperation between different popular movements, which had previously often operated in complete isolation from one another. At the same time, local governments themselves gained legitimacy and prestige in the eyes of the population, if only as efficient instruments in the struggle to address its basic demands.

From Protest to Proposal: The Shift to a Radical-Democratic Strategy

The five leftist municipalities managed to push the frontiers of popular participation further than D.L. No. 051 and the ruling Acción Popular party had ever intended, but they did not overcome certain limitations. For one thing, popular participation essentially remained restricted to neighborhood organizations, which had played an important role in the mass struggles of the 1970s. Other popular movements and their concerns, particularly survival movements and other women's movements, were effectively excluded, in part because they were still relatively weak. As a consequence, relatively narrow demands related to urban services and infrastructure predominated, while more complex problems were rarely tackled, and the difficult question of how to use popular participation to democratize the municipal administration itself was not even addressed.

In addition, the participatory structures developed between 1981 and 1983 were poorly institutionalized and therefore lacked permanence. The municipal councils and especially the mayors had important discretionary powers over when to activate them, and there were instances in which the municipal authorities demonstrated a certain *verticalismo,* or in other words, a tendency to interfere with the autonomy of popular movements and impose some political control on them from above (Rojas Julca 1989, 12).[18] The position of the district mayors was particularly strong, and some of them tried to use participatory mechanisms to shore up their own personal support bases (Chirinos 1991, 106). Their relative freedom to develop such practices was substantially enhanced by the fact that the local committees of Izquierda

18. Consequently, Luis Chirinos qualifies this kind of popular participation as "collaborative" and not truly democratic (Chirinos 1991, 105). He distinguishes between four different kinds of participation, namely, participation by delegation (i.e., elections), subordinate participation, collaborative participation, and democratic participation (Chirinos 1991, 89–94).

Unida proved to be almost inoperative after the elections and therefore could exercise only little control (Salcedo 1981, 94–95).

In a political culture permeated by deep-rooted authoritarian and clientelist traditions, such tendencies are perhaps not surprising, and they were certainly not confined to the political parties of the Left. However, at least to some extent, they flowed directly from the vanguardist ideological orientations that dominated the thinking of the Peruvian left at the time. As was explained above, these orientations entailed a certain paternalism or what José Távara, the district mayor of Carabayllo from 1981 to 1983, called a "pedagogical and constructive . . . relation" with popular movements (Távara 1983, 253), in the sense that the Left considered it its responsibility to build and lead them. It is not hard to see how such attitudes could enter into conflict with the otherwise professed respect for the absolute autonomy of popular movements (Távara 1983, 252–53), especially in cases of disagreement over goals and strategy. The fact that the five district mayors themselves had been members of urban popular movements before running for public office did little to change these attitudes and did not significantly increase the weight of these movements in their relations with the local administrations.

More so than the inherent contradictions in its view of popular participation, the underlying strategic dilemmas of the revolutionary approach proved decisive for its ultimate undoing. As I have explained, the revolutionary approach was based on the assumption that meaningful changes in the situation of the popular majorities were impossible within the framework of representative democracy. Consequently, in order to be plausible, the revolutionary approach had to show that democratic institutions did not and could not produce the desired results. As long as the Left was operating on the margins of the political system, such a stance was relatively unproblematic, but it became increasingly difficult to maintain once the Left had decided to become a part of the very system it had disparaged. This is of course the situation that the five leftist-controlled district governments found themselves in. To maintain a credible antisystem stance under these conditions, the Left had little choice but to opt for a confrontational strategy vis-à-vis the central government, highlighting deficiencies and shortcomings instead of offering practical solutions.

The main difficulty with this perspective was that it proved to be unable to address the problems that the inhabitants of the five districts were faced with every day. Given the urgency of these problems, it became less and less possible to defend a confrontational strategy that essentially postponed practical solutions to the distant future. Consequently, a more pragmatic, reform-oriented approach slowly began to replace the old antisystem stance. This change was helped along by the fact that the Left, which before 1980 had never been involved in institutional politics, was now able to look back on some concrete experiences and was less equivocal in its condemnation of representative democracy. Furthermore, by 1983 the political panorama had significantly changed. Popular support for Acción Popular had dwindled and Izquierda Unida began to look more and more like a serious contender in the upcoming municipal and maybe even the next national elections. With its electoral prospects looking brighter, the Left began to tone down its antisystem rhetoric and to move away from some of its more radical positions. Grooming themselves for a possible future role in government, leftist politicians put more and more emphasis on concrete policy proposals and stressed the capacity of the Left to govern within the existing representative democratic system.

This shift, which has been labeled the move from protest to proposal (see Calderón and Valdeavellano 1991, 13–30), had important consequences for the Left's view of local government. With the likelihood of revolutionary change seeming ever more remote, and a leftist municipal administration or even a leftist national government being a distinct possibility, it no longer made much sense for the Left to see local governments merely as platforms in its struggle against a political system that it had found difficult to penetrate and impossible to topple. Instead, the Left began to portray itself as capable of governing from inside the existing political institutions. This new approach to local government became the hallmark of the new administration of Metropolitan Lima following Izquierda Unida's victory in the 1983 municipal elections.

five

the barrantes administration of metropolitan lima, 1984–1986

The municipal elections for new provincial and district councils of November 1983 continued the upward trend in the electoral fortunes of the Peruvian left that had begun with the municipal elections of November 1980. Izquierda Unida was able to increase its overall share of the popular vote from 23.90 percent to 28.83 percent (Tuesta 1985, 117) and to win twenty-two new provincial councils—the most significant of them being Lima and Cuzco—while only losing four it had held previously, among them Arequipa. With this triumph,

Izquierda Unida stabilized its position as the second-strongest electoral force in the country, only slightly behind APRA, which had made even more significant gains to replace Acción Popular at the top of the electoral pyramid.[1]

Without any doubt, the Left's victory in Metropolitan Lima was one of the most significant outcomes of the elections. Led by its chairman and mayoral candidate Alfonso Barrantes, Izquierda Unida took 36.63 percent of the popular vote at the metropolitan level, as well as nineteen of forty-one city districts (Tuesta 1985, 176).[2] By winning the nation's capital, which concentrated a third of the country's population and an even larger share of its industrial and financial resources, the Peruvian left, for the first time in its history, had a relevant institutional forum to put its political program into practice. Moreover, given the centrality of the national capital in the overall political framework, its special status among Peruvian municipalities according to the Ley Orgánica de Municipalidades, Ley No. 23853, and the almost inevitable repercussions political events in Lima had on the national political scene, many leftists saw in the municipal elections a warm-up for the struggle for overall political hegemony that was shaping up between APRA and Izquierda Unida in anticipation of the national elections of 1985. Not surprisingly, therefore, the IU victory in Lima was greeted enthusiastically by the leaders of the leftist alliance, many of whom took the defeat of the ruling center-right Acción Popular as proof that the popular masses had at last come to accept the Left as their natural political representation, even as they acknowledged that APRA also had a claim on the popular vote (Bernales 1983, 86).[3]

However, if it wanted to win nationwide elections in the future, the Peruvian left first had to meet a twofold challenge in the more immediate term. On the one hand, it needed to demonstrate its ability to govern from within the institutional framework of representative democracy. What this meant was that the Left had to find pragmatic solutions for the main problems facing the Peruvian capital, particularly in the fields of public nutrition and health, public hygiene and garbage disposal, water supply, transport, and informal com-

---

1. The strong showing of APRA in 1983 foreshadowed Alan García's victory in the presidential elections of 1985 and APRA's subsequent dominance of Peruvian politics from the mid-1980s to the end of the decade. See Graham 1992 for a more detailed analysis of this period.

2. According to electoral law, the winning party was accorded the mayoralty as well as the absolute majority of seats in the municipal council, even if its share of the popular vote was below 50 percent.

3. Not all leaders of Izquierda Unida shared this optimism. Alfonso Barrantes, for example, opined that "not all of those who protest against the economic policy of the government can be identified with the ideas of the left" (Barrantes 1984, 222).

merce. Only if the Left could demonstrate that it was capable of administering the *gobierno chico*, or the small government, of Metropolitan Lima, was there a chance that the electorate would later entrust it with the greater responsibility of leading the national government. Seen against this background, it is no surprise that Alfonso Barrantes, the new mayor of Lima and presidential hopeful of Izquierda Unida, was at pains to dispel the public image of the Left as a force of confrontation and disorder, promising instead to lead a government of "order, discipline, and responsibility" (Barrantes 1983a, 30).[4]

Furthermore, in order to win elections at the national level, the Peruvian left needed to broaden its support base beyond the popular sector. Even in the municipal elections of 1983, the Left failed to attract more than one-third of the popular vote nationwide. Consequently, if it wanted to gain a majority across the country, it had to try to attract votes from other social groups, particularly the middle classes, and to strike alliances with other political actors. In order to achieve these goals, it was imperative for the Left to convince others of its willingness to compromise and to work for the broadest possible consensus. Its campaign slogan, *Lima—una ciudad para todos*, as well as the fact that the new municipal administration favored democratic openness and professional efficiency over political allegiance, clearly expressed such a willingness.[5]

4. As a highly visible public figure, Barrantes has given numerous interviews to periodicals such as *Caretas, Debate, La República,* and *Quehacer,* some of which are included in Barrantes 1984. From the early 1980s on, these interviews show him progressively moving away from a revolutionary position to espouse much more moderate views. While continuing to use fairly radical language, describing himself at various points as a Marxist-Leninist and an admirer of Joseph Stalin, he defines himself first and foremost as a follower of José Carlos Mariátegui, indicating a commitment to pluralism and tolerance of opposing viewpoints. Interestingly, Mariátegui is claimed by *all* factions of the Peruvian left as an intellectual precursor (Vanden 1986; Mariátegui 1971). Furthermore, when probed on the depth of his loyalty to some basic tenets of Marxism-Leninism and Stalinism, his loyalty often seemed tenuous at best. In one interview, for example, Barrantes concedes that he is willing to adopt from Stalin only the "positive sides," that is, his contribution to the resistance against Nazi Germany and the construction of socialism in the Soviet Union (Barrantes 1983a, 29). In another interview, he admits that he sees in Marxism-Leninism merely a method of analysis, without necessarily subscribing to some of its key principles, such as the dictatorship of the proletariat or the one-party state (Barrantes 1983b, 28–29).

5. Obviously, while tactical considerations with respect to its electoral fortunes undoubtedly played a role in what Neira has called the "legitimization" of the Peruvian left (Neira 1984), it would certainly be too simple to attribute this shift to tactical considerations alone. As we have seen in the previous chapter, it represented a genuine redefinition of the ideological orientations of large parts of the Peruvian left, which can only be properly understood against the background of a highly complex and conflictive process of ideological change, in which the Latin American left as a whole thoroughly redefined its stance toward representative democracy.

At the same time, however, it was clear that such an approach implied a certain trade-off of popular sector interests against those of other political actors. In fact, it was maybe the most obvious risk of the leftist strategy that in order to gain respectability and legitimacy, it would have to go too far in compromising its agenda for change, which in the end would make it indistinguishable from other political forces.[6] Obviously, the Left could not be content with proving its capacity to govern, if this meant nothing more than being as good an administrator as other political forces. Likewise, it was of little use for the Left to demonstrate its ability to arrive at compromises with others, if it ended up sacrificing most of its ideas and goals. Consequently, the second major challenge facing the Left was to prove that despite the limitations of an institutional strategy, as well as the relative weakness of local governments in the overall institutional framework, it was nevertheless possible to achieve fundamental political, social, and economic changes in the interest of the popular majorities. Apart from the implementation of a number of wide-ranging social and economic reforms, the Left also needed to show that an institutional strategy would substantially widen the possibilities for popular participation.

Given these inherent risks and trade-offs, it is perhaps not surprising that significant sectors within the Peruvian left opposed a shift to an institutional strategy and continued to advocate a more radical approach to municipal politics. The resulting conflicts pitted the radical wing of the Left, espousing what was previously called a revolutionary approach to local politics, against those advocating a reformist or radical-democratic agenda. In the run-up to the 1983 elections, these conflicts produced some bitter splits and divisions within Izquierda Unida over the selection of candidates for municipal office, with each of the seven member organizations fighting over the nomination of candidates for councillors and mayors on the IU slate. In several cases, such as in Arequipa, Tacna, and Moquegua, these conflicts could not be resolved, and Izquierda Unida ran two or even three separate lists, presenting the political right with some unlikely victories (Taylor 1990, 110). Even after the elections, tensions between radical and moderate forces continued to fester, producing a major crisis in Izquierda Unida's National Committee over the question of how to react to a string of urban land occupations and violent student demonstrations in Lima. Barrantes and his supporters within the Partido Socialista Revolucionario (PSR) and the Partido Comunista Revolucionario (PCR) argued that these events were costing the Left support and allowed the Right to mount

---

6. This is a common dilemma for leftist political parties. See Przeworski 1985.

a hostile propaganda campaign, while his detractors in the Vanguardia Revolucionaria (VR) insisted that the homeless and students were in need of support. The conflict escalated when Barrantes attempted to relegate the National Committee to monthly instead of weekly meetings and threatened to resign from the IU presidency and the mayoralty of Lima when his proposal was rejected. He later agreed to continue in both offices (Taylor 1990, 110).

Underlying these quarrels were deeply conflicting views over the role of the municipal government in the overall political strategy of the Left, as well as differing views over the correct tactic to adopt in the run-up to the 1985 presidential and parliamentary elections. While Barrantes and his backers, notably deputy mayor Henry Pease, defended a pragmatic approach, focusing on the Left's capacity to govern and its ability to strike pragmatic alliances with others around limited goals,[7] radicals such as Javier Diez Canseco, the leader of Vanguardia Revolucionaria (VR) and later of the Partido Unificado Mariateguista (PUM), continued to advocate a strategy of confrontation with the central government. According to Diez, the popular support that the Left had received in the 1983 municipal elections should have been used to "impose [the Left's] triumph in the streets" (Diez 1983, 88). In other words, it should have been channeled into street mobilizations that would have forced the ruling AP government to abandon its neoliberal economic policies, as well as helped the Left to concentrate forces for the 1985 elections and beyond. Diez's views were echoed by PCP leader Guillermo Herrera, who saw in the 1983 municipal elections merely a first, if crucial step on the "vía de la revolución peruana" (Herrera 1983, 90), that is, on the way to the Left's takeover of power at the national level and the subsequent road to socialism.

What finally tilted the balance in favor of an institutional strategy was the fact that the prospect of electoral victory nationwide and a future leftist government lent unity of purpose to the delicate endeavor that Izquierda

7. Overall, Barrantes's and Pease's political views were quite different. In a personal interview with the author (Barrantes 1991), Barrantes portrayed himself as a realistic and pragmatic politician for whom ideology came second to concrete achievements. Consequently, he opposed attempts by radical sectors of the Left to use municipal resources for partisan ends—for example, by placing loudspeakers on the balcony of the Lima city hall during party rallies—stood up to leftist unions whose wage demands threatened to undermine the policies of the municipal government, and cultivated good relations with the president and other holders of high public office. While generally supporting these policies, Henry Pease placed much greater emphasis on a radical-democratic agenda and the expansion of popular participation in local politics. For him, these "new ways of doing politics," rooted in a dense social network of popular movements and sustained by decentralist policies, contained the seed of an alternative political project that could usefully complement representative democracy.

Unida was at the time. Alfonso Barrantes, who was probably the most influential figure on the Peruvian left in the mid-1980s, played a crucial role in this regard. While he was not himself a member of any of the parties that comprised Izquierda Unida, it was precisely his status as an independent that enabled him to stay above the fray of ideological struggles between different member parties and to rally the considerable number of militants without party affiliation within the alliance. In fact, it would probably not be an exaggeration to see in Barrantes the linchpin that held Izquierda Unida together, at least until the latter part of the decade when he himself took sides and contributed to its decline.[8] In sum, focusing on immediate electoral challenges helped to paper over internal controversies and to stave off the danger of reopening the divisive and sectarian debates of earlier years. At the same time, the internal conflicts continued to fester, and some prominent representatives of the radical wing, such as Javier Diez Canseco, continued to criticize the policies of the municipal government and the programmatic orientations of Izquierda Unida as a whole.

Effective Local Government, Social Reform, and Protagonismo Popular: A Radical-Democratic Approach to Local Politics

The Peruvian left's radical-democratic approach to local politics, which informed the political program of the new municipal government of Metropolitan Lima (Izquierda Unida 1983), rested on three principal pillars: an emphasis on the need for an effective and efficient local government in

---

8. In a personal interview with the author (Pease 1992), Henry Pease laid the blame for the breakup of the Izquierda Unida in 1989 squarely on Alfonso Barrantes. For Pease, Barrantes committed a fundamental error in exaggerating the programmatic and strategic conflicts within Izquierda Unida, overlooking the fact that most "radical" councillors were in fact loyal to him and that Izquierda Unida had proven its capacity to govern: "Demostramos una cosa que Barrantes no aprendió, que Izquierda Unida era capaz de gobernar." Consequently, instead of using his prestige as an independent and his considerable electoral appeal to keep the alliance together, Barrantes actively contributed to its breakup, siding with the reformist faction and against the majority of radicals and independents. His personal aloofness and reluctance to deal with intraleftist squabbles further undermined his stature. The breakup became unavoidable when the various groups failed to mend fences at Izquierda Unida's first congress in 1989 and subsequently ran two separate tickets in the presidential election of 1990, which was won by independent Alberto Fujimori. As in 1980, the results of intraleftist factionalism were devastating: Izquierda Unida's share of the vote was slashed in half, with Izquierda Socialista under Barrantes obtaining only 4.7 percent of the vote, and Izquierda Unida under Pease little more with 8.2 percent. For further details on the breakup of the Izquierda Unida and its consequences, see the following chapter.

order to address the principal problems facing the Peruvian capital; the *Programa Popular de Emergencia,* a social emergency program that was geared to alleviate the critical social and economic situation of a large part of the inhabitants of Lima; and an insistence on the need to democratize the municipal administration itself and widen the scope of popular participation in local government.

With respect to its diagnosis of the principal problems confronting Metropolitan Lima, Izquierda Unida differed surprisingly little from other political parties. In fact, since many of these problems were of a technical nature, there was relatively little quarrel between *técnicos,* or specialists, across the political spectrum over the policies that would best address them (Barrantes puede ganar 1983, 9–10).[9] The Left seemed well prepared to tackle these problems in a pragmatic and efficient manner: for over a year, a team of specialists, many of whom later became part of the municipal administration, had been involved in the elaboration of detailed policy proposals, an effort which resulted in the formulation of the *Programa de Gobierno Municipal* (Izquierda Unida 1983). But the new administration was also ready to work with officials from the existing municipal administration. In a personal interview with the author,[10] former mayor Barrantes recalled: "This is a tradition, when a [new] mayor comes in, all the directors hand in their resignations. [But] we said: All those directors stay who are honest and efficient. We don't care if they are from the Right, if they are antisocialist or anticommunist, we only require efficiency and honesty" (Barrantes 1991). The intention of the new local government to put pragmatism and professional efficiency above political criteria was further evidenced by its decision to appoint opposition councillors to head some commissions or newly created municipal secretariats if they seemed better qualified than their counterparts from the governing party. This stance was not unopposed within Barrantes's own coalition: "The big discussion was, now that we are going to have commissions, we are going to give concrete responsibilities to the APRA party, to Acción Popular, to the Partido Popular. And here we had exchanges . . . it's a sort of culture, a sort of behavior on the part of the Left . . . I always say, the Left has the vocation of a policeman—it wants to capture everything" (Barrantes 1991). Finally, the Barrantes government emphasized a spirit of cooperation and compromise with the opposition: for the most part, decisions in the municipal council were taken with votes from one or several

---

9. It is no surprise, therefore, that leftist leaders often give credit to the ex-mayor of Lima, Eduardo Orrego, for his administration from 1981 to 1983. Naturally, this does not mean they endorse the political program of his party, Acción Popular.

10. All translations in this chapter are mine.

opposition parties, despite the fact that Izquierda Unida held the absolute majority (Barrantes 1991; Pease 1992). The only party that turned down this offer was APRA, most likely because it competed with Izquierda Unida for some of the same segments of the electorate (Barrantes 1991).

In several other important respects, however, Izquierda Unida's approach to local government was fundamentally different from that of other political actors. First, the Left did not content itself with measuring the success of a municipal administration simply in terms of the *obras*, or public works, that it accomplished during its term in office. Instead of focusing exclusively on material results, the Left put more emphasis on the creation of the political and economic preconditions that would make the running of an efficient and effective local government actually possible. Apart from a thorough administrative restructuring of the municipal government of Lima itself, this basically meant confronting the central government over the reappropriation of powers and resources which the Constitution of 1979 had assigned to the municipalities, but which in practice had never been fully devolved. As I will explain later, Izquierda Unida was clearly more willing than other political parties to take a firm stance against the central government in order to increase the institutional weight of local governments.

Furthermore, the Left differed from other political actors in its determination to use local government as much as possible for social reform and the democratization of the state. On the one hand, it planned to make full use of local public institutions in order to alleviate the drastic social and economic inequalities of Peruvian society, which in its view prevented a majority of Peruvians from fully exercising their democratic rights as citizens (Barrantes 1984, 250). Among other things, it intended to prioritize public works to improve the infrastructure in popular neighborhoods and to speed up the distribution of land titles to squatters. Additionally, it planned to implement its social emergency program, which was designed to improve nutritional and public health standards, especially with regard to children (Izquierda Unida 1983, 15–24; Barrantes 1984, 187). The Vaso de Leche scheme, which will be discussed in more detail below, can be regarded as the centerpiece of this program.

Beyond these more traditionally reformist goals, the Left also planned to democratize the municipal administration by throwing it open to direct popular participation. Over and above the implementation of new and improved mechanisms to consult and inform the inhabitants of Lima about municipal policy, this involved giving urban popular movements decision-making powers in certain fields, even turning over to them the administration of entire programs, as well as putting urban popular movements in charge of supervising and controlling certain aspects of the municipal administration (Izquierda Unida 1983, 10–13). This attitude, which was described before as radical-democratic and which Henry Pease and others have labeled *protagonismo popular* (Pease 1983b, 27), grew out of the conviction that without such democratic input from the grassroots, the new leftist city administration would not only be unable to achieve its goals, but that before long, it would exhibit the same familiar traits of bureaucratic inefficiency, corruption, and authoritarianism as other public institutions at the local and national level.

In more specific terms, popular participation in municipal politics was to be expanded in four different ways, which can be distinguished according to the amount of decision-making power that they transfer to urban popular movements.[11] First, the Barrantes administration planned to implement an "open door policy," that is, to adopt an attitude of dialogue and consensus and to institute improved mechanisms for the information and consultation of the population about municipal policy. In so doing, it was hoped that the municipal administration would be made more accessible to the population as well as more receptive to its concerns. Second, representatives of urban popular movements were to be given limited control functions (*fiscalización*) in a number of fields that fell under municipal jurisdiction, such as public hygiene and garbage disposal, the administration of public markets, and so on. The purpose of these "public inspectors" was to either act as a substitute for municipal officials in cases where the municipal administration did not have enough personnel to carry out these functions, or to monitor municipal officials themselves. It was hoped that by subjecting municipal officials to such supervision from below, corruption and inefficiency in the municipal bureaucracy could be alleviated. Third, in a number of cases, urban popular movements were to coadminister entire programs together with the municipal government of Metropolitan Lima or with one of the district municipalities in the province. The most notable examples of this practice were the distribution of land titles to urban squatters and the Vaso de Leche program. By participating in joint program management, urban popular movements would exert considerable influence over the way these programs were run, while at the same time

11. See Chapter 2 for a discussion of the concept of participation. Rojas Julca (1989) and Chirinos (1991) provide comprehensive accounts of the specific policies that were enacted under the Barrantes administration in order to enhance popular participation.

relieving municipal administrations that were strapped for qualified personnel and financial resources and could not have administered these programs alone. Finally, the potentially most far-reaching aspect of popular participation was a variety of mechanisms that would allow urban popular movements to participate *directly* in the running of the municipal administration and in decisions that affected the overall direction of municipal policy. In the case of Metropolitan Lima, the *agencias municipales* in the central district of El Cercado were the most significant examples of this practice. It was hoped that these "municipal agencies" would unite the various neighborhood movements of the district and thereby serve as permanent interlocutors for the municipal administration.

All three elements of the leftist platform hinged for their success on the achievement of a common objective, namely, effective political decentralization and a substantial elevation of the institutional stature of local governments. As I explained in more detail in Chapter 2, the effectiveness and efficiency of local administrations depend to a large extent on the prior devolution of powers and resources from the central government, as well as on firm guarantees for their autonomy from central government interference. Clearly then, if Izquierda Unida wanted to make good on its promise of effective and efficient local government, as well as tackle its ambitious social reform program, it needed to be successful in its struggle with the central government to effectively appropriate the powers that local governments had only theoretically gained in the Constitution of 1979. Furthermore, the new municipal government had to brace itself for a protracted struggle with the central government and its agencies in fields of shared jurisdiction, such as urban services, urban transport, and so on. Finally, the new leftist administration had to make sure that any transfer of powers was backed by a corresponding transfer of resources. In other words, it had to be guaranteed that the central government would not simply divest itself of bothersome obligations by passing them on to local governments, without at the same time enabling them to actually fulfill their new responsibilities.

In order to accomplish its participatory goals, the new leftist city administration likewise depended on the prior strengthening of local governments as such. A stronger role for popular participation in local affairs did not make much sense without a meaningful devolution of powers and resources to local governments. Otherwise, there would be few programs worth participating in, and popular participation would risk remaining an empty ritual. Furthermore, as I explained in Chapter 2, popular participation needed to be given explicit legal and institutional content. In particular, existing urban popular movements needed to be recognized by the local administration as legitimate interlocutors, in order to better protect their autonomy. Furthermore, permanent and binding mechanisms had to be instituted that would make popular participation independent from political circumstances and the support of specific allies.

The main question was of course how these objectives could be achieved from within an institutional system that in the past had worked quite well to prevent such changes, by concentrating power at the top and by protecting the interests of the political and economic elites. The obstacles to such a project were considerable. In particular, the task of leading an efficient and effective local government, which was made complicated enough by the reluctance on the part of higher levels of government and other political actors to accord the municipalities the necessary powers and resources, was made even more difficult in a time of severe economic crisis. Given that resources were low and shrinking for all levels of government, a redistribution in favor of the municipalities would likely run into even fiercer opposition than usual. Naturally, this was also bound to affect the capacity of local governments to accomplish social reforms.

The participatory agenda faced even greater obstacles. Any genuine increase of popular participation, be it in the form of improved mechanisms for consultation and information or in the form of joint program management, was bound to increase the power of previously excluded social groups and was therefore likely to be opposed by the political elites. Moreover, popular participation that went further than that and included a transfer of decision-making powers from elected authorities to urban popular movements, could be seen as exceeding the confines of representative democracy as established in the Constitution of 1979. It was therefore likely to arouse even stiffer political resistance than the realization of other goals of the Barrantes administration, such as the reshuffling of prerogatives and resources between central and local institutions of government and the prioritization of popular concerns. The political compromises needed to overcome such resistance might very well leave popular participation stunted, which would raise some fundamental questions about how well an institutional strategy can promote popular participation in a hostile political environment.

However, despite the magnitude of these obstacles to a successful implementation of its political program, the position of the Barrantes administration was not quite as bad as it might seem. In fact, two major developments toward the beginning of its tenure significantly altered the legal and economic context of local politics in Peru. On the one hand, a new law governing municipal politics, the Ley Orgánica de Municipalidades, Ley No. 23853, considerably increased the institutional stature of local governments. Furthermore, the Barrantes administration was quite successful, against all odds, in its attempts to secure new and increased resources for local governments.

Local Organs of Government or Local Service Enterprises: Ley No. 23853 and the Struggle for Increased Local Resources

In comparison with the previous legal framework governing local politics in Peru, the new Ley Orgánica de Municipalidades, Ley No. 23853, significantly strengthened the position of local governments vis-à-vis the central authorities. Ley No. 23853 was enacted on 8 June 1984 to replace the short-lived D.L. No. 051, which had met with universal opposition from municipal governments across the political spectrum since it had been passed as a decree law by the national government on 15 March 1981.[12] The new law contained a number of important changes to the legal situation of the municipalities. Most importantly, Ley No. 23853 broke with the guiding principle of D.L. No. 051, which, as I explained in Chapter 4, considered local governments to be "service enterprises" that were essentially dependent on the central government. Contrary to this rather restrictive view of local government, article 2 of Ley No. 23853 explicitly recognized the character of the municipalities as "local organs of government" that are democratically elected and represent the political will of the inhabitants of a given locality. In so doing, Ley No. 23853 provided a much closer approximation of the principles that were expressed in articles 252 and 253 of the Constitution of 1979. Not only that, by recognizing the municipalities as local organs of government, Ley No. 23853 also sanctioned the view that power within the Peruvian political system did not emanate solely from the central government, but that it was shared to a certain extent by other organs of government.

12. As Castro-Pozo and Delgado point out, D.L. No. 051 unleashed a veritable "tide of profound discontent" (Castro-Pozo and Delgado 1989, 41), not only because it severely limited the powers of local governments, but also because the national government had failed to consult mayors and councillors over the new law, including those that belonged to the ruling party, Acción Popular. One of the most prominent opponents of D.L. No. 051 was Eduardo Orrego, then-mayor of Lima. See also Chapter 4.

Consistent with this view, the new law provided stronger guarantees for the autonomy of local governments and delineated their powers more clearly. Without recognizing the *political* autonomy of local governments explicitly, the municipalities were nevertheless accorded economic and administrative autonomy with regard to matters that fell within their jurisdiction.[13] Local governments were most notably put in charge of the development of their respective constituencies and the elaboration of corresponding development plans, in addition to the responsibilities that had traditionally fallen under the municipal purview, such as the administration of local public services, public hygiene and garbage disposal, and urban transport. Furthermore, local governments were made accountable for the management of their own financial resources, as well as given the right to determine their own internal administrative structures.

Despite these advances, Ley No. 23853 also presented a number of serious limitations. Maybe the most important drawback of the new law lay in its failure to separate clearly the prerogatives of the municipalities from those of other levels of government. Basically, Ley No. 23853 merely listed the responsibilities of local governments, often simply by restating the relatively general provisions of the Constitution of 1979. What the law did *not* do was to explain if and how the prerogatives of local governments would be affected in cases where other levels of government had been accorded similar responsibilities by different legal norms. Such cases of overlapping jurisdiction were numerous. Since Ley No. 23853 did not furnish clear legal guidelines for the resolution of interinstitutional conflicts, such conflicts had to be solved through negotiation.

The consequences of these omissions were serious. For one thing, because of a lack of joint planning, the activities of local and central government authorities were often uncoordinated or contradictory, if they did not duplicate one another. For example, former mayor Alfonso Barrantes complained in an interview with the author: "One of our major projects was to build the *troncales* [trunk roads] between the city and the popular districts. . . . Frequently, shortly after they were built, these roads were dug

13. Local governments were not explicitly given *political* autonomy in the Constitution of 1979, because a number of legislators in the Constituent Assembly feared that doing so would endanger the unity of the state and introduce a federalist element into the Peruvian political system. However, as Castro-Pozo and Delgado rightly remark, the fact that local governments exercise at least some of their functions and prerogatives independently goes to show that they enjoy a certain degree of *practical* political autonomy (Castro-Pozo and Delgado 1989, 39). By giving local governments economic and administrative autonomy, they were in fact put in a position to exercise the role of government in these fields.

up again by central government agencies in order to install water pipes, electricity lines, etc." (Barrantes 1991). More importantly, the failure of Ley No. 23853 to clearly define and delimit the respective prerogatives of different levels of government allowed the central government to bring its superior political and economic resources to bear and to shape the relationship in its favor. In more concrete terms, the lack of a clear delimitation of these prerogatives provided the central government with a pretext either to delay the devolution of powers to local governments, or more frequently, to continue interfering in municipal affairs. Obviously, this constituted a serious threat to local governmental autonomy and limited the capacity of the municipalities for integrated urban planning. The central government had several instruments at its disposal to carry out this practice: the administrative organs of the central government proper, such as the *prefecturas,* public enterprises; existing central government agencies; and new agencies specifically created for this purpose.

The examples of central government interference in municipal affairs during the Barrantes administration are legion. For instance, while the provision of local public services fell under local jurisdiction according to Ley No. 23853, the most important public services in the capital, particularly water supply, sewers, and electricity, continued to be provided by central government agencies such as SEDAPAL and ELECTROPERU. Consequently, these agencies were in a position to control the extent and the quality of service provision in the different *barrios* of Lima and could either thwart or at least hamper the efforts of the Barrantes administration to achieve improvements for the popular neighborhoods. Such interference in municipal affairs was not just the result of reluctance on the part of the central government to relinquish some of its powers or simple bureaucratic inertia. Rather, what was at stake, particularly in the capital city of Lima, which comprised about a third of the national electorate, was the political fallout from the success or failure of specific policies.

This was particularly evident in another notorious case of central government interference in municipal affairs, the so-called *tren eléctrico* (electric train). While urban transport was clearly a responsibility of the municipal government, the central government under Alan García proceeded to implement its own project of urban mass transportation in Lima without sufficiently coordinating its design and implementation with municipal authorities. According to former deputy mayor Henry Pease, this led to serious coordination problems and put in jeopardy a major World Bank credit that the city had secured previously:

This wasn't just a legal problem. In the agreement with the World Bank, we had a clause stipulating that any investment of more than 10 million U.S. dollars had to be agreed by both sides if it referred to an aspect of the urban development program. Now, exactly in the most important area, infrastructure, the World Bank obviously did not want to invest in roads if afterwards these would be destroyed again to make room for the electric train. I spoke to an exasperated World Bank official in 1986 who had just come out of a meeting ... and who told me: This is a country in reverse! First they execute something and *then* they modify it. (Pease 1992)

Again, the conflict was not just over who wielded authority over matters of urban transport, but also about the political capital that could be gained from a project of this magnitude.

Apart from often politically motivated interference in municipal affairs by the central government and its agencies, the lack of adequate resources did its part in preventing the municipalities from fully assuming their newly won powers and from living up to their role as autonomous local organs of government as prescribed in Ley No. 23853.[14] At the very beginning of its tenure, the Barrantes administration of Metropolitan Lima was immediately confronted with an acute crisis in the financial situation of the municipality. In part as a result of the economic downturn of the early 1980s, municipal revenues were at their lowest level since 1965 (Municipalidad de Lima, n.d., 55) and the deficit carried over from the previous administration under Eduardo Orrego amounted to almost 30 percent of the budget for 1984 (Delgado Silva 1991, 156). The immediate problems created by this financial shortfall seemed almost insurmountable; nevertheless, the Barrantes administration desperately needed to find solutions quickly if it did not want to risk its credibility at the very outset of its term in office. As conservative observers noted, not without glee, what was on the line was the proof that the Left was indeed fit to govern (Delgado Silva 1991, 152).

In addition to the financial difficulties inherited from the Orrego administration, Barrantes and his team had to contend with another familiar problem. Following the adoption of Ley No. 23853, the central government immediately delegated a series of responsibilities to the municipalities, without at the

---

14. For a detailed analysis of the financial situation of the Municipality of Metropolitan Lima, see Arnao and Meza 1990, as well as Delgado Silva 1991. Mejía (1990, 161) provides a list of laws and decrees regulating municipal financing from 1980 through 1987.

same time transferring the corresponding resources. The administration of Metropolitan Lima, for example, was suddenly saddled with the responsibility for several hundred employees in fields such as urban development and the maintenance of urban parks and gardens, but it was in no position to actually pay their salaries. Former deputy-mayor Henry Pease recalled in an interview with the author: "The municipality . . . had to come up with the salaries for all these people without having any additional income. We therefore proposed a series of twenty-two laws that assigned resources to the municipalities. We did not achieve this until December 1984" (Pease 1992).

After having been precarious during the first year in office of the new administration, the financial picture therefore changed somewhat in 1985, when the local government financing was put on a new footing by the Ley del Financiamiento, Ley No. 24030. The Barrantes administration had lobbied hard for the new law and for this purpose had joined forces with local governments of various political stripes from all over the country. Apart from the creation of several other new sources of income, the most notable change contained in Ley No. 24030 was the replacement of direct transfer payments by the central government with the Impuesto de Promoción Municipal, which consisted of a one-percent share of the Impuesto General a las Ventas (IGV), a value-added tax levied nationally. Until then, direct transfer payments had provided an essential supplement to resources raised by the municipalities themselves, such as various local taxes, service fees, and fines. By making the resource base of local governments less dependent on the budgetary discretion of the central government and by putting it on a more constant footing, Ley No. 24030 helped strengthen local autonomy and therefore increased the governmental capacity of the municipalities.

In addition to the new revenues created by Ley 24030, local governments gained another important source of income from a major World Bank loan, which had been negotiated before the municipal elections of November 1983 and which was finally signed by President Belaúnde after much foot-dragging at the end of 1984 (Pease 1992). Out of a total credit volume of about U.S.$140 million, more than 40 percent or U.S.$60.1 million was destined for Metropolitan Lima; U.S.$7.8 million was actually disbursed in 1985 and U.S.$16.3 million in 1986 (Pease and Jibaja 1989, 367; Portocarrero 1991, 187). Together with somewhat higher matching funds from the municipal government of Metropolitan Lima (Municipalidad de Lima, n.d., 55–56), most of which stemmed precisely from the new tax revenues created by Ley 24030, the funds provided by the World Bank were instrumental for a substantial increase of the capital basis of the municipal Fondo de Inversiones Metropolitanas (INVERMET).

Thanks to this boost of its resource base under the Barrantes administration, INVERMET, which had been created in 1979, took on increasing importance as the principal venue for municipal investment in the capital region. INVERMET funded investments in fields as diverse as culture, education, and sports, but most of its resources went into urban infrastructure projects, particularly new roads linking popular districts with other parts of Lima, the so-called *troncales,* and the refurbishing of existing roads in the city center (Allou 1989, 152–55). At the same time, the investment priorities of INVERMET were changed. While the more affluent districts continued to receive a sizable share of overall investments, a much higher portion than under the previous AP administration now went to the popular districts (Allou 1989, 152–55). As a result of its efforts to channel most of the new municipal resources directly into investments, while at the same time holding the line on operational expenses and salary increases, the Barrantes administration managed to significantly alter the traditional distribution of municipal expenses during the last two years of its tenure. While operational expenses had taken up the lion's share of municipal budgets from 1980 to 1983, leaving only slightly more than 20 percent for capital investments, this percentage rose to 43 percent in 1986 (Pease 1988, 51–52, 55; Allou 1989, 136–37).

On the downside, this budgetary firmness produced labor relations between the municipal government and its employees that were never easy. In total, there were seven strikes by unionized municipal employees during the Barrantes administration, more than under the previous or the two subsequent city administrations (Pease 1991, 34). In an interview with the author, Alfonso Barrantes criticized the unions for putting the immediate interests of their members, and especially their salaries, over the interests of the popular sector as a whole: "The first strike was very painful for me. . . . Despite the dialogue the workers struck. . . . Some leftist parties supported this strike. . . . The workers are interested only in their salaries. This is a deformation for which the 'irresponsible' Left is to blame. We as the municipality said . . . we are going to build a school for the children of the workers . . . but they don't see this as a demand. The only demand they have is for a raise in their salaries" (Barrantes 1991). Former deputy mayor Henry Pease echoed this view: "Those that called themselves leftists didn't act as such here. It was the same miserable pettiness as always" (Pease 1991, 34).

In spite of the relative amelioration of local government financing brought about by Ley No. 24030 and the World Bank loan, Peruvian municipalities in general continued to operate with extremely limited resources that left them far from being able to actually live up to their role as true local organs of government. In most cases, municipal resources were still barely sufficient to cover operational expenses as well as the most basic public services. Likewise, most Peruvian municipalities remained unable to hire qualified personnel in sufficient numbers to actually perform the tasks assigned to them by Ley No. 23853 (de Althaus 1986, 22–26). Even in the case of Metropolitan Lima, which had always attracted a disproportionate share of municipal resources and where the financial crisis was less severe, about 45 percent of all public investment in 1987 continued to be undertaken by the central government and its agencies (Mejía 1990, 171). Furthermore, the very fact that local government finances had depended more directly on taxes and fees since 1984 and no longer relied on direct transfer payments from the central government presented a novel problem. Aside from widespread tax evasion, about half of the population were simply too poor to pay any taxes at all (Pease and Jibaja 1989, 368). This situation persisted throughout most of the 1980s because of the economic crisis and severely limited the capacity of the municipalities to raise sufficient revenue. Consequently, any fundamental change in the financial situation of the municipalities hinged on a redistribution of public sector spending as a whole. In this respect, change was slow in coming, and the share of Peruvian local governments in overall public spending remained below 4 percent for most of the 1980s (Mejía 1990, 167).

Popular Participation Under Barrantes: Implementing the Radical-Democratic Agenda

Openings and Barriers to Popular Participation

Despite the remaining limitations of the legal framework for local politics and the still precarious state of municipal finances, the conditions for enlarging the scope for popular participation in local affairs were clearly more favorable than in previous years. While it was true that under the terms of Ley No. 23853, local governments did not have exclusive jurisdiction over certain aspects of municipal politics and often had to face central government interference, they obviously were in a better position than their predecessors at the district level. Moreover, in terms of popular participation, a shortage of resources can actually be a blessing in disguise, since it limits the scope for bureaucracy and clientelism. The fact that the Barrantes administration was strapped for cash meant that it could not simply set up a new administrative structure to deal with the needs of the popular sector, which sometimes creates new dependencies and reduces program beneficiaries to passive recipients of state support ("assistentialism"). Instead, the municipal administration had a strong incentive to delegate certain responsibilities to urban popular movements and to make use of their organizational structures. This was bound to strengthen their administrative capacities, as well as make them more relevant to the population at large.

At the same time, there existed certain legal, political, and institutional obstacles to an enlargement of popular participation in local politics. At the legal level, the most important difficulty lay in the fact that Ley No. 23853 did not go much beyond the restrictive framework provided by D.L. No. 051.[15] More specifically, Ley No. 23853 failed to stipulate clear and binding mechanisms for popular participation, and it did not recognize existing urban popular movements as its legitimate agents. Instead, it reiterated the provisions contained in D.L. No. 051, which prescribed the creation of new organizations for this purpose by the municipality, the so-called *juntas de vecinos*. As I explained in Chapter 4, these organisms were rejected by the population and never acquired much significance, since they lacked autonomy and were almost completely dependent on the municipal government. In a sense, therefore, Ley No. 23853 was an attempt to continue a longstanding tradition in Peruvian politics, in which the elevation of status and the potential material benefits popular participation entailed were coupled with a loss of autonomy for the organizations involved and the creation of clientelist links to the political authorities.

In order to break with these traditions and to guarantee the autonomy of urban popular movements participating in municipal politics, Izquierda Unida had promised during the electoral campaign that it would recognize existing urban popular movements as the legitimate interlocutors of the municipal government.[16] Obtaining some kind of legal recognition, which

15. Chirinos points to three minor advances of Ley No. 23853 over D.L. No. 051: its recognition of the *cabildos abiertos*, albeit in a very limited form and restricted to communities with no more than 3,000 inhabitants, the provision that rural communities formed on the basis of traditional customs can fulfill the functions of municipal agencies, and the right of local governments to consult the inhabitants of their jurisdiction over municipal policy (Chirinos 1991, 98–99).

16. This promise was contained in a proposal for a municipal by-law, which was part of a series of legal norms proposed by Izquierda Unida during the previous years. See Delgado Silva 1982b.

was a precondition for putting their participation on a more permanent and stable basis, had also been a long-standing demand on the part of urban popular movements, and the new municipal government needed to keep its campaign promise if it wanted to retain the support of the popular sector. However, given the limits of existing laws, especially the newly passed Ley No. 23853, the granting of full legal recognition, or *personería jurídica*, to all urban popular movements was impossible. Instead, the Barrantes administration decided to confer legal recognition only on neighborhood movements, and only with respect to their dealings with the municipal government of Metropolitan Lima. This was achieved by way of passing the municipal Ordenanza (by-law) No. 192 on 6 June 1984, which was based on a novel legal category somewhat at the margins of the law, the so-called *personería municipal*. In a personal interview with the author, Luis Chirinos Segura, then an adviser in the General Office for Neighborhood Participation, explained the rationale behind this measure as follows: "The main purpose [of Ordenanza No. 192] was to give legal recognition to neighborhood associations, which was not foreseen by the law. Accordingly, we 'invented' the concept of the *personería municipal*, which also enabled us to recognize not just one, but several associations in the same settlement" (Chirinos 1992). However, since Ordenanza No. 192 was not binding for other political actors, particularly the central government and its agencies, these actors could continue to challenge the legitimacy of the urban popular movements they were dealing with or set up competing organizations that they could hope to co-opt and control.

At the political level, Ordenanza No. 192 was greeted with a barrage of criticism, particularly in the conservative media. In several editorials in the conservative press, the municipal government was attacked for flaunting existing laws (Ordenanza Objetable 1984; ¿Ordenanza con contrabando? 1984); *El Comercio* in its edition of 27 June 1984 even accused it of creating a network of "soviets." The vehemence of this critique can serve as an indication of the degree of suspicion with which conservative political actors regarded even small increases in popular participation. It also explains why plans to extend legal recognition to women's and survival organizations as well were later shelved (Chirinos 1992).

Another potential problem of Ordenanza No. 192 was contained in its provision that neighborhood organizations had to meet certain organizational criteria in order to be recognized by the municipal government (Rojas Julca 1989, 81–101). Given the problems plaguing many neighborhood organizations, for example, internal conflicts pitting one part of the membership against another or unrepresentative and unaccountable leaders, many of these criteria were reasonable. By and large, they were designed to ensure that the respective neighborhood organization was not defunct, that it was democratically organized, and that its leaders actually represented the membership. Consequently, the organizational standards imposed on neighborhood organizations were in fact intended to "strengthen" them (Chirinos 1991). Obviously, though, the fact that the municipal government could interfere with the internal structures of popular organizations and withhold recognition if these criteria were not met, provided it with a tool that it could have used to exercise political influence. By and large, however, this appears not to have happened, and the organizational guidelines were used mainly to resolve conflicts between popular organizations, such as over which one actually represented a particular settlement or neighborhood (Chirinos 1991, 112).

The highly centralist and hierarchical structure of the local government apparatus itself constituted one of the most significant institutional barriers to increased popular participation in municipal politics. Again, Ley No. 23853, at least in its basic outline, did not differ much from D.L. No. 051, which severely restricted the influence of the municipal council on the executive and placed most decision-making power in the hands of the mayor. According to Ley No. 23853, the execution of municipal policies was the exclusive responsibility of the *alcalde,* who usually would be assisted by the *director municipal,* the highest functionary within the municipal bureaucracy. The role of the municipal council, on the other hand, was to determine the general direction of municipal policy and to approve the municipal budget; at the same time, councillors were prevented from exerting any effective control over the municipal bureaucracy or from playing an active role in the execution of municipal policies.

The lack of democratic control over the municipal bureaucracy and the concentration of decision-making powers in the hands of the *alcalde* fostered authoritarian tendencies within local governments and lessened their administrative efficiency. Neither of these conditions were conducive to an expansion of popular participation.[17] On the one hand, the provision that at least in theory, all important decisions had to be approved by the mayor, worked against a delegation of decision-making powers even to the municipal administration

17. As Borja has pointed out, *a minimum* of democratic openness and administrative efficiency on the part of the municipal administration is in fact a central precondition for an expansion of popular participation (Borja 1988b, 26). Conversely, popular participation is crucial for any *more profound* democratization of local governments.

itself, let alone to urban popular movements. Apart from being undemocratic, this was also detrimental to administrative efficiency. Not only was it highly improbable that the mayor would always have all the information he needed to govern wisely; the concentration of decision-making power at the top made municipal employees less receptive to the demands of the population. Instead of taking the initiative themselves, they were more likely to wait for directions from above. On the other hand, in the absence of effective control mechanisms, it was improbable that municipal bureaucrats would have abandoned their habitual authoritarian behavior in their dealings with the population. Instead of making the municipal administration more accessible to the population and effectively sharing decision-making power with urban popular movements in the joint administration of municipal programs, it is more likely that municipal officials would have shielded themselves from popular input altogether and exploited their offices for personal gain.

The Barrantes administration tried to tackle these problems in two innovative ways, through administrative reform, and through the creation of a new administrative subunit to promote popular participation, the Oficina General de Participación Vecinal. To restructure the municipal administration, Izquierda Unida made use of a novel provision in Ley No. 23853 that allowed the mayor to delegate some of his decision-making powers to seven newly created administrative subunits, the so-called *secretarías municipales,* or municipal secretariats (Mejía 1990, 130–36; Villarán 1991). The *secretarías* were headed by city councillors and put in charge of the management of local services. As opposed to the model described above, in which the municipal council and the bureaucracy were completely separate and executive control rested entirely with the *alcalde* and his *director municipal,* the new structure favored political criteria over narrowly technical-administrative ones.[18] Decision-making powers were now more broadly shared, and the rigid line separating the municipal legislature from the executive became blurred. As was mentioned before, the Barrantes administration went even further than that: to improve the cooperation with other political parties represented on the municipal council and to augment overall administrative efficiency, it offered qualified councillors from the opposition the opportunity to chair a number of secretariats.

The Oficina General de Participación Vecinal, for its part, was created in 1984 with the specific purpose of advancing and coordinating the efforts of

18. According to Mejía, most provincial municipalities in Peru adhere to the technical-administrative model, whereas most district municipalities, as well as the Municipality of Metropolitan Lima, apply the political model (Mejía 1990, 134).

the different branches of the municipal government of Metropolitan Lima to promote popular participation and popular organizations at the neighborhood level (Chirinos 1991, 109; Rojas Julca 1989, 18–23). As one of its first tasks, the Oficina General de Participación Vecinal helped to set up branch offices at the district level and to train municipal officials there, since the districts were considered to be a "privileged space for the development of participatory policies" (Chirinos 1991, 109). Subsequently, the Oficina assisted in the registration of neighborhood organizations according to Ordenanza No. 192 and in the resolution of conflicts that arose during this process. The Oficina General de Participación Vecinal then turned its attention to the organization of communal work projects and finally, to the establishment of the *agencias municipales* in the downtown district of El Cercado.

Experiences with Popular Participation, 1984–1986

Once the administrative and legal groundwork had been laid, the municipal government began to implement participatory policies in fields as diverse as land titling and municipal housing, social services, and the municipal decision-making process itself. Not all these policies—which are examined below—had the same reach and ambition. Some simply entailed a transfer of functions from the metropolitan level to urban popular movements. Taken together, they show how far the municipal government was prepared to go in fostering popular participation in local politics, as well as how it structured its relations with urban popular movements.

Distribution of Land Titles and Municipal Land Development Schemes
The distribution of land titles to urban squatters and the municipal land development schemes have to be seen in the larger context of urban development policies (Driant 1991; Calderón and Olivera 1989). Ley No. 23853 had strengthened local governments in this regard by making them responsible for the control of land use in urban areas, the elaboration of urban development plans, and the restructuring of existing as well as the planning of new *asentamientos humanos,* or popular settlements. As a result of this transfer of powers from the central government, the municipalities found themselves faced with an extremely difficult situation that had repeatedly defied solution in the past, and that the central government itself had not been able to control. Especially in the case of Lima, the city had followed a chaotic pattern of urban development since the onset of massive migrations

to the capital in the 1940s, a pattern that was driven more by uncontrolled invasions and real estate speculation than by coordinated planning. All attempts in the past, be it by forced evictions or by the force of law, to put a stop to invasions and to establish a more controlled pattern of urban development had failed. Successive laws, beginning with Ley No. 13517 in 1961, had done little more than legalize existing settlements, without, however, stemming the tide of new invasions. The resulting problems for the urban area were massive, not only with respect to the popular settlements themselves, which were often established in locations that were unfit for human habitation, making living conditions extremely precarious and complicating the eventual provision of urban services. In addition, because of the combined effect of uncontrolled invasions, often unclear property relations, and real estate speculation, any attempt at controlling land usage in the metropolitan area appeared doomed to fail, while the pressure to convert the remaining agricultural land into human settlements led to grave environmental problems.

To address the crisis of urban development in Metropolitan Lima, the primary concern on the part of the municipal government had to be to put some order into the existing chaotic settlement pattern. One principal way of achieving this objective was to restructure and to consolidate settlements that had sprung up as the result of invasions and to issue land titles to the invaders.[19] Under the previous municipal administration headed by Eduardo Orrego, as well as under the central government, which had been in charge of the distribution of land titles before 1980, this policy had been implemented and controlled from above. As a result, the process often appeared heavy-handed, and since municipal officials were usually unaware of the local context, it frequently created more problems than it solved.

The Barrantes administration, on the contrary, delegated most of its respective functions to the district administrations (Castro-Pozo, Iturregui,

---

19. Normally, this process consists of several separate steps (Serrano 1987, 230–31). It begins with the legal recognition of the new settlement, after its outside boundaries have been determined and conflicts with the previous landowner and with adjacent settlements have been resolved. If this is impossible, the settlement is usually relocated to a new site. As a second step, a precise plan of the new settlement is drawn up, which in many cases involves completely redrawing the original boundaries of the individual plots, as well as making provisions for roads, sewers, communal facilities, etc. This second step is usually performed with technical help from the municipality or from NGOs. Subsequently, a detailed census of the inhabitants is taken to determine who actually has the right to remain in the settlement. Only after the completion of this phase and the resolution of outstanding boundary or ownership disputes, are land titles finally distributed to the individual *pobladores*.

and Zolezzi 1991, 302–3). Some of these, particularly those that were also controlled by the Left and had established links to urban popular movements in the past, cooperated in turn with neighborhood movements and/or NGOs. Consequently, the procedure not only became more efficient,[20] but also more democratic. For example, in the case of the settlement Rafael Belaúnde in the district of Carabayllo (Serrano 1987),[21] close cooperation between the district administration, neighborhood movements, and an outside NGO made it possible to solve two crucial problems often associated with the restructuring of popular settlements. For one thing, the active participation of the *pobladores* in the restructuring process made it easier to separate those settlers that were actually living on their lots from those who were not. In this way, it became possible to determine who actually needed a place to live and was therefore allowed to stay from those who did not, and had presumably participated in the invasion for the simple purpose of selling his or her plot at a later date for a profit. Lots belonging to absentee occupants were reappropriated and redistributed to settlers in need. Furthermore, by participating directly in the restructuring process, the membership of existing neighborhood associations could exert greater control over their leaders, many of whom had exploited their position of power to become involved in land trafficking themselves.

Obviously, the ex-post-facto recognition of popular settlements that had resulted from invasions in and of itself was not enough to break the pattern of chaotic urban development; for that, the municipal government needed to prevent invasions from happening in the first place and to provide alternative housing for the popular sector. The five urban land development programs initiated under the Barrantes administration—Huaycán, Laderas del Chillón, Frente Unico de Chillón, Pampas de San Juan, and Arenal de Canto Grande (Castro-Pozo, Iturregui, and Zolezzi 1991, 299–301)—were a step in this direction. All of them followed a basic pattern: the municipality provided the necessary land,[22] as well as organizational and technical

20. The Barrantes administration granted 112,000 land titles from 1984 to 1986, as opposed to 46,500 that were given out from 1982 to 1984 under Eduardo Orrego. During the entire period from 1946 to 1980, the central government distributed a mere 25,500 land titles (Castro-Pozo, Iturregui, and Zolezzi 1991, 303).

21. A similar case is the Comisión de Saneamiento Físico-Legal (COSFIL) in the district of El Agustino (Derpich 1986, 105), a predecessor to the *micro-areas de desarrollo* (MIADES). See Chapter 6.

22. While local governments technically controlled the use of land in urban areas, the actual process of appropriating unused land for municipal land development schemes was often very complicated. See Castro-Pozo, Iturregui, and Zolezzi 1991, 305–8.

support, while the actual development of the plots as well as the construction of the homes was performed by the settlers themselves. While it was clear that the five projects, which in 1986 accommodated a mere 20,000 families (Castro-Pozo, Iturregui, and Zolezzi 1991, 300), would not be sufficient to put a stop to invasions and therefore could not be considered a substitute for a coherent urban development policy, they did constitute a new approach to the problem in the sense that they stressed the participation of the organized population in the process. For this purpose, various mechanisms were set up to maintain close links between the *pobladores,* the technical support staff, and the municipal administration, so that the projects would be jointly managed by all parties involved.

In terms of its social organization and the extent of popular participation in the project, the settlement of Huaycán went a step further than the other schemes. It was based not on the individual family unit, as most other popular settlements, but on the so-called *unidad comunal de vivienda* (UCV) (Calderón and Olivera 1989, 27–66; Pease 1988, 87–89). The UCVs, each of which comprised sixty families that owned a plot of land collectively, were intended by the urban planners of the Barrantes administration to evolve into the center pieces of the communal life of the new settlement. According to this design, the UCVs would collectively oversee the development of the settlement, they would organize the construction of communal facilities as well as build homes for the settlers themselves, and they would manage communal programs. To lend the UCVs organizational support and to ensure the coordination between the municipality and the settlers, a *comité de gestión* (management committee) was set up, which was composed of representatives of the organized population and of the municipal administration.

Despite some initial successes, the design of the project soon proved to be too ambitious for the reality that it faced. For one thing, the relationship between the *técnicos,* or technical advisers, of the municipal government and the settlers proved to be more problematic than expected. In particular, the settlers were slow to accept the collectivist approach centered around the UCVs that the municipal advisers proposed to them. For example, the *técnicos* generally advocated collective solutions to the provision of communal services, such as communal toilets or water wells, whereas the *pobladores,* for cultural and other reasons, often favored individual solutions centered around the family dwelling, even if those were less efficient (Calderón and Olivera 1989, 63–64). Furthermore, the process of *co-gestión* (joint program management) suffered from some serious deficiencies and never got off the ground. Partly, this can be attributed to the weakness of the neighborhood movements themselves, which, as Calderón and Olivera (1989, 61–62) have noted, often lacked the organizational capacity necessary to participate fully in the process. In addition, the *comité de gestión* itself was poorly institutionalized, which not only limited its effectiveness, but also made it susceptible to being influenced by politically motivated struggles between different neighborhood movements. This became particularly noticeable in July 1986, when neighborhood leaders sympathetic to APRA established a new district-wide neighborhood association, the Asociación de Pobladores. "The new leadership looked toward the APRA-controlled central government as an alternative source of institutional support. Its objective was to achieve *obras*, more so on the basis of clientelism than on the basis of joint management" (Calderón and Olivera 1989, 65). As a consequence, the *comité de gestión* for all intents and purposes ceased to exist, and it remained defunct even after neighborhood leaders sympathetic to the Left had finally regained control of the Asociación de Pobladores.

In the case of Laderas del Chillón, which is similar to the remaining three housing programs, the project did not even reach the stage of joint program management (Calderón and Olivera 1989, 67–99). Here, the relationship between the settlers, on the one hand, and the technical advisers and the municipal administration, on the other, remained at the level of what can be characterized as an improved consultation process. In other words, Laderas del Chillón in most respects resembled a settlement that was the product of an invasion, with the important difference that it received technical assistance from the municipal government and was therefore more organized and structured. As a result, Laderas del Chillón, as well as the other three projects, could be characterized as a *barriada ordenada*, or organized settlement. In other words, while they differed from ordinary popular settlements, or *barriadas*, by being somewhat more orderly and organized, they never became alternative public housing projects in the sense envisaged in Huaycán.

In sum, the efforts of the Barrantes administration to expand popular participation in the field of urban development proved to be a mixed success. On the positive side, the administration achieved its objective of improving the information and consultation of the population about municipal policy in this regard, and popular participation made the implementation of some of these policies more efficient. However, with respect to a stronger involvement of popular organizations in the joint management of such policies, success was limited. While problems in the relationship between technical advisers and settlers played a certain role, most of this lack of success was due to the weakness of neighborhood movements themselves. A fundamental problem in this context, which I discussed in more detail in Chapters 1 and 3, was the periodic nature of popular participation at the neighborhood level and the fact that such participation was often narrowly oriented toward the achievement of fairly limited goals. As Mario Zolezzi Chocano, the director of the municipal urban development secretariat under Barrantes, remarked in a personal interview with the author: "Participation at the neighborhood level was always strongest when specific benefits, particularly land titles, could be obtained, but it rarely extended to more complex issues where benefits were less clearly defined and less certain" (Zolezzi 1991).

The Vaso de Leche Program
The second example for popular participation under the Barrantes administration, the Vaso de Leche program, has to be seen against the background of the critical economic situation in Peru in the early 1980s. As a result of the economic crisis, which had persisted more or less without interruption since the mid-1970s, as well as the adjustment policies of the early 1980s, the living standards of the popular classes had fallen steadily. Particularly in the shantytowns around Lima, nutritional and health standards were becoming dangerously low (Haak 1987, 58–59). To address this dramatic situation, Izquierda Unida developed a social emergency program, the *Programa Popular de Emergencia* (Izquierda Unida 1983, 15–24; Ugarte and Haak 1991) and began implementing it after winning the municipal elections in Lima in 1983. As the cornerstone of the social emergency program, the Vaso de Leche scheme was designed to improve the diet of the most vulnerable of the poor by delivering a protein supplement in the form of one glass of milk daily to all children under six years of age, as well as nursing mothers and pregnant women.

The Vaso de Leche program, which marked the first time that a Peruvian local government had made a major foray into the field of social policy, differed in several ways from previous social assistance programs. Traditionally, social assistance had always been the domain of the central government and had usually been administered from above in a clientelist and co-optive way, exchanging material benefits for the promise of political support. The Vaso de Leche program, on the contrary, adopted a different approach, which was centered around the principle of *co-gestión*, or joint program management. This approach was characterized by the delegation of responsibilities from the provincial to the district administrations as well as the active participation of independent urban popular movements in the administration of the project. While this program design was consistent with the political and ideological outlook of the Barrantes administration, it was also the result of the severe material constraints put on the municipal government. Most importantly, the municipal government of Metropolitan Lima was in no position to set up the bureaucratic apparatus that would have been necessary to control the daily milk distribution to hundreds of thousands of beneficiaries. Consequently, if the municipal government wanted to implement the program in all popular districts and reach all potential beneficiaries, it had no choice but to share control of the program with the district-level municipal governments and, more importantly, with the existing network of neighborhood organizations and survival movements. Former deputy-mayor Henry Pease explained in an interview with the author: "In the *pueblos jóvenes*, women's organizations and women's clubs were multiplying. What we did was to organize them in 1,500 Vaso de Leche committees, starting with the women themselves. We did not set up a big bureaucracy, we worked with [only] twenty-nine people . . . and a couple of old trucks. The municipality did not have more resources, not even for the milk itself. That was done through NGOs" (Pease 1992). By the same token, the possibilities of exploiting the program for political gain and of exchanging material benefits for political support were reduced.

In more specific terms, the Vaso de Leche program was organized in the following way. The overall policy guidelines, setting out the organizational framework of the program and determining who would benefit from it, were established by the municipal government of Metropolitan Lima. The municipal government of Metropolitan Lima was also responsible for providing the milk, most of which it received in the form of powdered milk from foreign donations, and for assuring its transport to the districts in which the program was being implemented. The district municipalities, for their part, distributed the milk among the various settlements and cooperated with their neighborhood associations in the elaboration of a list of beneficiaries. The neighborhood associations, finally, took on the task of preparing the milk and of handing it out to the recipients. All these arrangements were backed by formal agreements signed between the parties (Barrig 1990, 183–85; Ugarte and Haak 1991, 247–48).

The final stage of the distribution process in the settlements themselves presented the greatest difficulties. In most cases, the task of preparing and distributing the milk was not assumed by the neighborhood association as such, but immediately delegated to its secretary of social affairs, a position which was "invariably held by a woman" (Barrig 1990, 184). The secretary of social affairs, in turn, cooperated with the Vaso de Leche committees, which were specifically created for this purpose at the street or *manzana* (block) level, and made up of the beneficiaries themselves. The main problem facing these committees, who were to plan and oversee the distribution process autonomously, was that they had virtually no resources for this purpose. In more practical terms, there existed no storage sites for the milk, there were no cooking facilities and no money to buy cooking fuel for the preparation of up to one hundred rations of milk daily, and there were no suitable localities where the milk could be distributed to the recipients.

These were considerable difficulties, and they would have been impossible to overcome without the prior existence of mutual networks of solidarity in the form of urban popular movements. As I explained in Chapter 3, so-called survival and other women's movements, such as *comedores populares* (communal soup kitchens), had sprung up all over the popular districts of the capital as a response to the economic crisis. Toward the mid-1980s, these movements, not only became more numerous, but also displayed increasing organizational coherence and dynamism, setting them apart from most neighborhood movements, which had entered a period of slow decline. The previous experience of the *comedores populares*, in particular, greatly helped to solidify the fledgling Vaso de Leche committees. During their participation in the *comedores populares*, many of the women who later became involved in the Vaso de Leche program acquired crucial organizational skills. Likewise, the *comedores populares* had gathered experience of how to raise and manage funds locally, which could be put to use by the Vaso de Leche committees. Most of these committees resorted to charging a small contribution from the recipients, a practice which proved necessary, even if it ran counter to the official program guidelines. The committees also raised funds from other activities, such as the sale of the cartons that had contained the plastic pouches of powdered milk.

The Vaso de Leche program became one of the big success stories of the Barrantes administration: toward the end of its term in office in 1986, about 100,000 women participated in 7,500 Vaso de Leche committees, and the program reached up to one million recipients daily in thirty-three districts of Lima (Municipalidad de Lima, n.d., 44–45; Barrig 1990, 186–87). To a large extent, this success can be attributed to the organizational skills and the considerable sacrifices in terms of time, work, and money made by the women involved in the Vaso de Leche committees at the base level. Without their efforts, it would almost certainly have been impossible to get the program off the ground, or at the very least, off the ground quickly enough to ensure that the milk reached its intended recipients. In other words, the participation of urban popular movements in the management of the Vaso de Leche program made its implementation, not only more efficient, but possible to begin with.

Aside from its material success, the Vaso de Leche program also helped strengthen the urban popular movements that participated in it. This sets it apart from "assistentialist" programs mentioned earlier and also from those self-help schemes that see in urban popular movements merely a source of cheap labor. The original Vaso de Leche committees were encouraged by the municipal government of Metropolitan Lima to establish higher instances of coordination, which resulted in the creation of a multitiered structure with coordinating committees, so-called *coordinadoras,* at various levels. In October of 1986, a meeting of the district-level *coordinadoras* elected a coordinating committee for all of Metropolitan Lima, the *coordinadora metropolitana,* which was then formally recognized by the municipal government as a partner in the management of the Vaso de Leche program. Aside from assuming an increasingly important role in the administration of the Vaso de Leche program, as well as in the management of other aspects of the social emergency program, the *coordinadoras* also organized several marches to demand resources from the central government.[23]

According to the available information, this process took place without infringements on the independence of the Vaso de Leche committees by the municipal administration. From the base level committees to the *coordinadoras* higher up, the organizational structure of the Vaso de Leche program remained open to all women, and at least in theory, also to all men, independently of their political orientation. Likewise, program participants did not have to be sympathizers of Izquierda Unida or take part in political activities in support of the municipal administration in order to qualify for program benefits.[24] Alfonso Barrantes was adamant about this point in an interview with the author: "To those leftists who came and wanted to use

23. These marches, which were among the largest popular mobilizations of the decade, resulted in the promulgation of Ley No. 24059 on 4 January 1985, which extended the Vaso de Leche program to all Peruvian municipalities and at the same time reserved funds for it in the national budget. On the negative side, Ley No. 24059 made the program susceptible to a certain degree of central government control; however, its actual administration remained in the hands of the provincial municipalities.

24. My analysis confirms the results of Carol Graham's study, who notes that the practice of Izquierda Unida compares favorably with subsequent efforts on the part of the APRA-led national government to establish a political support base in the popular sector. In the case of

the Vaso de Leche program for partisan ends [I said]: This is for all children, be they children of an *aprista,* be they children of a member of the PPC, it doesn't matter, this is for all children" (Barrantes 1991). At the same time, it is obvious that the Vaso de Leche committees, and the administration of social policy in a more general sense, constituted a means for Izquierda Unida to win the support of urban popular movements and to establish popular support bases. Not surprisingly, many participants of the Vaso de Leche program, and especially its leadership, were in fact IU sympathizers or militants (Barrig 1990, 195). Moreover, some of the most significant activities of the Vaso de Leche committees, particularly the mobilizations against the central government mentioned above, were coordinated with the municipal government. Nonetheless, it appears that the municipal administration respected the autonomy of the Vaso de Leche committees and did not resort to co-optive tactics in order to win their support.

Despite these achievements, the Vaso de Leche program was also limited in a number of ways. An obvious constraint was the program's initial concentration on survival needs, which was later somewhat remedied when the Vaso de Leche committees became the basis for other initiatives, such as in the field of public health (Pease 1988, 86). More importantly, the degree of participation in the program differed greatly between program organizers, or *dirigentas,* and program beneficiaries. Participation was clearly strongest on the part of the *dirigentas,* most of whom did not belong to the poorest strata within the popular sector and could therefore afford not to work and instead invest their time into organizational activities. For many of these women, becoming involved in the Vaso de Leche program constituted an important step on the way to their own personal and political empowerment. Yolanda Giraldo, a city councillor and member of the coordinating committee for the Vaso de Leche program in the district of El Agustino, explained this in an interview with the author:

> The most important thing [about the Vaso de Leche program] is the way in which women have organized and also how they have tried to overcome their predicament. . . . Before the program came into existence, many women remained behind the four walls of their

---

the PAIT and PAD programs, which were designed to create temporary employment opportunities in the informal sector, top jobs in the program administration were often reserved for APRA members, and program participants were urged to participate in rallies to support APRA leader Alan García (Graham 1991, 123).

houses. Today, you see in the *directivas* many women who had a lot of problems . . . who went to meetings with black eyes after fighting with their husbands. . . . Now, with the help of the organization, they assert themselves, resolving two issues: the problem of hunger and their own self-development. (Giraldo and Berna 1992)

In other words, the participation in the Vaso de Leche scheme enabled many women to first shake off the limitations of the traditional female role that had tied them to their children and the household, to acquire managerial experience, and often to assume increasingly important positions in the administration of the program. For some *dirigentas,* this experience even served as a stepping-stone into the realm of politics, at the local level and above, which before had been an almost exclusively male domain.[25]

The same cannot be said about the majority of simple program beneficiaries, many of whom continued to view the Vaso de Leche program in terms of a traditional "assistentialist" logic. Many beneficiaries participated in the Vaso de Leche committees only as much as was necessary to keep them operational, since the benefits that the program provided were often crucial for the survival of their families. As the economic crisis became more acute, it became all the more difficult to make the participatory logic of the program take root. Many beneficiaries simply could not afford to spend much time on unpaid volunteer work, since they had been forced to take up employment, usually in the informal sector, in order to help support their families. From 1985 onward, clientelist schemes, such as the APRA-sponsored PAIT program, which offered a small remuneration to its participants, acted as an additional drain on the level of participation in the Vaso de Leche committees.

In sum, mainly as a result of the economic crisis and the competition from clientelist schemes sponsored by the APRA-led central government, the existing distance between the leadership and the bases of the Vaso de Leche program became more pronounced, and only a minority of *dirigentas* participated fully in the management of the program. While this posed at least a potential threat to the democratic character of the program and limited its overall efficiency, the municipal administration of Metropolitan Lima could do little to remedy these problems. Obviously, it was beyond its

25. The best-known example is probably María Elena Moyano, who rose from the ranks of the Federación Popular de Mujeres de Villa El Salvador to become vice-mayor of the district. Ms. Moyano was also a leading member of the Movimiento de Afirmación Socialista (MAS) and a likely future candidate for the Senate, before she was murdered by Sendero Luminoso on 15 February 1992.

power to end the economic crisis or to eradicate the roots of political co-optation; therefore, it had to limit itself to supporting ongoing efforts to strengthen the organizational structures of the Vaso de Leche committees, and of urban popular movements as a whole.

The Municipal Agencies in the District of El Cercado
The third example of popular participation under the Barrantes administration, the *agencias municipales*[26] in the downtown district of El Cercado (Barrantes 1986, 94–96; Pease 1988, 89–90; 1990, 71–72; Pease and Jibaja 1989, 371; Rojas Julca 1989, 22–23), differed in important respects from the two cases discussed previously. Whereas in those cases, the emphasis was put on improved consultation and information about municipal policy, as well as joint program management, the purpose of the *agencias municipales* was to increase the direct participation of the population in the municipal decision-making process and the democratization of the municipal administration itself. As such, the *agencias municipales* can be considered the potentially most far-reaching forms of popular participation implemented by the Barrantes administration.

The *agencias municipales* have to be seen against the backdrop of the specific situation of the downtown district of El Cercado. Comprising a population of approximately 400,000 inhabitants, the district was structurally very heterogenous, encompassing the historic city core, but also residential and industrial zones, as well as popular neighborhoods. Consequently, the concerns of its inhabitants varied greatly. Unlike the other districts in the province of Lima, El Cercado did not have a separate municipal administration at the district level, but had traditionally been administered by the provincial municipality directly, that is, by the municipal government of Metropolitan Lima. As a result, the distance between the inhabitants of the district and the administration was greater than usual, and their specific concerns risked being swamped by the interests of the metropolitan area as a whole.

To remedy this problem, El Cercado was subdivided into six separate municipal agencies, to decentralize the municipal administration and to better address the specific problems of the district. The *agencias municipales* were conceived as joint decision-making organs, in which functionaries of the municipal government together with representatives of the population would decide upon municipal policy. It was planned to successively delegate

---

26. As explained previously (Chap. 4, n. 4), Peruvian legislation governing the municipalities allows for the creation of such administrative subunits at the level below districts.

all those functions to the *agencias municipales* that were usually performed by the district administrations. In the long run, it was hoped the municipal agencies would become permanent interlocutors of the provincial administration as well as assume increasingly important decision-making powers.

When the *agencias municipales* were formally created in April of 1985 under the provisions of Edicto No. 021, they were not set up simply by delegating functionaries from the provincial administration to the newly created municipal agencies. On the contrary, the Barrantes administration decided to construct them from the ground up, starting with neighborhood committees at the block or street level. A fundamental problem in this context was the lack of a strong tradition of urban popular movements in the district and the fact that only very few neighborhood committees existed. Consequently, the first task of the *promotores* (promoters) from the Oficina General de Participación Vecinal, which had been put in charge of the implementation of the project, was to raise the level of popular organization. By the end of 1986, these efforts had been quite successful: about 350 neighborhood committees had been registered by the municipal government, and in each of the six agencies, neighborhood assemblies, so-called *asambleas vecinales,* had been held, which were to serve as permanent venues of coordination for the individual committees (Pease and Jibaja 1989, 371). Among other things, the *asambleas vecinales* discussed and approved the Plan de Obras 1986 (plan of public works).

However, despite these partial advances, the overall impact of the *agencias municipales* remained marginal. Neither the individual neighborhood committees nor the neighborhood assemblies acquired much organizational cohesion, and as a consequence, the *agencias municipales* never fully consolidated. Furthermore, the transfer of decision-making powers from the provincial administration was slow, partially because of resistance by the municipal bureaucracy (Pease 1988, 90), and the *agencias municipales* never lived up to their potential as interlocutors of the municipal administration and as true decision-making organs. To some extent, these shortcomings were due to the fact that the *agencias municipales* were extremely short-lived: after APRA's victory in the municipal elections of November of 1986, the project was ended, and subsequently, the neighborhood committees disintegrated.[27] Nevertheless, the experience of the *agencias municipales* can

27. The *juntas distritales de planeamiento* (district planning boards), which were established toward the end of 1986 and in which representatives of neighborhood organizations participated together with mayors and councillors in the elaboration of the Plan Director de la Ciudad (i.e., the master plan for the urban development of Lima), suffered the same fate (Pease 1988, 91; Chirinos 1991, 114–15; Iturregui 1990).

serve as proof at least of the willingness of Izquierda Unida to open up the municipal administration to democratic participation from below, up to and including popular participation in decision-making at the municipal level.

Conclusions

The experience of the IU administration of Metropolitan Lima is instructive with regard to the potential and the limitations of the radical-democratic approach to local politics. On the positive side, Izquierda Unida proved to be an able municipal administrator, thereby demonstrating its readiness to govern also at higher levels. Faced with difficult starting conditions, the leftist city government was able to secure greater powers and responsibilities for itself and for local governments in general, and it successfully led the fight to wrest greater autonomy and financial resources from the central government.

Most significantly, the Barrantes administration substantially widened the room for popular participation in local politics. Equipped with limited powers and resources and faced with considerable legal obstacles to an enlargement of popular participation, the Barrantes administration succeeded in improving the information and consultation of the population about municipal policies, it transferred almost the entire management of some crucial municipal policies, particularly the Vaso de Leche program, to urban popular movements, and it demonstrated its willingness to devolve decision-making powers over the running of the municipal administration to urban popular movements. At the same time, it successfully encouraged and promoted the development of the popular organizations that participated in municipal politics, by lending organizational and technical support and by encouraging the development of higher levels of organization.

Remarkably, these efforts were not accompanied by parallel attempts to co-opt urban popular movements. All the available evidence suggests that urban popular movements did not have to be IU sympathizers to participate in municipal programs or to receive benefits from the municipal administration. Of course, this is not to deny that the municipal government regarded its participatory programs as a means to strengthen its popular support; in fact, some urban popular movements, and especially their leadership, were strong supporters of Izquierda Unida. Nevertheless, it deserves to be pointed out that the municipal government refrained from violating the autonomy of urban popular movements. In fact, in terms of the basic options mentioned in Chapter 2 that are available to popular movements in their relations with other actors, the Barrantes administration seems to have been one of those rare cases in which an alliance with a political party did not result in co-optation. Rather, the political left acted as a "benevolent ally" for popular movements, providing critical support and widening spaces for their activities, without at the same time infringing on their independence.

On the negative side of the balance sheet, the limits of the radical-democratic approach became equally obvious. This is particularly true with regard to the efforts of the Barrantes administration to enlarge the scope for popular participation in municipal affairs. A first and obvious limitation resulted from the institutional weakness of local governments. While in theory, they had considerable powers and responsibilities thanks to Ley No. 23853, in practice, they often had to compete with the central government and its agencies over the jurisdiction for urban public services, urban transport, and the like. This lack of real political clout, together with a shortage of economic resources, considerably lessened the attraction of participating in municipal affairs and made it more likely that urban popular movements would seek to establish direct clientelist links with the central government. As was shown, this is precisely what happened in the case of the municipal land development scheme of Huaycán, where the APRA-dominated settlers association tried to obtain improvements of urban services directly from the APRA-led central government.

A second reason why popular participation did not evolve further was related to the deficiencies of urban popular movements themselves. As was explained, these movements suffered from some critical shortcomings, such as institutional fragility and fluctuating levels of participation, which were exacerbated by the economic crisis. Among other things, this heightened the propensity on the part of some to seek individual solutions to the problem of survival, and it reduced the time available for unpaid organizational activities. As a result, the ability of urban popular movements to participate in the decision-making process at the local level, or even only in the joint management of municipal policies, was often quite limited. With the notable exception of some survival movements, particularly the Vaso de Leche committees and the *comedores populares,* urban popular movements did not become the driving force behind the democratization of the local administration, as the radical-democratic project had assumed. Consequently, the transfer of real decision-making powers to urban popular movements halted almost before it had begun, which considerably lessened their influence on the running of the municipal administration as such.

Finally, a number of legal and political barriers likewise militated against popular participation in local politics. Most notably, Ley No. 23853 restricted the space for popular participation, and as a consequence, most initiatives that the Barrantes administration undertook in this area remained at the margins of the law. Furthermore, as was shown in the case of the Ordenanza No. 192, there was often intense political resistance on the part of the conservative elites to any further expansion of popular participation. As a result of these legal and political barriers, the inroads for popular participation that were created during the Barrantes administration were never formally institutionalized and always remained precarious.

Had Izquierda Unida remained in office after 1986, these obstacles might have been overcome. In fact, a victory in the 1986 municipal elections would have given Izquierda Unida a chance to build on its prior achievements, to consolidate its alliance with urban popular movements, and to continue its struggle for more powers and resources for local governments, as well as increased possibilities for popular participation. An electoral victory at the national level, which did not seem impossible at the time, would have put the Left in an even better position to implement its radical-democratic agenda. Such a scenario, which would have provided close to ideal conditions for the implementation of the radical-democratic agenda, would also have allowed urban popular movements to mature, to solidify their organizational structures, as well as to continue acquiring vitally needed administrative and managerial experience. However, what happened was precisely the opposite: Izquierda Unida lost the municipal elections of 1986, albeit by a narrow margin,[28] and subsequently entered a long period of decline. As a result, most forms of popular participation at the local level were replaced by a more conventional clientelist approach on the part of the new municipal government led by APRA.

Most observers would agree that Izquierda Unida's defeat in 1986 was not due to its record in office.[29] On the contrary, as mentioned above, its performance had been fairly good, considering the adverse conditions and the short time frame to implement any substantial changes. Political circumstances may have played a role: APRA leader Alan García, still immensely popular after his stunning victory in the presidential elections a year earlier, intervened personally in the municipal campaign and gave a highly controversial speech from the balcony of the presidential palace in

28. APRA won with 37.6 percent of the vote, Izquierda Unida followed with 34.8 percent, and the Partido Popular Cristiano (PPC) came in third with 26.9 percent.

29. Allou (1988) expresses this consensus. See, however, Taylor 1990, 111.

favor of his party's mayoral candidate, Jorge del Castillo. Alfonso Barrantes, by contrast, was accused of running a lackluster campaign and not really wanting to win, because of his differences with the radical sectors of Izquierda Unida. But more importantly, Izquierda Unida's loss exposed some fundamental weaknesses in its political strategy. Unable to increase its overall share of the vote, Izquierda Unida also failed to keep APRA from making major inroads into its principal electoral base, despite its overtures to urban popular movements. To some extent, this may have been due to its failure to satisfy the high expectations of some of its constituents, in large part because of a lack of resources.[30] At the same time, its relatively good performance as a municipal administrator and its insistence on democratic government, moderation, and consensus failed to bring in the expected middle-class votes, much of which likewise went to APRA. Attempts to strike alliances with other political parties, especially Alfonso Barrantes's project of forming a popular front with APRA, proved equally fruitless. For Izquierda Unida's radical wing, all this provided further proof that an institutional strategy emphasizing political moderation and the search for consensus around pragmatic goals was pointless and detracted from the real goal of building grassroots strength and mobilizing forces for the struggle against the regime.

In short, Izquierda Unida's defeat in 1986 cast doubt on whether a radical-democratic, institutional strategy would be able to deliver the expected results and bring the Left to power at the national level. As a consequence, the old ideological and strategic differences between the various factions within the leftist alliance, which had barely been papered over in the past, again came to the fore. The resulting infighting all but immobilized it, leading to frustration and withdrawal on the part of many militants and popular sector voters, until the alliance finally broke up in 1989.

30. This is a common problem faced by leftist local governments all over Latin America (Castañeda 1993, 152, 368).

six

revolutionary and radical-democratic approaches in conflict

APRA's victory in the municipal elections of November 1986 radically changed the political and institutional environment for local politics, ushering in a return to clientelism and strengthening the role of the central government in municipal affairs. Eager to dry up what it perceived as political support bases for Izquierda Unida, the new APRA administration brought the participatory policies of its predecessor to an

An earlier version of this chapter was published under the title "Local Politics and the Peruvian Left: The case of El Agustino," in *Latin American Research Review* 33, no. 2 (1998): 73–102.

abrupt halt. Rather than replace them with a new set of policies at the municipal level, the new city government decided to take part in existing programs run by the APRA-led central government, PAIT and PAD (Graham 1991). Focusing on public works and providing paid employment for its participants, these programs clearly functioned according to a clientelist logic aimed at increasing support for APRA among the popular sector. Opening the door to central government intervention at the local level, the new APRA administration also dealt a blow to the institutional autonomy of local governments, so strenuously defended by its predecessor.

These changes made themselves felt in the district-level municipalities in and around Lima, particularly those that were still controlled by the Left. The new APRA administration drastically cut the resources previously transferred to the districts and proved much more reluctant than Izquierda Unida had been to share or devolve decision-making powers. Since the persistent economic crisis prevented the district municipalities from raising additional revenue on their own, their operating budgets plummeted and their capacity to implement participatory and other policies was greatly reduced.

At a different level, Izquierda Unida's defeat in 1986 fueled the ideological and strategic divisions within the Peruvian left, which had widened since Alfonso Barrantes's loss in the 1985 presidential elections and his attempted rapprochement with APRA. As I mentioned in Chapter 5, some sectors of the Left took the municipal defeat as additional proof of the nonviability of a strategy that attempted to use democratic elections as the main road to power and stressed the Left's capacity to govern within the existing political institutions. Other sectors continued to defend this strategy, and as a consequence, the viability of the leftist alliance was increasingly questioned.

Inevitably, this trend affected the Peruvian left's stance toward local politics by intensifying the struggle between what I earlier called the revolutionary and the radical-democratic approaches. While the radical-democratic approach attempted to continue the tradition of the Barrantes administration, stressing the potential of urban popular movements to democratize political institutions and parties and the need to respect their autonomy, the revolutionary approach insisted on the need to "construct" these movements from above, assigning a crucial role to the party in the process. As the competition between these two approaches intensified, co-optive pressures on urban popular movements mounted and existing forms of popular participation became increasingly politicized. Along with other low-income districts in Metropolitan Lima, El Agustino in the northeast of the capital was a social laboratory to observe how these developments played out in practice.[1]

El Agustino—Portrait of a "Typical" Popular District

El Agustino is one of the oldest of Lima's popular districts. Bordering the Río Rímac on the north side, the districts of Santa Anita on the east, Ate-Vitarte on the south, and La Victoria and El Cercado on the west, El Agustino lies only a few kilometers east of the historical Plaza de Armas, the heart of colonial Lima. When the first settlers arrived in the 1940s, leaving behind their overcrowded inner-city dwellings in La Victoria and Barrios Altos, they found an area consisting mainly of farmland belonging to a few large agricultural estates, as well as some steep hills or *cerros* leading up to the Andes to the east. Lima itself was still a pleasant, if slightly sleepy, colonial city, with large swathes of agricultural land separating the historical center with its presidential palace, city hall, and cathedral clustered around the Plaza de Armas from the seaside resorts of Miraflores and Magdalena.

With the arrival of successive waves of migrants from the central highlands, setting up their makeshift settlements in the city itself or squatting on land in the surrounding countryside or desert, this tranquil picture began to change. Attempts to evict them or to stem the migratory tide were unsuccessful; and over the years, many of the precarious clusters of straw huts huddled around a Peruvian flag would eventually make way for more permanent settlements with brick homes, paved roads, water, and electricity. As a result, Lima's population shot up from a few hundred thousand in the 1940s to over eight million today, and the city pushed its tentacles far into the desert plains along the coast to the north and the south, as well as up the valley of the Río Rímac to the east (Driant 1991, 29–60). These so-called *conos* or "cones," as they became known, now contain most of Lima's popular districts. While some of them, notably Villa El Salvador,

---

1. The main source of data for this chapter is a series of open-ended, semi-structured interviews with representatives of urban popular movements, political parties, and local government. I have also drawn on participant observation in a number of cases and on printed sources such as newsletters and material provided by the municipal administration, NGOs operating in the district, and others. A few of the interviews were held in the neighboring district of Santa Anita, which was carved out of El Agustino in 1989. See also the interviews conducted by the Servicios Educativos El Agustino (SEA) in 1993 and 1994 (SEA 1995, 1996).

were not founded until the 1970s, El Agustino came into existence much earlier. In fact, the invasion of the Cerro El Agustino in 1947, along with several other hills in the area, can be seen as a harbinger of the coming migratory wave from the Andean highlands (Matos 1977, 68). Like other popular districts, El Agustino has continued to grow in area as well as population and is beginning to run out of space for further expansion (Calderón and Valdeavellano 1991, 142; CENCA and SEA [1991], 18).

One of El Agustino's defining characteristics is the poverty of its inhabitants. In the period under study, the late 1980s and early 1990s, only 4 percent of the labor force of the district were adequately employed. Only this tiny percentage received at least the minimum wage and enjoyed the protection of valid labor laws, while 80 percent of the inhabitants were underemployed and 16 percent were unemployed (Calderón and Valdeavellano 1991, 142; CENCA and SEA [1991], 20; Tuesta 1989, 16–17). Employment was overwhelmingly concentrated in services, with about a third of the labor force being self-employed workers in the informal sector. More than 53 percent of the dwellings in the district lacked access to drinking water and sewers, whereas over 21 percent had no electricity (CTIC [1991], 2). The poverty of the district was also reflected in the state of its municipal finances. For much of the 1980s, the budget of the municipal administration amounted to only two to five U.S. dollars per year and person (Allou 1989, 139–40).

Even though overwhelmingly poor, the district is by no means uniform. In fact, another of its basic features is its structural heterogeneity, stemming from a somewhat chaotic settlement pattern over the years and the virtual absence of urban planning (Ruiz et al. 1987, 13–24). Some neighborhoods in El Agustino are now fully consolidated, boasting paved roads, sidewalks, and brick houses equipped with drinking water, sewers, and electricity. Certain of these areas, tucked away at the foot of the Cerro El Agustino in the central *Zona Plana*, with their carefully maintained homes and front yards, quiet streets, and the occasional little park, would not appear out of place in one of Lima's middle-class neighborhoods. But only a few blocks away, just off the bustling Avenida Enrique de la Riva Agüero, with its bumper-to-bumper traffic, small shops, businesses, and public institutions, streets are dusty and partly unpaved, sidewalks are missing, and the homes are in various states of disrepair. In these parts, street life is busy, with small children and dogs mingling freely, street vendors hawking their wares, and people coming and going on their various errands. Further away from the center, in the outlying pueblos and particularly on the *cerros*, living conditions are more dire. Large expanses of the district consist of desolate shantytowns perched precariously on the hillsides, often lacking even the most basic amenities. The most recently erected shantytowns are usually the most desolate, consisting of little more than straw huts offering little protection against the elements, but many of the older settlements in the *cerros* are also in a critical state. Often severely overcrowded, their location on the slopes of steep hills makes the provision of urban services extremely difficult and expensive, if not outright impossible.

What makes El Agustino a particularly interesting case in the context of this study is the fact that it shares many similarities with other low-income districts in the Peruvian capital, as well as elsewhere on the Latin American continent. Settlement patterns and basic socioeconomic characteristics are comparable. More importantly, the sustained presence of urban popular movements and leftist political parties in El Agustino, which served as an impetus for the development of participatory policies by the municipal government, has parallels elsewhere.[2] Given these commonalities, the experience of El Agustino should be considered, not an isolated case, but rather an example of more universal trends in relations among urban popular movements, leftist political parties, local government, and other actors such as NGOs.

Urban popular movements in El Agustino look back on a long history of struggle which began in the late 1940s with the formation of the first neighborhood organizations that spearheaded the occupation of the *cerros* or hills. This history continued throughout the 1950s and 1960s, when new land occupations led to renewed and often violent confrontations with landowners and police (Calderón 1980b; Fernández and Núñez 1986). In the 1970s, these struggles attained a new quality when the committees that emerged in connection with the restructuring of the central *Zona Plana* challenged the traditional clientelist relationship between *pobladores* and state agencies like SINAMOS.[3] Victor Abregú, a neighborhood leader who at age twenty became a central figure in this conflict, explained in an interview at his home in El Agustino:[4]

> In the 1970s, there was a great mobilization in this part of the *Zona Plana*, with the goal of remodeling the places where we lived. At this

---

2. See, for instance, Calderón and Valdeavellano 1991 on San Martín de Porres, Comas, and El Agustino and Stokes 1995 and Pomar Ampuero 1997 on Independencia.

3. See Chapter 3 for more detail on the relationship between the military government and the popular sectors. See Chap. 5, n. 19, for further information on the restructuring of popular settlements.

4. All translations in this chapter are mine.

> time, the military government had a new, very interesting discourse that gave legitimacy to the rights of the poor, the *pobladores,* [stressing themes like] dignity and the improvements that had to be made to their habitat. . . . We pushed for a remodeling process that was very different from all others in the *Zona Plana,* because from the beginning, we demanded a degree of autonomy in the elaboration of the plans for the urban restructuring of our community. This led to confrontation with the government's proposal put forward by SINAMOS. We set up our own technical support group in order to be able to promote new forms of organization and we gave a very strong push to the participation of women and youth. . . . As a result, the remodeling of our *pueblo* was not limited to the handing over of newly marked plots, but was part of a proposal to construct homes, including the commercialization and production of some building materials, with the participation of the community. (Abregú 1992)

Building on this experience, El Agustino witnessed the formation of neighborhood movement coalitions throughout the 1970s, which played a key role in the street mobilizations against the military government at the end of the decade. The most noteworthy one was the Federación Distrital de Pueblos Jóvenes y Urbanizaciones Populares de El Agustino (FEDEPJUP) (Calderón 1980b, 95–110; Calderón and Valdeavellano 1991, 143; CENCA and SEA [1991], 20).

Women's movements likewise have a long tradition in El Agustino, dating back to the *clubes de madres* or mothers' clubs of the 1960s. These early women's clubs, focusing on literacy work, handicrafts, and the like, were often instrumental for the formation of other women's movements later on. Gloria Libia, a member of a soup kitchen and at the same time a neighborhood leader in her *pueblo,* remembers:

> At first, we were a sort of women's club. For example, we taught the *señoras* to read and write, we did literacy work. Then we saw the needs of our *pueblos,* for example, myself and others left very early in the morning to work at [the market] La Parada. . . . We left our children at 5 A.M. and only returned at 1 P.M. to cook for them. . . . In one of our meetings, an idea was raised by one of our members who had seen a *comedor* in another neighborhood. We thought, why don't we start one ourselves? (Libia 1992)

During the crisis years in the late 1970s, new forms of women's movements emerged, the *movimientos de sobreviviencia* or survival movements, breaking with the clientelist tradition represented by some of the earlier *clubes de madres* and stressing organizational autonomy as well as democratic forms of participation (CELATS 1983; Montes 1987). El Agustino was at the forefront of these developments; for example, the soup kitchen *Sembrando la Alegría* may have been the first *comedor popular* in Lima (Cuadros 1992). Zenaida Zúñiga, its first coordinator, recalls the difficult first years during an interview at the busy neighborhood center of the *Zona Plana*, where she is now the president:

> When the remodeling was finished . . . we found ourselves without other tasks and the idea of forming a *comedor popular* came up. We had to save to build our houses but our husbands' salaries would not be enough for food as well. Maybe, with a *comedor popular*, we would be able to save for a brick here, steel rod there. . . . At first, we were in a park. We did not have a place, so someone gave us a little room in his house to keep our things. That went on for about a year. . . . [Later] a neighbor gave us a room in his house one block further down and we stayed there for another year. . . . In the meantime, we tried to get into the neighborhood center, . . . but at that time, the leadership was reactionary and did not recognize women. [Finally], the leadership changed and in 1983 we could get in. (Zúñiga 1992)

Both the politicization resulting from the remodeling of the *Zona Plana* and the social work carried out by the Catholic Church were crucial in this process. Irene Cáceres, who participated in the early days of the *comedor* and later became a member of Association of Self-Administered Soup Kitchens of El Agustino (Comedores Populares Autogestionarios de El Agustino), explained in an interview at her home in El Agustino:

> In this period we were involved in all the work related to the remodeling of the *Zona Plana*. . . . It was very difficult to face up to the remodeling and at the same time to the needs that also existed in our households, basically related to food. Therefore, we thought about what we could do. . . . At first, we wanted to set up a consumption cooperative but then we decided a *comedor* was better, because it

would also give us a space for reflection. . . . During the remodeling process we had realized that we did not know much about life. . . . Support from the parish was fundamental, because the parish facilitated contacts among ourselves, since we all worked. (Cáceres 1992)

During the crisis years of the 1980s, the number of *comedores populares* in Lima increased exponentially, followed by the establishment of the Vaso de Leche committees under the Barrantes administration of Metropolitan Lima. Both of them achieved an impressive degree of organizational consolidation, uniting in federations at the district level and forging links with other districts all over Metropolitan Lima.

The rise of urban popular movements in El Agustino was paralleled by the growing strength of leftist political parties, particularly those belonging to the New Left, which emerged in the 1970s under the reformist military regime. To a large extent, the Left owed its influence among the *pobladores* of the district to its early involvement in neighborhood organizations and its participation in the conflicts opposing the settlers to the state, particularly the restructuration of the *Zona Plana* and other parts of El Agustino already mentioned. In the late 1970s, the nationwide general strikes that ushered in the end of the military regime represented a further milestone in the relations between the Left and popular organizations. As in other low-income districts, neighborhood organizations in El Agustino participated alongside leftist groups and trade unions in organizing the strikes and were instrumental in ensuring a high turnout.

The Left's involvement in the struggles of the 1970s and its recruiting of activists among popular movements laid the foundations for its subsequent strength as an electoral force in the district. This was reflected first in a share of more than half of the popular vote for various leftist parties in the 1978 Constituent Assembly elections and subsequently in a string of electoral victories for Izquierda Unida at the municipal level. Within Izquierda Unida, first the Unión de Izquierda Revolucionaria (UNIR) and later the Partido Unificado Mariáteguista (PUM) succeeded best in translating popular backing into political influence at the district level. Izquierda Unida formed the first democratically elected local government in El Agustino after obtaining 33 percent of the popular vote in 1980,[5] and went on to win

---

5. As mentioned previously, according to Peruvian electoral law, the party with the largest share of the popular vote was accorded the mayoralty and the majority of seats in the municipal council.

the three following municipal elections in 1983, 1986, and 1989 (Allou 1989, 88–91; Roncagliolo 1989/1990, 16). In 1983, riding the wave of Alfonso Barrantes's triumph in Metropolitan Lima, Izquierda Unida could increase its share to 53 percent, dipping only slightly to 47 percent in 1986, despite APRA's strong showing. In 1989, by contrast, Izquierda Unida was reduced to only 27 percent of the vote after it had broken up into two competing camps shortly before (31 percent including the breakaway Acuerdo Socialista). Following this near defeat, Izquierda Unida was finally swept from office in February 1993 by the independent OBRAS movement.[6]

Because of the long-standing cooperation between leftist political parties and urban popular movements in the district, the consecutive leftist administrations in El Agustino were fairly responsive to demands for more popular participation.[7] In fact, the municipal government of El Agustino began to experiment with new forms of popular participation between 1981 and 1983 and actively supported the efforts undertaken in this regard by the city government of Metropolitan Lima between 1984 and 1986. By launching the Micro-Areas de Desarrollo (Microareas of Development, or MIADES)

---

6. The resounding victory by OBRAS in twenty districts of the capital, as well as in the mayoral contest at the metropolitan level, represented not only a vote of no confidence in the Left but a clear indication of the electorate's growing dissatisfaction with all "traditional parties" and the increasing prominence of independents in Peruvian local politics. See the conclusion for more detail.

7. As explained in more detail in Chapter 3, this kind of cooperation was viciously attacked by the armed guerrilla movement Sendero Luminoso, particularly during its campaign in the early 1990s to infiltrate and take over (or at least to disable) the popular organizations operating in the popular districts surrounding the Peruvian capital. Sendero Luminoso regarded any cooperation with the institutions of the existing political system as counterrevolutionary and contrary to its own goals and thus considered its opponents as legitimate targets for violent attacks. Typically, Sendero Luminoso would first spread rumors and launch slander campaigns to undermine the legitimacy of popular movement leaders in the eyes of their constituents, coupled with threats on their lives. If this approach did not ensure compliance, Sendero would assassinate targeted leaders, often in a gruesome fashion. The most infamous example of this tactic was the killing of Maria Elena Moyano, the deputy mayor and long-time organizer of women's groups in Villa El Salvador, on 15 February 1992. But despite Sendero's presence in El Agustino dating back to the early 1980s and a series of attacks on individuals and public installations, the guerrilla movement did not seem to consider the district a priority and was concentrating its activities elsewhere, for example, in Ate-Vitarte or Villa El Salvador. During the period under study, urban popular movements in El Agustino continued to function and to entertain links with the municipal administration, albeit on a more limited scale. However, attacks by Sendero Luminoso took an increasing toll in the two years that followed, resulting in the death of at least six popular movement leaders (J. Tovar 1996), even though they leveled off somewhat following the capture of Sendero's leader, Abimael Guzmán, in September 1993. As a result, popular movement activity in the district was severely curtailed and coordinating forums such as the MIADES or the Comite de Gestión were virtually shut down.

project in 1987, the municipal administration tried to continue the legacy of cooperation between urban popular movements and leftist local governments, despite a political environment that had deteriorated significantly after APRA's victory in the 1986 municipal elections. In fact, the MIADES project went a step further than previous instances of popular participation, which were relatively sporadic und unconnected. Adopting an integrated approach, the MIADES created a forum where urban popular movements could cooperate with one another and with the municipal administration on a variety of issues.

Constitution and Partial Consolidation of the Micro-Areas de Desarrollo (MIADES) in El Agustino

The MIADES project in El Agustino originated from two prior studies on the feasibility of urban development in the district, both commissioned by the municipal government (Acosta 1986; Domenack 1987). Starting from the shared premise that the structural heterogeneity of the district constituted one of the principal obstacles to its overall development, the studies recommended the district be subdivided into several zones sharing common characteristics. These zones could then have policies tailored to meet their specific development needs.

The original MIADES proposal, adopted by the municipal council on 25 June 1987, embraced most of the technical considerations of the two prior studies, but also added an unmistakably political twist to the project. As Mayor Jorge Quintanilla described the project: "What we are proposing is a model within the framework of the official scenario—the state, the municipalities—that would allow the people to organize in small spaces, which we call microareas of development. In these spaces, we try to see to it that the people centralize, begin to make decisions and exercise functions of government" (Quintanilla 1991).

As a first step, it was hoped, the MIADES would act as a catalyst for consolidating and unifying the district's urban popular movements, which were considered relatively weak and dispersed by the municipal administration, despite their long history of struggle (Quintanilla 1987, 4; 1991). The second stage was intended to unite the individual MIADES in a federation of MIADES at the district level, which could then assume increasingly important decision-making powers, including deliberation over the municipal budget. Not unlike the Comunidad Autogestionaria de Villa El Salvador (CUAVES), this district-wide federation of MIADES would act as a sort of "popular parliament," with its decisions being enacted by the municipal administration. For the longer term, the mayor and his party had even more ambitious plans for the MIADES project. As Quintanilla explained: "Of course, the project has a greater importance. It is a political project of self-government. Therefore, it cannot be implemented only in a district, it has to be national" (Quintanilla 1991). It was hoped that the MIADES experience would spread to other districts, making it possible to establish regional alliances and federations of MIADES, which would then form the base for an *Asamblea Nacional Popular* (National Popular Assembly) at the national level (Atúncar 1991, 6). Viewed from this angle, it could indeed be said that the purpose of the MIADES was to "gestar las bases del poder popular" (Quintanilla 1988, 6), meaning to lay the groundwork for popular self-government outside of the established institutions of representative democracy.

In the initial phases of the MIADES, however, the radical political goals of the project and its hoped-for future role as the nucleus of an alternative political system were little more than theoretical pronouncements. They were clearly overshadowed by more immediate and pragmatic concerns for consolidating the MIADES. When municipal community workers or *promotores* explained the project to the population, they emphasized the public works or *obras* that it was supposed to make possible.

In December 1987, municipal *promotores* fanned out to the individual settlements of the district and held a series of meetings, most of them with the leaders of neighborhood organizations, to explain and promote the MIADES project. Parallel to that, and without the active involvement of the municipal government, so-called *talleres de autodiagnóstico* (self-diagnosis workshops) took place in the proposed MIADES. These workshops were essentially general assemblies attended by urban popular movement leaders and the population at large. Their purpose was to delineate the boundaries of the proposed MIADES, to decide which settlements should be included, to deliberate the common concerns of the respective settlements, to draft a list of public works that were accorded priority, and finally to elect a *junta directiva provisional* or provisional leadership body of each MIADE. By the end of this process, around November 1988, eight MIADES had been constituted.

Subsequently, women's or survival organization were integrated into the project. Again, municipal *promotores* held meetings with the leaders of these organizations and independent workshops were organized. The integration of women's organizations into the MIADES was completed when first the *comedores populares* (in March 1988) and then the Vaso de Leche committees (a year later in 1989) adapted their district-level organizations to the MIADES structure (Calderón and Valdeavellano 1991, 158). Following the integration of women's organizations, a number of other organizations began to participate more actively in the MIADES, such as youth groups and associations of microentrepreneurs (CENCA and SEA [1991], 27).

Another significant event in the development of the MIADES project was the creation of the *Fondo de Desarrollo Comunal* (FODECO). This municipal fund served as the main source of funding for the public works previously identified in the *talleres de autodiagnóstico* by the individual MIADES. Given that the municipal administration initially considered public works to be the main factor motivating the population to participate in the MIADES, it is no exaggeration to see in the FODECO the centerpiece of the project. Essentially, the FODECO consisted of funds taken from the municipal budget,[8] which were deposited in separate bank accounts and put at the disposal of the individual MIADES. The legal status of the MIADES was unclear, however; and in order to avoid accusations of financial mismanagement, each payment still had to be approved by the municipal council as well as by the municipal administration. In 1988 payments were made in installments of about U.S.$800, which could be replenished after the funds had been used (Calderón and Valdeavellano 1991, 154).

Finally, greater involvement by nongovernmental organizations also shaped the development of the project. The NGOs, or *centros,* as they were commonly called, helped organize the *talleres de autodiagnóstico* and provided crucial technical support for realizing some of the public works that the assemblies had agreed upon. More importantly, the NGOs drew up an integrated development plan for the district on behalf of the municipal government, the *Plan Integral de Desarrollo* (CTIC [1991]). While stressing the importance of increased popular participation in urban development and building on the efforts undertaken by individual popular organizations and MIADES, this plan sought to coordinate these activities, infuse them with professional urbanist criteria, and link them to the urban, social, and economic development of the district as a whole. At the same time, the *Plan Integral de Desarrollo* emphasized the necessity for increased political decentralization, that is, the transfer of powers and resources from the central to local governments. The plan also linked the development of El Agustino with that of the *Cono Este* (Eastern Cone) of Lima and with the entire metropolitan region.

---

8. In 1988, FODECO amounted to 8 percent of the municipal budget, rising to 9 percent in 1989 (CENCA and SEA [1991], 26; Calderón and Valdeavellano 1991, 154).

By mid-1989, two years after the official announcement of the project, the MIADES in El Agustino had achieved a certain degree of consolidation. Eight *micro-áreas* had been formally constituted in all parts of the district, following a lengthy process in which the population had reshaped their physical outlines, established their organizational structure, and defined the goals they hoped to reach. Most neighborhood organizations were represented in the MIADES, women's or survival organizations had been included, and other popular organizations had also begun to participate in the project. Moreover, the functioning of the FODECO had been formalized, and it had financed a number of projects in various MIADES. Finally, the three main NGOs active in El Agustino had agreed to work together on an integrated development plan for the district while continuing to lend organizational and technical support to the individual urban popular movements they had been working with all along.

Despite these achievements, the project was plagued by difficulties, particularly a critical shortage of resources on the part of the municipal administration.[9] When it became clear that the funds provided by the FODECO, limited to begin with, were decreasing and often insufficient to realize even minor projects, a certain disenchantment with the MIADES began to set in, and the level of participation slowly began to decline. A striking example of such disenchantment was observed by the author on 9 January 1992, when the MIADES Cerros Unidos staged a march down the central Avenida Enrique de la Riva Agüero to the city hall of El Agustino. A mixed crowd of men, women, and children demanded the release of certain funds that had been promised under the FODECO, but not made available by the municipal government. After a tense standoff, during which the demonstrators again voiced their demands, the mayor finally called in police who dispersed the crowd with the help of tear gas, dodging rocks thrown at them in the process.

The realization that it was unable to satisfy all the expectations it had raised could not have come as a surprise to the municipal administration. In fact, municipal officials had probably known all along that their resources were insufficient to attain their ambitious goals for the urban development

---

9. Accounting for inflation, E. Guerrero (n.d.) documents a drop of 52 percent in municipal spending between 1988 and 1989. In addition to the effects of the economic crisis in Peru during these years, another reason for the difficult financial situation of most district administrations was that after 1986, the new APRA-controlled government of Metropolitan Lima was much less willing than the previous IU administration to grant resources to the districts, particularly if these were controlled by the Left.

of the district. But they apparently believed they could redirect the expectations created around the MIADES project toward the APRA-controlled provincial and central governments and use them as part of a confrontational strategy for demanding increased financial resources for the district. If this was the strategy adopted by the municipal government, it clearly backfired. Moreover, disillusionment with the MIADES project contributed to a loss of popular support for the municipal government itself, a trend that became evident in the municipal elections of November 1989.

While these setbacks did not alter the main actors' conviction that the MIADES were essentially a political project and that material concerns would eventually make way for a more political outlook, they helped intensify the debates over exactly what such a project would entail in practice. At the same time, the debates around this issue were fueled by political struggles within the Peruvian left at the national level, which began to make their effects felt in the district. At the heart of these debates lay the question of how the relations between the respective actors involved in the MIADES project should be structured and who was to be the project's main protagonist. Put more precisely, disagreement was growing over the question of whether the MIADES and the urban popular movements composing them indeed needed to be "constructed" and led from above, as the municipal government seemed to believe, or whether autonomous urban popular movements should be the main driving force behind the project, albeit assisted by other actors. These disagreements radically altered the character of the MIADES project and fostered the emergence of a counterproposal, the Comité de Gestión Distrital, while slowly destroying the unity of the actors involved.

The Politicization and Decline of the MIADES

It would be impossible to understand the politicization and ultimate decline of the MIADES project in El Agustino without at least making reference to the political and ideological struggles that ravaged the Peruvian left at the end of the 1980s.[10] As I explained in Chapters 4 and 5, the first half of the decade had been a period of relative calm and unity, marked by the formation of Izquierda Unida in 1980 and a string of electoral successes in the following years. For a while, this made the Left look like a serious contender at

---

10. For further detail, see Taylor 1990; Rojas Samanez 1991, 403–56; Haworth 1993; and particularly Roberts 1996 and 1998, chaps. 7 and 8.

the national level, not least because of Alfonso Barrantes's record as mayor of Metropolitan Lima between 1984 and 1986. But Izquierda Unida's defeat in the 1986 municipal elections reversed this upward trend and revived old internal tensions and contradictions.

In the following years, marked by an economic crisis that was rapidly spiraling out of control, widespread institutional decay brought about by the nepotism and corruption of the APRA government, and a mounting challenge to the political system from the Sendero Luminoso guerrilla movement, the rift separating the Izquierda Unida's radical and moderate wings widened. While the radicals around PUM and UNIR claimed that the bourgeois system was "exhausted" and in need of revolutionary change, Barrantes and his allies saw the solution to the crisis in a broad national pact with the political center, a strategy that required moderation, compromise, and the building of coalitions with other political actors. Barrantes's aloof personal style and his reluctance to become involved in intraleftist conflicts, combined with a tendency to rely on his own personal appeal with the alliance's supporters, did not make matters easier and further infuriated his radical opponents. The tensions between moderates and radicals, who were better organized and could therefore mobilize their adherents more easily, finally came to a head following Izquierda Unida's first national congress in January 1989. Pressed by the large neutral bloc within Izquierda Unida, which included representatives of the Christian Left such as Henry Pease and Rolando Ames, as well as the Communist Party (PCP), to renew his commitment to the alliance and to submit his presidential candidacy to an internal primary, Barrantes refused, arguing that his candidacy had broad popular support and could not be held hostage by a small group of party militants.

In September 1989, Izquierda Unida finally split into two competing camps when Barrantes and his supporters presented a separate ticket under the heading Acuerdo Socialista (Socialist Agreement) for the municipal elections of 1989 and the presidential and legislative elections a year later. If any side had hoped to turn this situation to their favor, the experience proved them wrong: as in 1980, the electorate spurned a divided Left, this time by shifting its preferences to independent candidates. Henry Pease, deputy mayor of Lima under Barrantes, and Michel Azcueta, the well-known former mayor of Villa El Salvador, polled only 11.5 percent for Izquierda Unida in the municipal elections of November 1989, while Enrique Bernales, running for Acuerdo Socialista, did even worse with only 2.2 percent. In the following presidential elections, Barrantes came in a distant fifth with not even

5 percent of the vote, and Henry Pease did little better with just over 8 percent. The elections were won by independent Alberto Fujimori, who beat out the heavily favored candidate of the Peruvian right, the writer Mario Vargas Llosa. Weakened further by Fujimori's right-wing populist attacks on political institutions and "traditional" political parties, the Peruvian left went through various alignments and realignments in subsequent years, and finally disintegrated into a number of competing factions and parties.

In El Agustino, three specific developments related to these intraleftist struggles had a particularly strong impact. The first dates back to November 1988, when a group of dissidents broke away from the Partido Unificado Mariateguista (PUM) and went on to form the Partido Mariateguista Revolucionario (PMR). This split was the result of the PUM's own internal contradictions, pitting those who wanted to build on the PUM's considerable strength at the grassroots and its involvement in popular struggles against others who favored a more orthodox conception of the party as a political vanguard preparing for the revolutionary struggle. When the latter tendency became dominant, as the PUM was struggling to reclaim political terrain it had lost on the far Left, particularly to Sendero Luminoso, the rupture became inevitable. While its impact at the national level remained relatively minor, the split seriously undermined the PUM's standing in El Agustino, where it had previously had the deepest roots and the strongest organizational structure among the leftist parties of the district. As a result of the breakup, the PUM lost most of its cadres and much of its support among urban popular movement leaders (Abregú 1992; Romero 1992), while the breakaway PMR became the main opposition within the Left.

The decision by Izquierda Unida to choose its candidates for the 1989 municipal elections for the first time by way of internal primaries likewise contributed to the intensification of tensions within the Left.[11] In El Agustino, two competing lists of candidates were presented. One was supported by the PUM and two smaller parties, the Unión de Izquierda Revolucionaria (UNIR) and the Frente Obrero Campesino y Popular (FOCEP), as well as some independents. An alternative list was backed by the PMR, the Partido Comunista Peruano (PCP), and some unaffiliated supporters. In a close vote, the list presented by the PUM and its allies carried the day,

---

11. As Jorge Castañeda has pointed out, "holding primaries to select candidates for elective office . . . can be a terribly fratricidal affair, pitting factions, regions, and personalities against each other without the healing postprimary reconciliation of other latitudes" (Castañeda 1993, 361). Nevertheless, there is no substitute for this if the Left wants to be serious about internal democracy.

amid accusations of vote-rigging and fraud. The municipal administration and the PUM were accused by their adversaries of using the municipal apparatus to hand out material benefits like food and building materials in exchange for political support, and of ferrying their supporters in buses to the election sites. Enrique Mendoza, city councillor for the Movimiento de Afirmación Socialista (MAS), explained in an interview at the city hall:

> These were elections that sharpened the crisis even more. . . . The PUM was much weakened, without a great number of cadres, but it still had the mayor's office and the municipal apparatus. . . . Therefore, the strategy they applied for winning the internal elections was one of clientelism, directed at those *pueblos* that had IU members. They gave them support, stoves, cement, food . . . they agreed to sign agreements for public works, provided the vote would go in the mayor's favor. . . . When the elections came, the mayor won again with only thirty to fifty votes . . . but the other sector was clearly very taken aback [*golpeado*] and challenged the results. . . . At this point the rupture became even more pronounced. (Mendoza 1992)

Rosario Romero, a researcher at the Centro de Investigación y Promoción Popular (CENDIPP), one of the NGOs operating in the district, made a similar observation: "It was an error to have internal elections, at least here. . . . Having a mobilizing zeal amounted to a form of harakiri, given that people were not prepared to embark on a more or less democratic game. In the head of party members, there was only confrontation and hegemony . . . you win or you die [laughs]" (Romero 1992). Izquierda Unida later went on to win the municipal elections for the third time in a row but garnered only 27 percent of the popular vote, less than the combined vote for the several independent candidates (Roncagliolo 1989/1990, 16). The price for this victory was high: the clashes during the internal elections had left deep wounds and made the rupture of the Left in El Agustino almost irreversible.

Finally, the PUM's withdrawal in July 1990 from the national coordinating committee of Izquierda Unida, the Comité Directivo Nacional, further undermined the viability of the leftist alliance. Following Izquierda Unida's defeat in the presidential elections the same year, the PUM's decision to suspend its membership in the Committee indicated a shift in its strategic calculations and ended the party's cooperation with other leftist forces representing more moderate positions, notably the large block of independents that had remained in the alliance. The PUM's gamble to galvanize the

Peruvian left and to reconstitute it on its own terms failed miserably: as Barrantes before, the PUM had grossly overestimated its capacity to rally the Left's supporters and to impose its own political strategy on the remaining parties. As a result, Izquierda Unida disintegrated even more at the national level, while in El Agustino, the PUM became further isolated. At the same time, the PMR, the remaining leftist parties, and the considerable number of unaffiliated leftist militants that continued to participate in Izquierda Unida's district committee were brought closer together in their joint opposition to the PUM-led municipal government.

It is hardly surprising that the intraleftist struggles in El Agustino would profoundly affect the relations between the Left and urban popular movements. In destroying the previous relative unity of the different leftist parties and groups in the district, these struggles accentuated their competition over "capturing" bases of popular support. Frequently, such increased political competition was accompanied by the emergence of a different attitude toward urban popular movements, in which previous respect for the autonomy of these movements and the absence of manipulation were replaced by a desire to dominate and to use these movements as vehicles for amassing political support. Although this new attitude toward urban popular movements was not restricted to any one actor in particular, it manifested itself most strongly in the new municipal government controlled by the PUM. After the local elections of November 1989, the new municipal administration clearly intended to impose its hegemony on urban popular movements, and on the other leftist parties of the district as well.

The success of this new strategy hinged on two crucial preconditions: first, the reconstruction of a sector within the municipal bureaucracy that would be loyal to the mayor and his party and could also be used as an effective administrative instrument for implementing new policies; and second, the reestablishment of the ties between the municipal government and urban popular movements, which had suffered badly. As a first step in meeting these preconditions, the new local government thoroughly restructured the municipal bureaucracy by creating a new unit to oversee relations with neighborhood and women's movements, the Oficina de Promoción y Desarrollo (PRODES). The new unit was staffed entirely by PUM supporters, most of whom had to be brought in from outside the district.

The influx of these activists profoundly affected the political dynamic of the district and changed how the municipal government conducted its relations with the population. Most of the new *promotores* had long track records as PUM militants, and many of them had university educations, but relatively few of them were qualified professionals. Consequently, they brought a much more ideological approach to the outreach activities of the municipal government, which they understood first and foremost as political work in support of their party. In the words of Victor Abregú, who became one of the most outspoken adversaries of the municipal administration: "They are very special intermediaries . . . they were party activists and now they have a different character [as representatives of the municipal government]. Logically, this creates great confusion on the part of the population" (Abregú 1992). As an unwanted consequence, the arrival of the PUM activists also undermined the control the mayor had previously exercised over his party in the district, which eventually prompted him to recall them from their duties.

For a while, however, PRODES became the main link between the municipal administration and the population. Apart from giving technical and sometimes legal advice, PRODES assigned several *promotores* specifically to each MIADE to work with neighborhood, women's, and youth organizations (Mendoza 1992). The *promotores* were usually the only local officials who actually visited the individual settlements. They informed the population about services and resources that could be obtained from the municipal government, but also collected information on behalf of the municipal administration, such as the level of public support for specific urban popular movement leaders. Yolanda Maraví, a member of a Vaso de Leche committee, said of these activities: "The municipality has its *promotoras* in all the MIADES. They work with the women and when they come [to us], they come with lies and unclear ideas . . . in the settlement itself they say that a *dirigente* is corrupt. Most of what the promoters do in the settlements is misinform" (Maraví 1992).

With the help of PRODES, the municipal government set up tighter political controls over the MIADES program and reined in the leaderships of the MIADES who had expressed opposition to the municipal government. In at least two cases (the José Carlos Mariátegui MIADE and the UPMIRR MIADE), the municipal administration cut off its financial support in order to discredit the MIADES leadership in the eyes of the population (Abregú 1992; Cancho 1992). In addition, municipal *promotores* attempted to manipulate the general assemblies of these MIADES into replacing the existing *juntas directivas* with new ones more sympathetic to the municipal government. When these measures were not enough, the municipal government went a step further and set up alternative organizations in opposition to the MIADES. Financial support from the municipal government was channeled through these new groups, in the hope of eroding the remaining legitimacy of the MIADES leaders. In several other cases, such as in the MIADE Zona Plana (Abregú 1992; Estrada 1992), the municipal administration circumvented the MIADES structure altogether to work directly with individual *pueblos* (settlements).

The fact that many MIADES were already debilitated by internal tensions facilitated these tactics on the part of the municipal government. Friction could be rooted in the personal ambitions of some urban popular movement leaders but were more typically due to political differences or prior cleavages between different urban popular movements. These divergences were sometimes of a long standing, going back to the very founding of the respective settlements. Such dissension made it easier to divide any particular MIADE by pitting one part of the population against another. Likewise, wrangling could render a MIADE inoperative and become a pretext to replace it with an alternative organization.

In sum, after the municipal elections of November 1989, the municipal government clearly abandoned its earlier policy of noninterference in the MIADES in the initial stages of the project. Instead, the municipal government and the PUM as the main political force behind it adopted a much heavier-handed strategy, openly using the MIADES structure to garner political support and strengthen their own position in the intraleftist struggles taking place in the district. The municipal government did not hesitate to employ clientelist tactics in order to achieve these objectives, trying to coopt the leaderships of certain MIADES and the urban popular movements supporting them. If these tactics failed, particularly in cases where the MIADES leadership opposed the municipal government on political grounds, the municipal government had no qualms about undermining the respective MIADES by cutting off their funding or employing other means to replace them with alternate organizations that it could hope to control. It is therefore fair to say that to a certain extent, the municipal administration undermined its own project for reasons of political expedience, but without ever officially abandoning it.

Beyond exacerbating the divisions among the various leftist factions of the district, the politicization of the MIADES debilitated the project itself. Many popular organizations did not want to be drawn into the political struggles taking place in many MIADES and either abandoned the project altogether or minimized their participation. Others who had distanced themselves from the municipal government earlier felt vindicated in their insistence on self-help strategies and organizational autonomy. Carmen Barnet and Amanda Collazos, both coming from a new generation of young neighborhood leaders in the settlement of Villa Hermosa, remarked in an interview with the author: "Here in our *pueblo,* we have always relied on our *dirigentes.* We have never had an intermediary or [municipal] *promotores,* because they inform in their own way and according to what suits them. It's a trick . . . if you don't do this, they won't give you that" (Barnet and Collazos 1992). Thus the political struggles surrounding the MIADES further diminished the level of popular participation in the project, which had already tapered off as a result of the economic problems plaguing it. Furthermore, the political conflicts surrounding the MIADES also accentuated latent conflicts between the municipal government and other actors involved in the project. This was particularly true in the case of the NGOs, which began to turn against the municipal government, notwithstanding their continued collaboration on projects such as the Plan Integral de Desarrollo.

The Emergence of a Counterproposal to the MIADES: The Comité de Gestión Distrital

In August 1990, amid intense political infighting and growing penury, a new organization appeared in El Agustino, the Comité de Gestión Distrital (CG), or District Management Committee. As in other municipalities, the CG in El Agustino was set up in response to the social emergency program announced by the newly elected president Alberto Fujimori. This program was to be part of his overall economic adjustment package (Carbajo 1990). The CG was intended to organize and oversee the distribution of the emergency relief funds expected from this program and therefore attempted to unite the broadest possible spectrum of actors to assist in this task. These actors can be categorized in three groups. The first consisted of the local government and other organizations that had traditionally maintained relations with urban popular movements and could therefore help with the distribution of resources, particularly the NGOs and the Catholic Church. Second, urban popular movements were represented on the CG via their respective district-level organizations: the MIADES in the case of the neighborhood organizations, the coordinating committees of the Programa del Vaso de Leche, the *comedores populares,* and the *clubes de madres,* as well as organizations representing street vendors, microentrepreneurs, and youth. Finally, central government agencies and other institutions from outside the district were invited to participate in order to coordinate their activities with those of the CG at the district level.

The CG in El Agustino soon began to be drawn into the political conflicts that were dominating the district. Shortly after it was constituted, a confrontation began to shape up over who would direct the new umbrella organization, pitting the municipal government against the other organizations represented on the committee. The issue was highly significant, because whoever presided over the CG and controlled the distribution of its resources would be likely to receive most of the political credit in the eyes of the public. The municipal government insisted on its primacy as the local government of the district and refused to share authority over the CG with the other organizations. The other members of the committee, wary of past instances of what was perceived as political manipulation on the part of the municipal government, feared that the CG would be dominated and used for partisan ends. They therefore argued that the presidency of the committee should be shared and rotate each month among all the organizations involved.

At a general meeting in September 1990, a rotating presidency was finally agreed on. Mayor Quintanilla assumed the presidency of the CG for the first one-month term. After his term ended, however, the municipal government sent only minor-ranking functionaries to participate in committee meetings. Several conflicts ensued in the following months over the distribution of certain resources (Calderón and Valdeavellano 1991, 172). They confirmed the municipal government's view that it was being marginalized within the CG and ultimately prompted it to leave the committee. Subsequently, the mayor accused the CG and the organizations supporting it, particularly the Catholic Church, of promoting "assistentialist" attitudes among the population and fostering political opposition to the municipal government by building a "reformist" alternative to the MIADES project. In Mayor Jorge Quintanilla's own words:

> This other form of centralization is a fraud. There you do have manipulation, you do have mercenary behavior on the part of the leaders. There, autonomy and independence are not guaranteed. . . . Support for the Comité de Gestión comes mostly . . . from organizations involved in matters related to health, survival, from the Vaso de Leche Committees, the soup kitchens . . . which are brought together by the Church, with a marked influence by the Church and some reformist political forces. . . . If we are talking about *protagonismo popular*, why doesn't the Comité de Gestión become a part of the MIADES and assume its proper tasks there. . . . (Quintanilla 1991)

After abandoning the CG, the municipal government redoubled its efforts to shore up the ailing MIADES and to lend credence to the claim that they were in fact the preferred forum for uniting the various urban popular movements in El Agustino. In particular, the municipal government encouraged the establishment in January 1991 of the Central Autónoma de MIADES, a coordinating committee bringing together the leaders of the individual MIADES. Before, such a district-wide agency had not existed and it was hoped that its creation would strengthen the MIADES and thereby enhance their legitimacy as the true representative of urban popular movements in El Agustino. This strategy was partially successful, in that the municipal government found some backing within the Central Autónoma for its views particularly regarding the CG and its supporters. But at the same time, the leadership of the Central Autónoma insisted on their own independence vis-à-vis the municipal administration. Julio Casanova, its president, explained in an interview:

> Up to a point, [the Comité de Gestión] wants to set up a parallelism . . . to the microareas . . . which in any case is not feasible, not possible, because they cannot elaborate a program. . . . But what they do have is economic power, they attract resources [leading to] assistentialism. . . . If it comes to this point . . . we as an organization will have to close the door and block this kind of access, not only to the Centros, but also to the *promotores* of the municipality itself. . . . There is sufficient autonomy and sufficient authority within the microareas to exercise it. (Casanova 1991)

The label "assistentialist" may have been appropriate for the CG in its early stages, given its rather narrow preoccupation with providing material assistance to the district's poor to alleviate the effects of Fujimori's economic stabilization program. But the focus of the committee soon widened considerably. Shortly after it was founded, three separate commissions were formed to coordinate the activities of the member organizations in the fields of nutrition, health, and the generation of employment. These commissions also sought to develop concrete policy proposals at the level of local government. Ultimately, it was hoped that these proposals would result in a coherent work plan that would address the problems related to urban development of the district in a comprehensive and integrated manner. The fact that the CG in El Agustino was able to make this transformation is significant, and it probably explains why unlike many other CGs elsewhere, it continued to exist when the resources promised by the central government failed to materialize (Carbajo 1990, 12; Abregú 1992).

The impression that the CG in El Agustino had achieved considerable programmatic maturity was reinforced at a meeting of CGs from all over Lima, held on 27 November 1991 on the initiative of the General Office for Neighborhood Participation of the municipality of Metropolitan Lima. One by one, representatives from the various popular districts stood up and presented their committee to the other participants, explaining its origins, structure, and relations to public institutions and other popular organizations, as well as its programmatic responses to the principal problems of the district. What was impressive about the CG in El Agustino was, not only the relatively advanced state of its organizational development compared to most of the others, but also the fact that it presented a more comprehensive and more detailed program. In an atmosphere slightly reminiscent of a political meeting, the participants, almost all of them women, politely applauded each speaker and exhorted one another to make progress in their respective activities. The organizers intervened only rarely, trying to distill a common core from the individual presentations. While sometimes short on specifics, the speakers' enthusiasm was nevertheless contagious, lifting the spirits of the participants in the face of the obstacles ahead.

In addition to fostering policy proposals and functioning as a coordinating body for its participants, the CG in El Agustino had limited resources at its disposal to fund concrete projects directly. These resources were provided by the Catholic Church and were used to establish two separate funds of U.S.$14,000 each: one to assist street vendors and another to support the economic activities of the district's microentrepreneurs. Similar funds were planned to support the Vaso de Leche committees, the *comedores populares,* and the *clubes de madres.* The money was loaned on a rotating basis, meaning that it was used and repaid by the first recipient, and then loaned to a different organization.

The emergence of an alternative to the MIADES worsened existing political tensions in the district and accentuated latent divisions between neighborhood movements and other urban popular movements. While popular organizations were generally represented in both the MIADES and the CG, they usually participated more actively in one or the other. Because the CG had a somewhat different focus than the MIADES and emphasized survival issues in the broadest sense of the term—nutrition, health, and job creation—survival movements and popular organizations representing street vendors and microentrepreneurs were more strongly represented on the committee.

The participation of neighborhood organizations, in contrast, remained strongest in the MIADES. The interests of these organizations revolved chiefly around improving the urban infrastructure of the district, as in building roads and sidewalks or providing a safe water supply, sewers, and electricity. These issues were not a priority of the CG, and limited resources continued to be provided chiefly by the local government (plus those given by other public institutions and central government agencies). Many neighborhood organizations had also cooperated closely with the municipal government in the past.

If the MIADES and the CG, despite certain discrepancies and differing appeals to individual popular movements, were essentially similar proposals targeting the same popular bases for support, what motivated the rivalry between the two? The obvious answer would be the political differences between the supporters of the two organizations. This interpretation was advanced by many of those interviewed, who usually blamed the other side for fanning the flames. Such an interpretation has some basis in fact, given that political support for the two projects came mostly from opposite sides: from the municipal administration through the MIADES and from its political opponents through the CG.

Yet it would be too facile to reduce the conflict between the supporters of the MIADES and the CG to a dispute between political opponents over the capture of popular bases and to view the two projects as mere tools in this struggle.[12] While it seems clear that the PUM-controlled municipal administration tried to use the MIADES project to build its own bases of political support among the urban popular movements of the district, the issue seems to be somewhat more complicated in the case of the backers of the CG. To be sure, there were those who, just like the municipal government, saw the CG as a springboard for their own political ambitions. For example, the PMR and another leftist group, the Movimiento de Afirmación Socialista (MAS), advocated building a *frente amplio* (broad front), based on the CG, the MIADES, and urban popular movements in general. Such a coalition would unite leftist opposition to the municipal administration with the urban popular movements of the district (Confluencia Socialista 1991).

---

12. This seems to be the view taken by Calderón and Valdeavellano. They contend that the ideological discrepancies between the two adversaries are negligible in that they see eye to eye on fundamental questions such as democracy and popular self-government. Rather, their differences boil down to divergent "political styles"—one more radical and uncompromising, the other less aggressive but still trying to marginalize the municipality (Calderón and Valdeavellano 1991, 180–81).

But the other supporters of the CG, and particularly the NGOs involved in the project, did not necessarily share these views. Several of those interviewed alleged that the NGOs were controlled by the political opposition and that some of their leading members sought to succeed Jorge Quintanilla as mayor of El Agustino (Atúncar 1992; Casanova 1991; de la Cruz 1992), but these accusations seem exaggerated and are in any case difficult to substantiate. Based on the available evidence, it appears that the NGOs as institutions did not take sides in the political struggles in the district and considered themselves to be nonpartisan. Furthermore, the political orientations of their members varied widely, ranging from independent sympathizers with the Left to supporters of the PMR, the MAS, and even the PUM. Of course, this does not mean that the relationship between these *centros* and the popular movements they were working with was unproblematic and free of tensions. On the contrary, it was highly complex and marked by contradictions, as pointed out by Carlos Escalante, an architect working for CENCA:

> The *centros* have a different approach, an approach characterized by respect toward popular organizations . . . but almost always when a *centro* works with a popular organization, that organization becomes dependent on the *centro*. On the one hand, the *centros* can exert influence via the technical expertise of their promoters. On the other hand, the *centros* can also facilitate things. . . . Furthermore, there are promotion styles that are very close, [down to] resolving personal problems of the *dirigente*. Obviously, this forges links, whether you want to or not. . . . Between the municipality and the population there is always a relationship of authority . . . this is not the case with the *centros*. A *centro* can have influence, but in the last instance it has to be earned. (Escalante 1992)

While not taking sides in the political struggles in the district, the NGOs did not abstain completely from mobilizing the population against the municipal administration. Francisco Chamberlain, the parish priest of the Virgen de Nazareth parish and director of Servicios Educativos de El Agustino (SEA) admits: "I don't deny my intention to undercut the leading role of the municipality a little, given what has happened in the past. But undercutting its leading role and wanting to marginalize it are two different things" (Chamberlain 1992). On the whole, what matters most is that the supporters of the CG did not seem to have a clearly defined political strategy, nor did they appear to unite around a single protagonist who could become a serious challenger to Mayor Quintanilla. It therefore makes little sense to view the CG merely as a tool in a struggle to win power in the district.

What appeared to unite the supporters of the CG was their shared antagonism to the municipal administration, seen as authoritarian and manipulative, and their common ideas about how relations between urban popular movements and other actors should be structured. They saw these principles expressed in the CG but no longer operative in the MIADES scheme. If this assessment is correct, then the disagreements between the supporters of the MIADES and those of the CG were rooted in the respective political projects underlying them rather than in the fact that they both could be integrated in a tactical way into competing political strategies. The basic features of these two projects, which were already outlined in the preceding chapters, can briefly be recapitulated as follows.

The MIADES scheme started out as a pragmatic policy proposal for enhancing the participation by urban popular movements in the planning and execution of public works, but it soon began to resemble what was earlier labeled the "revolutionary approach" to local politics. Declining municipal resources made pragmatic solutions from within the system appear less and less feasible and were aggravated by intensifying political tensions within the Left of the district. As a result, the underlying political rationale of the project prevailed, and the MIADES were increasingly touted as the nucleus of an alternative political system of popular self-government.

The role of the PUM-led municipal administration as the principal champion of the redefined MIADES scheme was twofold. First, in order to create a popular mass basis for the project (and for its more far-reaching political ambitions), the urban popular movements of the district had to be strengthened. Increasingly, this goal implied interfering with their autonomy and trying to "construct them from above." Even more important, in order to maintain control over these movements, the municipal administration had to convince them to forgo other forms of centralization and accept the MIADES as the exclusive link between themselves and other actors, such NGOs, other state institutions, and the like. The municipal government went as far as to use clientelist methods in trying to achieve this goal. If successful, such a strategy would have secured the dependency of urban popular movements on the municipal administration in material as well as political terms, particularly because the MIADES had no official legal status and their continued existence depended entirely on the goodwill of the municipality.

The CG, in contrast, demonstrated a different emphasis than the MIADES and resembled the radical-democratic approach to local politics mentioned before. Instead of trying to lay the foundations for an alternative political project led by a revolutionary municipal administration and drawing its mass base from the urban popular movements of the district, the CG's main function was to serve as a *convocatoria* within the existing political system.[13] In other words, it was to serve as a coordinating body among various organizations of civil society and state institutions at different levels, uniting all relevant actors to find pragmatic solutions for the pressing needs of the popular sector. Consequently, the relations between urban popular movements and the other participants on the CG were much more open than those between the municipal administration and the MIADES. Most important, the NGOs, which had established the closest links to urban popular movements of all actors in the CG, generally abstained from political manipulation and clientelist tactics, while providing organizational and material support.[14] The CG had also accepted the existence of parallel forms of centralization by urban popular movements, as well as their establishing direct links with other actors. While the supporters of the MIADES scheme insisted on MIADES being the exclusive representative of urban popular movements in the district, the backers of the CG saw no problem in sharing this role and regarded the MIADES and the CG as complementary rather than competing organizations.

Conclusion

The case study presented in this chapter highlights the main difficulties and dilemmas of the two approaches to local politics delineated previously. The inherent problems of what has been called the revolutionary approach to

13. Not all CG backers unequivocally favored a system-immanent strategy. The PMR and the MAS, for example, continued to express their support for the idea of popular self-government (Confluencia Socialista 1991). Unlike the municipal administration, however, they did not seem to be entirely clear on whether this would entail a complete break with the existing political system or merely the introduction of some mechanisms of direct democracy. This attitude reflected a more general ambivalence within the Peruvian left toward representative democracy at the time.

14. As mentioned before, members of the municipal administration and their sympathizers nevertheless accused the NGOs of politically motivated interference, but generally without providing concrete examples (Atúncar 1992; Casanova 1991; Giraldo and Berna 1992; Quintanilla 1991). Atúncar stated that SEA offered the president of the MIADE UPMIRR a camera and a trip to Spain.

local politics became most apparent in the case of the MIADES project, particularly after its politicization following the breakup of Izquierda Unida and the ensuing intraleftist struggles in El Agustino. It proved to be extremely difficult for the municipal administration, the main backer of the MIADES project, to reconcile what was essentially an antisystem stance with the fact that it was a part of this very system and therefore shared responsibility for the results it produced, at least in the eyes of its constituents. For example, when the municipal government tried to blame the crippling lack of resources for the MIADES project on the provincial and central governments, it was held accountable for its own shortcomings and began losing popular support. Likewise, when the municipal administration attempted to distract it constituents from the more immediate shortcomings of the MIADES project by stressing the long-term character of the project as the core of a new form of popular self-government, most urban popular movements remained skeptical and were more concerned about tangible improvements in their dismal living conditions.

Another fundamental problem faced by the municipal administration concerned how it handled relations with the urban popular movements of the district. After an initial phase of the MIADES project marked by noninterference and respect for the movements' autonomy, the municipal administration changed its tune and began to apply increasing pressure, sometimes trying to co-opt the movements' leaders and win their support. This strategy failed. Most urban popular movements took pains to preserve their autonomy and avoid involvement in intraleftist struggles, but without abandoning the MIADES project altogether or openly siding with the political opponents of the local government.

The Comité de Gestión, which can be considered an expression of the radical-democratic approach to local politics, did not face the same difficulties in its relations with urban popular movements. Adopting a much more open approach, the CG actively encouraged their participation in the committee and elsewhere in the local arena, and it accepted the fact that some of them also had independent ties with other actors and with one another. In fact, the character of the CG as an open forum for all actors that could contribute to the economic and social development of the district and its adoption of the format of a rotating presidency prevented any one actor from asserting dominance over the others.

But while the CG had some success in uniting the relevant actors around a common platform for developing the district (with the important exception of the municipal government), it achieved few concrete results. Compounding the lack of cooperation from the municipal administration was the fact that CG members could provide little or no resources. Urban popular movements had few resources to contribute, being themselves in dire need of assistance. Representatives of the central government agencies did little more than participate in some of the meetings of the committee, and resources provided by the NGOs were just enough to finance two modest rotating funds for street vendors and microentrepreneurs. Given these political and economic obstacles, the CG could do little more than serve as a coordinating body for its members and make proposals for the integrated development of the district. The fact that the CG could do so is an important achievement in itself. But it falls well short of the main objective of the radical-democratic approach to local politics: to show that solutions for the most pressing concerns of the popular sector can be found within the existing representative democratic system.

Three main conclusions follow from this analysis. First, leftist local governments cannot escape responsibility for governing, that is, they cannot forgo the difficult task of trying to find workable solutions for the urgent needs of the popular majorities within the framework of the existing political institutions. Attempts to use local governments as "Trojan horses" and to foster a revolutionary project from inside the political system are likely to fail, not only because of the unfavorable political climate for such projects, but also because popular constituencies will not tolerate neglect of their everyday concerns.

At the same time, it is clear that an institutional strategy also faces several major obstacles and may also fare poorly at the polls.[15] Like most other local governments, those controlled by the Left often face an acute shortage of resources that prevents them from fulfilling even their most basic responsibilities. Most central government are reluctant to rectify this situation and to devolve additional resources to local governments. They are especially hesitant with leftist-controlled municipalities for fear of enabling the Left to use a successful experience in local government to mount a challenge at higher levels. For similar reasons, leftist local governments are likely to encounter problems when trying to forge political alliances with other

---

15. This point was illustrated in the 1989 municipal elections by the dismal showing of the Acuerdo Socialista (AS), the breakaway group around Alfonso Barrantes and Enrique Bernales, its mayoral candidate for Metropolitan Lima. In El Agustino, AS obtained less than 5 percent of the popular vote, while Izquierda Unida despite its internal problems could at least hang on to the mayoralty for one last time. At the same time, there was mounting evidence for a generalized fatigue with the Left as a whole as well as political parties in general, including the newly resurgent independents: the number of invalid and blank ballots increased to almost a third of the electorate, far surpassing the share of the valid vote received by any of the competing parties.

actors, which may be necessary to push through policies locally, or to pressure higher levels of government. Leftist local governments are also more likely than others to run into resistance from local elites, who will perceive any attempt to improve the living conditions of the urban poor as a threat to their own privileges. In short, while the imperative to govern is inescapable, it is not at all clear that leftist local governments following an institutional strategy will actually be able to achieve their objectives or manage to retain the support of their constituents on election day.

The second conclusion is that urban popular movements are willing to throw their support behind actors that promise to tend to their concerns—or to withdraw it from those who do not deliver on their promises. On the one hand, these findings seem to confirm the existence of "pragmatist attitudes" on the part of urban popular movements which have often been described in the literature as continually vulnerable to co-optation. The integration of urban popular movements into participatory schemes—even if this takes place in a nonhierarchical or "horizontal" context—may in fact accentuate co-optive pressures by bringing these movements into contact with other actors and by making them rely, at least in part, on outside resources. But my findings also show that urban popular movements no longer succumb to co-optation almost automatically. On the contrary, the movements I studied were generally able to withstand such pressures and proved very reluctant to sacrifice their autonomy to powerful patrons in return for material rewards. They often did so by striking several limited alliances with an array of other actors, gratefully accepting the resources they offered but refusing to provide unconditional support to any single actor and give up their own autonomy. In adopting such a strategy, these movements were able to take advantage of the fact that several actors were vying for their support and thus did not have to commit themselves unconditionally to get their concerns addressed.

Finally, the case presented here shows that leftist local governments would be ill-advised to take the support of urban popular movements for granted. These movements seem to have become more hesitant in recent years to back leftist political parties that promise to take up and defend their demands, and they seem especially reluctant to be drawn into intraleftist struggles that could jeopardize their own autonomy. Thus if leftist local governments want to form stable alliances with urban popular movements, they will have to take on some of these movements' concerns, respecting their independence and their right to establish links with other actors. That is to say, local governments will have to accept some degree of ideological pluralism.

Yet it should not be forgotten that urban popular movements themselves have a lot to gain from an alliance with leftist political parties. While generally successful in defending their autonomy, at least some of the movements studied reacted to co-optive pressures by retreating into themselves and by reducing their relations with others to a minimum. Such an "excess of autonomy" can actually be harmful, since it hinders the cooperation between different urban popular movements and therefore keeps them from acquiring higher levels of centralization and a greater influence on others (Olivera, del Carmen, and Vergara 1991, 93–97). Partially as a result of this failure to unite, the influence of urban popular movements on the institutional makeup and the political practices of public institutions, political parties, and other actors in El Agustino remained fairly limited.

Political parties and particularly the Left can play a crucial role in this regard, by transcending the often limited and particularistic demands of urban popular movements and integrating them into an overarching political project. The Left continues to be the actor that is most likely represent these movements' concerns in the political arena, other than populists, who prefer to establish traditional clientelist relations with the popular sector.[16] Moreover, many urban popular movements would benefit from assistance by leftist political parties (or by other actors such as NGOs) for developing and consolidating their organizational structures. In short, mutual alliances appear to be beneficial for leftist political parties and for urban popular movements alike. If so, the challenge remains for the Left to construct a political alliance capable of integrating urban popular movements and their concerns in a nonmanipulative way, while addressing their impulses for democratizing political institutions and the political arena as a whole.

16. See the conclusion for an assessment of the potential role of political independents, at the local level and beyond.

conclusions and epilogue

This study began by setting out a theoretical framework for analyzing popular participation in local government. I argued that the collective identities and practices of urban popular movements, the main agents of popular participation in the urban realm, contain a democratic potential that could serve to democratize other political actors and make local political institutions more democratic and more efficient. For this to happen, several crucial conditions need to be met, namely, effective political decentralization and the creation of institutional openings for popular participation at the local level, as well as the formation of alliances between urban popular movements and other actors, such as political parties. Urban popular movements were seen as having a range of options in their dealings with these actors, so as to minimize the risk of being co-opted while at the same time maximizing their own influence on the direction the alliance would take. This theoretical framework was then applied to an analysis of popular participation under several leftist-led municipal governments in Lima during the 1980s and early 1990s.

From this analysis, it is now possible to draw up a balance sheet of these experiences and relate them back to the main research questions that were developed at the outset. To begin, there can be little doubt that the expansion of various forms of popular participation at the local level had a significant impact on the leftist-controlled local governments examined. For one thing, as a result of increased popular participation in local affairs, these local governments became more open and more responsive to popular concerns and demands. For example, the Barrantes administration implemented an open-door policy to render the municipal bureaucracy more transparent. Moreover, various leftist local governments convened popular assemblies and so-called *cabildos abiertos* in order to consult the population about their needs and to receive popular input on municipal policy. In addition, the fact that popular demands, which had previously been made chiefly from outside the political system, were now backed up by local political institutions, gave them greater clout and invested them with greater legitimacy.

Second, popular participation contributed to making local governments more efficient and more accountable, essentially as the result of a transferral of functions to urban popular movements and the joint management of municipal programs. At the same time, this expansion of popular participation permitted the respective leftist-led local governments to take on a number of tasks that they would not have been able to fulfill otherwise with the resources and qualified personnel they had available. For instance, members of urban popular movements performed control functions in fields such as public hygiene or the administration of public markets, either as substitutes for municipal inspectors or to monitor municipal officials themselves. Furthermore, so-called *comisiones mixtas*, or joint committees, were established in several instances, bringing together representatives of urban popular movements and the municipal administration, in order to devise strategies vis-à-vis the central government, to develop proposals for municipal policies, or to oversee their implementation. Finally, in a number of cases, leftist-controlled local governments shared the administration of municipal programs with urban popular movements, who often exerted a considerable influence on their planning, execution, and evaluation. The most notable example of this was the Vaso de Leche scheme, which was put in place by the Barrantes administration.

Third, participation by urban popular movements made local governments more democratic, in the sense that over and above the transferral of certain functions from the municipal administration or the joint management of municipal programs, decision-making powers in certain fields of the municipal administration were put in the hands of urban popular movements. Most notable in this regard were the *agencias municipales,* or municipal agencies, in Metropolitan Lima and the Micro-Areas de Desarrollo (MIADES), or microareas of development, in El Agustino. As we have seen in the previous chapters, these programs enabled the inhabitants of certain neighborhoods of the Peruvian capital to determine the specific needs and the development priorities of their constituencies autonomously, as well as to assign limited funds for their realization.[1]

Overall, however, popular participation played a relatively minor role in the cases studied and the impact of urban popular movements on the institutional makeup of local governments and on the strategies and political practices of other political actors remained fairly limited. In part, this was due to the weaknesses of local governments themselves, whose institutional autonomy was constantly threatened by central government interference and whose finances were in a chronic state of crisis. Attempts to enhance popular participation by stretching existing legal norms to the limit remained at the margins of the law and the resulting policies were often poorly institutionalized and severely underfunded. The worsening economic crisis at the end of the 1980s and the drying-up of financial transfers from the provincial government to the districts further undermined the viability of participatory policies. Most local governments scraped by on a budget that barely covered their day-to-day operating expenses, leaving them with little to spare on programs meant to further urban development or the health and well-being of their constituents—simply put, there was often nothing left to participate in.

The inherent shortcomings of urban popular movements were another important factor. Hampered by highly fluctuating levels of participation,

---

1. See García and del Carmen 1998 for some more recent examples of popular participation in Peruvian local governments, often continuing earlier experiences.

unstable and sometimes contradictory collective identities, and weak organizational structures, urban popular movements were not always able to fully exploit even the existing limited openings to participate in local politics, much less push for their further enlargement. A crucial factor in this regard was the desperate economic situation of the urban poor toward the end of the decade, many of whom lost their regular jobs and were forced to work longer hours for less pay in the informal sector, if they could find work at all. With less time available for organizational activities, many began to doubt their effectiveness and instead started looking for "individualist" solutions to their problems.[2] Regarding the so-called survival movements, such as soup kitchens and Vaso de Leche committees, the economic crisis proved especially damaging, in the sense that it contributed to a growing rift between the leadership and the rank and file. While the leaders were often highly politicized thanks to a long trajectory of popular activism, many ordinary members tended to see the respective movements as little more than an extension of an "assistentialist" state that they held responsible for the provision of certain resources. When the survival movements' capacity to provide these resources declined toward the end of the decade, participation levels dropped off as well. In addition, cases of fraud and mismanagement of funds, sometimes involving autocratic and unaccountable leaders, further undermined their credibility. These conflicts were skillfully exploited by Sendero Luminoso when it launched its campaign on Lima's popular districts in the early 1990s. Generally unable to make major inroads into existing popular movements, aside from spectacular exceptions such as in the districts of Ate Vitarte and Villa El Salvador, its slander campaigns and its murderous attacks on their leaders nevertheless succeeded in disabling many of them.

Finally, the relations between urban popular movements and other actors were full of pitfalls and only rarely amounted to alliances between equal partners. Some leftist-led local governments used the municipal bureaucracy and the resources at their disposal to build political support bases, while keeping firm control of the way the municipal government was run. In other words, they tried to absorb popular movements into their own political strategies and projects, often trying to restrict their autonomy, while being deeply distrustful of any contacts they might wish to establish

---

2. Distinguishing between different modes of participation, Henry Dietz (1998) claims that only "state petitioning" declined in the crisis period, in response to declining state capacities to address the needs of the urban poor. By contrast, "community problem-solving" and "local involvement" remained relatively constant over the years.

with others. This attitude was typical for what I have termed the revolutionary approach to local politics adopted by parts of the Peruvian left. By contrast, the radical-democratic approach that became dominant in the mid-1980s allowed urban popular movements much greater leeway. Relations with the municipal administration were more equal and pluralist, allowing for links also with other actors and giving urban popular movements wide-ranging responsibilities for running municipal programs, with little interference from the municipal bureaucracy. However, these experiences were short-lived and soon swept away when the Peruvian left broke up amid mutual recriminations and renewed ideological battles at the end of the 1980s.

Politically motivated interference on the part of the Left as well as other actors, particularly APRA in the latter half of the decade, clearly damaged the participatory policies implemented during the period studied. Undermining their pluralist character and posing a potential threat to the autonomy of urban popular movements, it pushed many of them to reexamine the options they had in dealing with other actors. As discussed in more detail in Chapter 2, there are basically four such options. As a first and basic one, urban popular movements can simply refuse to entertain any contacts with other actors, be they state institutions, political parties, NGOs, or others. Instead, they may rely on self-help strategies or try to put pressure on these actors from the outside, for example, by staging marches or demonstrations. In the cases studied, there was some evidence of such strategies, but never in isolation from others. In other words, while many—if not most—urban popular movements will resort to self-help strategies at some stage in their development and be keen on trying to pressure public institutions into attending to their needs, most of them will also explore other options in their dealings with others. They will do so because of the inherent limits of this first course of action: given the limited resources of urban popular movements and the urban poor in general, self-help strategies only go so far, while public institutions are often quite impervious to their demands, unless they are made through other channels. For example, even the leftist-led municipal government of El Agustino called in police when a protest march to city hall by one of the MIADES threatened to get out of hand.

The second option mentioned was for urban popular movement leaders to "infiltrate" political parties or institutions and then wield power from within in the interest of their constituencies. In the political climate of the late 1980s and early 1990s, the chances of success for this strategy became increasingly remote. Aside from the common dilemma faced by all social movement leaders entering political institutions, namely, the need to chose between defending the interests of their former comrades or that of the citizenry at large, they were more and more at risk of becoming embroiled in political infighting and partisan struggles and thereby losing touch with their constituents. Once identified with a particular faction or grouping, they were often no longer able to represent the movement they came from, especially when that movement was itself riven by ideological or strategic disputes. The pressure to take sides and to defend the stance of a particular faction or grouping was often so strong that it overshadowed the need to come up with practical solutions to the needs of the urban poor. Alternatively, leaders who tried to remain on the sidelines were often presumed to belong to one side or another anyhow, by virtue of their contacts or associations, or simply on the basis of hearsay.

The third option, an alliance between urban popular movements and a preferred partner, such as the political left, had likewise become untenable. More and more, such an alliance carried the risk of turning the respective movements into dependent support bases with little influence of their own. Dependency was sometimes created using material resources in a clientelist fashion. For example, following the breakup of Izquierda Unida at the national level and the increasingly bitter infighting among leftist parties in the district of El Agustino, the municipal government resorted to handing out benefits and favors with the goal of buttressing its popular support bases. The MIADES scheme, which had begun as a nonpartisan, participatory program open to all, more and more fell victim to these tactics. At a more general level, linking the fortune of urban popular movements too closely to that of the Left was clearly a problematic proposition in Peru in the late 1980s and early 1990s, given the rapid decline of the Left as a political force. Unfortunately, no other political actor was ready to fulfill the same role, a point to which I will return.

In this complex situation, some urban popular movements withdrew from programs that had been politicized and generally scaled down their contacts with others, including other popular movements. This clearly damaged the efforts at coalition building promoted by previous participatory politics. Some movements, however, opted for a fourth course of action, trying to counter co-optive pressures by establishing alliances with not one but several actors simultaneously. In so doing, they tried to benefit from the resources each of these actors had to offer, such as institutional support and help with infrastructural projects in the case of the municipal government of El Agustino, or technical and organizational assistance from one of the NGOs. At the same time, they were careful not to be associated too closely with any one of them, skillfully maintaining their distance and insisting on their own independence. As shown in the case of the Comité de Gestión in El Agustino, this strategy had some success in protecting the movements' autonomy, but it resulted in partial alliances that were mostly defensive and did little to broaden what little influence urban popular movements had.

Of course, this is not to say that co-optation was universal and that urban popular movements were incapable of shaping public policy or influencing other actors. Popular movements can take at least partial credit for the shift of the Peruvian left away from its vanguardist stance of the 1970s toward a partial embrace of political pluralism and the so-called new forms of doing politics. This programmatic shift became particularly relevant under the Barrantes administration of Metropolitan Lima, which largely abstained from trying to co-opt urban popular movements, and it also influenced the policies of district governments such as in El Agustino. Furthermore, the strength of regional popular movements toward the end of the 1970s and the crucial role they played in the mass mobilizations to end military rule, led to the inclusion of decentralist reforms in the Constitution of 1979 and the democratization of local governments. More often, however, rather than influencing other actors, urban popular movements were themselves under pressure and had to defend their independence against various forms of co-optation.

In sum, then, the democratic potential of urban popular movements appeared genuine enough, but in the cases studied it could not be fully realized because of the existence of institutional, economic, and political barriers, as well as the weaknesses of urban popular movements themselves. As long as such obstacles exist, the democratic potential of urban popular movements will probably remain unrealized, and the idea of establishing a new social contract at the grassroots, so often evoked in the literature, will remain an elusive goal. To become a reality, several important changes would be needed, and it is instructive to list them. To begin, existing openings for popular participation at the local level would have to be widened and new ones created. This would require widespread and far-reaching political decentralization, leading to a real devolution of powers and resources to lower levels of government. At the same time, clear mechanisms for popular participation would have to be put in place, backed up by institutional provisions and legal guarantees. Second, urban popular movements themselves would have to be strengthened. They would need to become more representative and enhance their programmatic and organizational capacities, possibly with help from other actors, such as NGOs. Urban popular movements would also need to unite around common goals, ideally integrating them into a comprehensive program. This would make it easier for them to influence public debates and to have an impact on other actors as well as public policy. Third, other actors, and especially political parties, would have to show a greater willingness to form alliances with urban popular movements on the basis of mutual respect, taking up and promoting the concerns of these movements, instead of trying to co-opt them and exploiting them for their own purposes. For this to happen, these actors would have to interpret such a nonco-optive strategy to be in their own best interests.

In Peru in the 1990s, such a scenario became increasingly unlikely, following the rise to power of a political outsider with authoritarian and anti-institutional leanings, Alberto Fujimori. Fujimori's victory in the 1990 presidential elections spelled the end for the decentralist policies of the previous decade, marking a reconcentration of the policy process at the national level. The centralist bias of the new government first became apparent in its draconian economic stabilization program designed to put an end to hyperinflation and economic chaos, as well as its approach to the struggle against Sendero Luminoso, which relied heavily on the Peruvian military and gave short shrift to concerns for the protection of civil and human rights.[3] But it manifested itself most clearly in the "self-coup" or *autogolpe* in April 1992, when Alberto Fujimori put an end to a long-standing battle with an opposition-dominated legislature by shutting down congress with the help of the military and assuming quasi-dictatorial powers. While the regime quickly bowed to international pressure and convened a constituent assembly later that year, it nevertheless managed to push through a new constitution in 1993 that greatly strengthened the power of the executive at the expense of the legislature. In so doing, it benefited from a wave of popular support due to an improving economy and a string of successes in the fight against Sendero Luminoso, particularly the surprise capture of its leader Abimael Guzmán in September 1992. In addition, the "traditional" parties had boycotted the constituent assembly elections, handing control of the chamber to Fujimori's backers and their allies. The new regime further consolidated its hold on power in the general elections

3. There is a large and growing body of literature on the Fujimori regime. See, for example, Grompone and Mejía 1995, Roberts 1995, Tuesta 1996, Cameron and Mauceri 1997a, Crabtree and Thomas 1998, and Tanaka 1998.

of 1995, when Alberto Fujimori won a resounding second term as president and the established political parties were virtually obliterated from the political map, failing to clear the 5-percent threshold required to maintain their registration with the National Electoral Board (Jurado Nacional de Elecciones).

As a central pillar in its strategy to maintain popular support, the regime handed out selective benefits to key constituencies, which was all the more crucial, given the devastating social impact of its economic policies.[4] President Fujimori could often be seen crisscrossing the country dressed in traditional garb, shaking hands with smiling farmers, handing out seeds and agricultural tools, or inaugurating roads, bridges, and other public works. The president's adept handling of the media (Tanaka 1998) ensured that coverage at these events was extensive, while the executive maintained a tight grip on the respective funds via the newly created Ministry of the Presidency, which acquired a growing role under Fujimori and managed an increasing share of the public budget. Obviously, independent regional and local governments had no place in this strategy, especially if they were controlled by political opponents that could one day become challengers to Fujimori himself. Consequently, the regime not only stopped the regionalization drive initiated under previous governments and promoted especially by APRA's Alan García,[5] it also set about undermining the status of local

---

4. See Wise 1997 and Figueroa 1998 for details. Socially regressive economic policies are not normally associated with populism. Traditionally, populist regimes have relied on alliances with specific social or economic groups ("rent-seeking combines") that received certain benefits financed by expansionary fiscal policies. By contrast, Fujimori's "neopopulist" regime derived its support from a citizenry often seen as amorphous and dispersed, and its austerity policies inflicted steep social costs instead of distributing benefits. The success of this model is variously attributed to the rampant social atomization and deinstitutionalization characterizing Peru in the early 1990s (Roberts 1995), providing a fertile breeding ground for political populism and economic neoliberalism alike, or alternatively, to Fujimori's adept handling of the mass media (Tanaka 1998). Other authors see it simply as an expression of a recurrent cycle of political populism and economic crisis brought about by the persistent weakness of representative institutions, albeit under different circumstances (Panfichi and Sanborn 1996). However, even the Fujimori regime had to resort to distributing selective benefits in the end, in order to retain popular support and head off potential discontent over its economic policies. Still, by favoring direct, personal interventions by the president and maintaining tight control over the distribution of funds, it managed to avoid the building of corporatist links to organized actors.

5. After President Fujimori's *autogolpe* of 5 April 1992, the existing regional governments were replaced by the so-called CTARs (Consejos Transitorios de Administración Regional) created at departmental level and controlled by the central government. The new Constitution of 1993 again provided for the creation of autonomous regions and the direct election of their presidents by universal suffrage. However, the Ley Marco de Descentralización (Ley No.

governments, particularly the larger ones such as Metropolitan Lima, which had remained in the hands of the political opposition despite concerted efforts to install a regime-friendly mayor.[6] Leaving the legal framework intact, this was done mainly by administrative decree, most notably Decree-Law (D.L.) No. 776 of 31 December 1993 (Delgado Silva 1994).

Presented as a measure to simplify municipal taxation, the main effect of D.L. No. 776 was to undercut the financial autonomy of local governments and to make them dependent on central government transfers. Aside from eliminating certain traditional sources of income and restricting the municipalities' right to charge a series of own levies, the decree abolished the practice of allocating a share of the national value-added tax and the gasoline tax (*rodaje*) to local governments. This meant that local governments lost their most important autonomous source of income, which they had won only in the mid-1980s, as a result of the concerted efforts of the Barrantes administration of Metropolitan Lima and the Asociación de Municipalidades de Perú (AMPE). In the case of Metropolitan Lima, for example, the municipal investment fund INVERMET, which had been created under Barrantes and used by successive administrations to finance infrastructure investments in the districts of the capital, lost 80 percent of its funding (Delgado Silva 1994, 37). To compensate for this, the central government established the nationwide Fondo de Compensación Municipal (FCM), which was controlled by the Ministry of the Presidency and distributed funds directly, mainly to district-level municipalities. Not surprisingly, this policy was fiercely resisted by the provincial governments and particularly the municipal government of Metropolitan Lima, whose mayor, Alberto Andrade, became one of the highest-profile challengers to Alberto Fujimori and a presidential candidate in the 2000 general elections.

The centralist, anti-institutional bias of the Fujimori regime was not without effect on urban popular movements, as well as other social actors. Still reeling from the corrosive effects of the economic crisis of the late 1980s, which were later compounded by the neoliberal economic policies

---

26922) adopted by the Congress on 30 January 1998 maintained the existing structure based on the CTARs, albeit on a transitory basis, placing them under the supervision of the Ministry of the Presidency. Not surprisingly, this law was criticized by the opposition and parts of the media, on the grounds that it obstructed decentralization and did not respect constitutional provisions.

6. In 1995 and 1998, Alberto Andrade, representing the opposition alliance Somos Lima that later changed its name to Somos Perú, beat the government candidates Jaime Yoshiyama (Nueva Mayoría) and Juan Carlos Hurtado Miller (Vamos Vecino).

of the Fujimori government, urban popular movements also had to cope with the aftermath of Sendero Luminoso's urban campaign in the early 1990s. Resulting in the death of about one hundred popular movement leaders in Lima alone and prompting many others to go into hiding, the attacks by Sendero Luminoso had severely curtailed participation by ordinary members. In addition, urban popular movements were now confronted by a populist regime that tended to bypass political institutions and organized civil society actors, in favor of establishing direct links between ruler and ruled. Crucially, this lessened their ability to obtain and distribute state resources, which had been an important source of legitimacy and a rallying point for its participants under previous governments. Such monies were now increasingly channeled through a variety of funds managed directly by the Ministry of the Presidency, such as the Fondo de Compensación Municipal mentioned earlier or the Fondo Nacional de Desarrollo y Compensación Social (FONCODES). At the same time, urban popular movements did not simply disappear, and the populist policies of the Fujimori regime did not result in the complete dissolution of the social fabric.

Obviously, in the absence of reliable empirical data, this is hard to know for certain. However, according to the evidence that is available (Sagasti et al. 1996), urban popular movements continue to function, even though they have certainly lost much of the dynamism of earlier years.[7] Some of them, particularly those run by women, have taken steps toward establishing more permanent structures, setting up productive enterprises such as bakeries providing inputs for communal soup kitchens or Vaso de Leche committees. What is more, urban popular movements are part of an increasingly complex and plural civil society (Sagasti et al. 1996; Lynch 1997), together with established actors such as labor unions, regional associations, and student organizations, as well as newer ones like chambers of commerce or associations of entrepreneurs or informal workers. Of course, this is not to deny that most of these organizations have serious shortcomings and deficiencies, among them their inability to unite around common

---

7. Given the circumstances, participation rates are quite respectable. The empirical study by Sagasti et al. (1996) shows that while 65.4 percent of those interviewed in Lima did not belong to any organization, 9.6 percent were members of a Vaso de Leche (Glass of Milk) committee. In the case of female interviewees, this figure rose to 14.1 percent, out of which 6.9 percent also participated in a communal soup kitchen. According to the same source, the Federación de Centrales de Comedores Populares Autogestionarios de Lima y Callao, established in 1991 at the height of the political and economic crisis, represented 39,982 women organized in 1,824 soup kitchens, with 74 representative bodies (*centrales*) at the zonal and 12 at the district level.

goals. In the words of the former mayor of Villa El Salvador, Michel Azcueta: "There is and there continues to be a level of participation . . . but the view of the whole by each organization has been lost. That is what is new. Everybody goes their own way" (García and del Carmen 1998, 310).[8] But the continued existence of these movements and organizations in very unfavorable circumstances casts doubt on the notion of a wholesale disintegration of civil society, which is sometimes voiced by political observers and in the academic literature. The real problem seems to lie not in the dissolution of the social fabric as such, but in the lack of suitable allies that could play the role of intermediaries between civil society and the state, especially political parties.

The disintegration of the traditional party system during the 1990s—one of the most striking features of the Fujimori regime—is of crucial importance in this regard. Beginning in 1989 with the election of an independent to the mayoralty of Metropolitan Lima, the TV personality Ricardo Belmont, and the victory of Alberto Fujimori himself in the 1990 presidential elections, this trend continued throughout the 1990s, culminating in the general elections of 1995. Even more astonishing was the fact that it affected all traditional parties across the board, from the extreme Left to the political center and the Right. The collapse of the Peruvian party system is usually attributed to the emergence of an independent or "floating" electorate (Roberts 1995, 1996; Cameron 1997), a result of the growth of the informal economy and the associated spread of pragmatist and individualist attitudes. Politically centrist and ideologically unbound, this electorate was no longer represented by the political parties on the Left or the Right, which increasingly espoused radical ideological positions and catered to specific constituencies. The resulting "crisis of representation" was exacerbated by the fact that successive "centrist" governments, first under Acción Popular and subsequently under APRA, had failed to provide solutions to the related problems of a worsening economic crisis, growing institutional decay, and an intensifying cycle of political violence. In this situation, the populist and antiestablishment discourse of political outsiders such as Alberto Fujimori rang true with a disillusioned and increasingly autonomous electorate.[9]

8. My translation.
9. In a variation of this argument, Tanaka (1998) contends that the traditional political parties continued to represent the established social and political actors throughout the 1980s, but not the population at large. The parties were overtaken by the key shift from an "electoral-movement driven dynamic" to a "media-driven dynamic," which revealed Alberto Fujimori's superior command of the mass media, as well their increasingly independent character. Grompone (1995) maintains that instead of a crisis of representation, there existed a more

The terrain vacated by the traditional political parties has been occupied by new political actors, often political independents trying to benefit from the deep public distrust of the old political parties and of politicians and politics in general. At the local level, this trend has been particularly pronounced: in the municipal elections in 1998, for example, virtually all candidates declared themselves independent of party links and connections to the political establishment. This included those running under the banner of the government-sponsored Vamos Vecino (Let's Go Neighbor) coalition, as well as the candidates of the opposition alliance Somos Perú (We Are Peru).[10] Many of the self-declared independents were in fact former party members who had abandoned their previous affiliation, using their personal charisma or successful track records as mayors or councillors in order to launch new movements or groupings. At the same time, particularly in the regions away from the capital, many of the candidates and movements that have surfaced over recent years express something genuinely new, standing up for local and regional concerns and fiercely independent of national political parties and groups (El Pulso Municipal 1998; A Medio Camino 1998). This not only highlights a growing schism between Lima and the rest of the country and the resentment felt by many toward a way of making politics in which decisions are made in the capital by an inner circle of leaders with little or no input by ordinary members (*política de*

---

deep-seated split between the social and the political realms. The retreat of the state and its drastic reduction under neoliberal auspices opened up spaces for groups such as the *rondas campesinas* (peasant self-defense leagues), leading to the emergence of a "new paternalism" under novel social leaderships based in family units or small communities. Of course, in the absence of reliable empirical data, it is difficult to know to what extent support for the regime was based on an underlying ideological shift within the Peruvian electorate or on pragmatist cost-benefit calculations. Henry Dietz (1998), for example, emphasizes what he sees as perfectly rational behavior on the part of the urban poor: after having exhausted all other options throughout the 1980s, they threw their support behind the newcomer Fujimori, all the more so when it became clear that he could deliver the key goods of economic and political stability. Conversely, they could easily withdraw their support if and when he ceased to do so. See also Panfichi 1997.

10. Somos Perú won a resounding victory in Lima, where its candidate for mayor, Alberto Andrade, received 59 percent of the popular vote against only 32 percent for his closest opponent, Hurtado Miller, representing the government-backed grouping Vamos Vecino. In addition, Somos Perú won in twenty-five of the forty-two districts of the capital, with fourteen going to Vamos Vecino and one each to APRA and Acción Popular. In the rest of the country, the picture was very different: independent candidates won in fifteen departmental capitals, with Vamos Vecino taking control of five and Somos Perú only three. At the provincial level, the dominance of the independents was less pronounced: they took control of eighty provincial councils as opposed to seventy for Vamos Vecino and just twenty-one for Somos Perú.

cúpula). In more general terms, the success of the "new independents" emphasizes the difficulties faced by any national-level political actor in Peru these days wanting to build stable political support bases and to integrate local or regional constituencies into a more universal political project.

At the time of writing, it was not yet clear what impact the sudden demise of the Fujimori regime would have on the situation just described. After a flawed election process in 2000 in which Fujimori won a constitutionally dubious third term as president, he was forced to step down amid revelations that his closest security adviser and political fixer, Vladimiro Montesinos, had masterminded an elaborate scheme to bribe politicians, army officials, judges, mayors, and others into supporting the regime and its often unconstitutional practices. With more and more evidence coming to light—Montesinos had assembled hundreds, perhaps thousands of videocassettes, called "vladivídeos," recording such exchanges—first he and then Fujimori himself had to flee the country, leaving behind a rapidly crumbling regime and a dwindling political support base. Pursued by international arrest warrants and reportedly having undergone plastic surgery, Montesinos was finally captured in Venezuela, while Fujimori took up residence in Japan where he was granted citizenship and thereby sheltered from prosecution. Back home, an opposition-dominated congress declared Fujimori "morally unfit" to govern and installed an interim government of highly respected technocrats under its president, Valentín Paniagua, including the former secretary general of the United Nations, Javier Pérez de Cuellar, as prime minister. The interim government's main task was to oversee the transition period, undo some of the more egregious deformations to democratic institutions under Fujimori, and especially to organize new and clean elections in the spring of 2001 under international auspices.

The first round of these elections on 8 April 2001 resulted in a victory by Alejandro Toledo and his movement Perú Posible, with APRA and its presidential candidate, former president Alan García, who had returned to Peru from political exile, coming in a surprisingly strong second. Both contenders promised to reinvigorate democratic political institutions and to reverse the effects of a decade of centralist and anti-institutional rule under Fujimori, but their programmatic platforms remained vague and sometimes overly optimistic. By all indications, the choice was between a political newcomer nagged by persistent doubts regarding his moral aptitude for high office, and a former president whose previous tenure in the 1980s had left the country reeling from hyperinflation, political violence, state-sanctioned human rights abuses, and pervasive corruption. More importantly,

Alejandro Toledo was backed by an untested political movement that was riven by internal differences and trying to shed its legacy as a loose opposition alliance against the Fujimori regime, whereas Alan Garcia's APRA—while being the strongest of Peru's remaining political parties—was a shadow of its former self and in any case had a track record in office that was less than reassuring. Alejandro Toledo went on to win the decisive runoff vote on 3 June 2001, vowing to pursue the reforms begun by the interim government before him. At the time of writing, he had been in office for only a few months, and it would have been too early to predict what course his government would finally take.

Seen from the perspective of popular movements and of civil society more generally, the upshot of these developments was that they were unlikely to find reliable allies in the political realm in the foreseeable future. In the case of Perú Posible, it still remained to be seen whether the movement could evolve into a more stable political force, with a clear programmatic outline and sufficient staying power on the political scene. APRA, on the other hand, had proved in the past to be highly manipulative, favoring co-optation and clientelism over more equitable relations with its partners. The political left, the preferred ally of popular movements during the 1980s, was unlikely to recover any time soon from its long decline since the mid-1980s and subsequent demise following the 1990 presidential elections.[11] Other political parties, such as Acción Popular (AP) or the Partido Popular Cristiano (PPC) had never shown much interest in establishing alliances with popular movements in the first place. In any event, they, too, had virtually disappeared from the political map, even though some of their components reappeared as parts of new political alliances, such as Lourdes Flores's Unidad Nacional.

Notwithstanding isolated cases at the local level (García and del Carmen 1998), the absence of reliable allies means that popular movements are unlikely to make great strides in Peru, at least for the time being. However, this is not to say that direct popular participation in politics, be it at the local level or further up in the political system, is impossible. In fact, Peru may be a special case, given that institutional decay and social disintegration went further there than in other countries as a result of a combination of exceptional circumstances at the end of the 1980s: an economic crisis of

11. For a debate on the future perspectives of the Peruvian Left, see Espinoza 1996, Haya de la Torre 1996, Lynch 1996, and Vilas 1997 in the journal *Socialismo y Participación*. Petras (1997) offers a more optimistic—and more radical—vision, referring to Latin America as a whole.

extraordinary depth, a national government engaging in mismanagement and corruption on an unprecedented scale, and a pervasive cycle of political violence.[12] Moreover, the almost total collapse of the party system has no parallels elsewhere in the region, with the possible exception of Venezuela. Other countries present more favorable conditions for popular participation in local politics (Castañeda 1993, 365–73; Fox 1994; NACLA 1995), and they could serve as examples for more successful cooperation between popular movements and other political actors.

Perhaps the most significant of these cases is that of Brazil. Experiences with popular participation in local government date back to the early 1970s, gaining momentum in the 1980s during Brazil's slow transition to democratic rule (*apertura*) (Assies 1993; Shidlo 1998). In 1988, when a new constitution eased the restrictions imposed on the municipalities by the military government, this tendency accelerated further. Aside from reintroducing direct elections of mayors in cities previously deemed of "strategic importance," the new constitution broadened the resource base of the municipalities, strengthened the position of municipal legislatures vis-à-vis the mayor, and created new possibilities for popular participation at the local level. Significantly enhancing the status of the municipalities versus other levels of government, this also created more favorable conditions for further experiments with participatory local governance, particularly under city councils controlled by the Workers' Party (PT).

The PT had been imbued with an "ethos of participation" since its emergence in the 1970s in the so-called ABC region around São Paulo, because of its close ties to labor unions and ecclesiastical base communities (CEBs), as well as rural urban popular movements forged in the struggles against the dictatorship (Keck 1992; Nylen 1997). Stressing autonomy and self-organization, one of the key tenets of this ethos was the belief that workers and the popular classes in general could not rely on elite actors to represent

---

12. I concur with Chalmers and his coauthors (Chalmers, Martin, and Piester 1997), who contend that in Latin America as a whole, popular movements are *more* likely than previously to become active participants in what they call "associative networks." See also McClintock and Lowenthal (1997, viii–ix), who agree with Cameron and Mauceri (1997b) that "given the strength of presidential power and the weakness of civilian political institutions," as well as the fact that Fujimori ruled de facto during the period between his *autogolpe* in April 1992 and his reelection in 1995, the Peruvian case goes beyond what O'Donnell has called delegative democracy (O'Donnell 1994). O'Donnell's term refers to a system in which traditional democratic criteria are maintained, notably with regard to clean elections, but which is majoritarian: for a given number of years, the president becomes the embodiment and the interpreter of the nation's interests, reducing voters ("delegators") to a passive but cheering audience.

their interests but had to participate in the political process themselves. Consequently, when PT candidates were elected to the mayoralty in various localities throughout Brazil, they strongly promoted the direct participation of these actors in the exercise of municipal government. One of the most visible examples was the controversial city government of São Paulo under Mayor Luiza Erundina (Assies 1993; Castañeda 1993, 151–52; Shidlo 1998), who supported the creation of "popular councils" that were to coexist with the municipal government and have "deliberative," that is, decision-making powers over municipal policy. Away from the PT's traditional heartland in the industrial areas of the southeast, cities such as Fortaleza, Icapuí, and Quixadá in the northern state of Ceará likewise experimented with popular participation (Nylen 1995; 1997). Finally, a particularly successful form of popular participation has been practiced in the southern city of Porto Alegre since 1989 (Tavares 1995; Rhodes 1998; Abers 2000). Labeled the participatory budget process, it involves the allocation of a sizable portion of the municipal budget for investment purposes, largely in poorer neighborhoods, following the deliberation of concrete investment proposals by sixteen regional and five thematic assemblies. Porto Alegre has been hailed as a showcase of pragmatic, fiscally responsible government by the Brazilian left, providing an alternative to the socially exclusionary policies of neoliberal governments.

Obviously, these experiences were not without problems (Fontes 1997), and some of them, such as the first PT government in Diadema in the mid-1980s, were clear failures (Assies 1993, 47). Popular expectations were often much too high and had to be scaled back in the face of inadequate administrative capacities and limited municipal resources, the result in part of financial mismanagement by previous administrations. In addition, the relations between popular movements, political parties, and institutions proved much more complex than initially thought, revealing a need for more explicit institutional arrangements and more permanent structures. For example, the newly created popular councils were soon reduced to a merely consultative role, and hopes for a more direct exercise of popular democracy were deferred. In addition, significant sectors of the PT regarded the expansion of participatory policies with suspicion, fearing an erosion of the traditional leading role of the party. Municipal bureaucracies were also recalcitrant and not easily convinced to adopt a more open, transparent, and responsive management style. As to popular movements themselves, they proved to be weaker and less representative than initially thought, despite their great visibility in the anti-authoritarian struggle, sometimes displaying familiar particularist and clientelist tendencies (Gay 1990). Overall, however, the PT's involvement in local government has yielded promising results. To a large extent, this was due to the adoption of a pragmatic, "heterodox" approach to local government, resulting from a process of party building and institutional learning (Nylen 1997).[13] While never acquiring hegemony in the party as a whole, this PT-specific mode of local governance, the *modo petista de governar,* has proved to be successful in combining efficient local management with a radical-democratic agenda for a more inclusive and democratic way of local governance.

The Uruguayan capital, Montevideo, has been the site of another important experience with popular participation in local government (Winn 1995; Winn and Ferro-Clérico 1997; Rankin 1998). Under its charismatic leader, Tabaré Vázquez, the leftist Frente Amplio coalition (Broad Front) won the municipal elections in 1989, breaking the dominance of the two traditional political parties, the Blancos and the Colorados, and taking control of the capital, in which live almost half of the nation's population. In government, the Frente Amplio quickly established a reputation for effective management of municipal affairs, addressing long-standing problems like the presence of street vendors in the capital, the decline in the quality of urban services, and the difficult relations between the city administration and its employees. More importantly, it launched an ambitious program to decentralize the municipal government and to increase citizen participation in local politics. For this purpose, the Uruguayan capital was subdivided into eighteen administrative zones, and a Centro Comunal Zonal (CCZ) with an associated committee structure was established in each. This consultative scheme resulted in a "big jump in participation" (Winn and Ferro-Clérico 1997, 460) around project proposals in fields such as housing, health, and urban services which later had to be approved by the municipal government. Subsequent efforts centered around the need to "develop a neighborhood movement that was not just a prisoner of immediate needs, but interested and capable of thinking in terms of the development of the zone, and able to mobilize other groups in the community around these goals" (Winn and Ferro-Clérico 1997, 461), leading to the establishment of directly elected neighborhood councils in each of the eighteen zones of the capital. As in Brazil, these efforts were not without problems, exposing a

---

13. It also helps to remember that Brazil has one of the highest degrees of political decentralization in Latin America, as reflected in the share of regional and local governments in total government expenditure (Peterson 1997; Willis, Garman, and Haggard 1999). Peru, by contrast, has one of the lowest.

rift between moderates within the Frente Amplio coalition favoring the empowerment of civil society via increased popular participation, and radicals clinging to a more conventional notion of political participation linked to political parties. Nevertheless, the decentralization initiative can be termed a qualified success, and it was continued after the Frente Amplio was returned to office for a second term in the municipal elections in 1994.

Clearly, though, creating more space for popular participation will always be an uphill battle, and truly ideal conditions for such an endeavor are unlikely to materialize. But this does not make it irrelevant. On the contrary, greater popular participation, at the local or other levels, remains a crucial means to tackle the exclusionary nature of many contemporary Latin American democracies.[14] Years after the return to civilian rule, the political systems of these countries often remain impervious to the pressing social and economic needs of the popular majorities, while most political parties are incapable or unwilling to represent their concerns in the political arena. Coupled with the inefficiency of public bureaucracies, the persistence of clientelist and populist traditions, and the social costs inflicted by structural adjustment policies, this has cast a shadow on the prospects for stability and democratic consolidation in the region. In fact, it is hardly surprising that several Latin American countries have been confronted by outbursts of social unrest and threatened by authoritarian coup attempts, and that the continuity of democratic rule seems to be threatened in some. As long as these problems persist, and as long as no other approach promises more feasible solutions, a strategy that aims at democratizing political institutions and political parties via an increase of popular participation at the grassroots still has its place. This study has left no doubt about the difficulties such a strategy faces; in fact, one of its principal contributions is to have highlighted the numerous obstacles that prevent popular participation from living up to its full potential. The challenge therefore remains for policymakers, social scientists, and social movement participants themselves to identify the conditions that would make popular participation viable.

---

14. As Roberts pointed out, the deepening of democracy and its consolidation need not be incompatible. On the contrary, the "self-containment or emasculation" of many current democracies in Latin America holds dangers for their stability (Roberts 1998, 280–81).

appendix: list of interviews

Interviews in the Districts of El Agustino and Santa Anita

Abregú, Victor. Neighborhood leader and member of the central committee of PMR. Lima, 21 January 1992.

Angulo, Neda. Community worker for SEA. Lima, 11 February 1992.

Atúncar, Jorge. PUM district councillor and head of the Oficina de Participación Vecinal (Neighborhood Participation Office) of El Agustino. Lima, 14 January 1992.

Barnet, Carmen, and Amanda Collazos. Neighborhood leaders in El Agustino. Lima, 21 January 1992.

Bazán, Pedro. Editor of the newsletter *Agenda Distrital* in Santa Anita. Lima, 19 February 1992.

Cáceres, Irene. Member of a *comedor popular* in El Agustino. Lima, 15 January 1992.

Cancho, Erasmo. Independent district councillor in El Agustino. Lima, 23 January 1992.

Casanova, Julio. Neighborhood leader and president of the federation of MIADES in El Agustino. Lima, 26 November 1991.

Castillo, Rosa. Member of the *clubes de madres* in El Agustino. Lima, 13 January 1992.

Chamberlain, Francisco. Catholic priest of the parish *Virgen de Nazareth* in El Agustino, head of SEA. Lima, 13 February 1992.

Cuadros, Carmen. Community worker for SEA. Lima, 8 January 1992.

de la Cruz, Jhon. APRA district councillor in El Agustino. Lima, 20 January 1992.

Durand Ríos, Elías. Neighborhood leader in Santa Anita. Lima, 19 February 1992.

Escalante, Carlos. Urban Planner working for CENCA. Lima, 9 January 1992.

Estrada, Lorenzo. Neighborhood leader and executive secretary of the Comité de Gestión in El Agustino. Lima, 27 February 1992.
Giraldo Flores, Yolanda, and Josefina Berna. Independent district councillor responsible for the Vaso de Leche program and district coordinator of the Vaso de Leche program in El Agustino, respectively. Lima, 8 January 1992.
Huarcaya de la Cruz, Valentín. Neighborhood leader in El Agustino. Lima, 11 February 1992.
Libia, Gloria. District coordinator of the *comedores populares* in El Agustino. Lima, 22 January 1992.
Lizarga, Carlos. Urban planner working for SEA. Lima, 6 February 1992.
Maraví, Yolanda. Member of a Vaso de Leche committee in El Agustino. Lima, 27 February 1992.
Martínez, Ana. President of the *clubes de madres* in Santa Anita. Lima, 26 February 1992.
Mendoza, Enrique. MAS district councillor in El Agustino. Lima, 22 February 1992.
Núñez, Celinda, and Maritza Jiménez. Head of the División de Bienestar Social y Participación Vecinal (Division of Social Welfare and Neighborhood Participation) and social assistant in the Oficina de Participación Vecinal (Neighborhood Participation Office) in Santa Anita, respectively. Lima, 20 January 1992.
Ortíz, Humberto. Community worker for SEA. Lima, 2 December 1991.
Palomino, Adelina. Member of the Vaso de Leche committee in Santa Anita. Lima, 21 and 25 February 1992.
Quesada, Carlos. Mayor of Santa Anita for Acción Popular. Lima, 7 January 1992.
Quintanilla, Jorge. Mayor of El Agustino for Izquierda Unida. Lima, 6 November 1991.
Romero, Rosario. Researcher for CENDIPP and CTIC in El Agustino. Lima, 15 January 1992.
Valencia, Gladys. Member of the district coordinating committee of the Vaso de Leche committees of El Agustino. Lima, 19 February 1992.
Véliz, Gustavo. Adviser to Mayor Jorge Quintanilla of El Agustino. Lima, 29 October 1991.
Zúñiga, Zenaida. Neighborhood leader and member of a *comedor popular* in El Agustino. Lima, 11 February 1992.

Interviews at the Level of Metropolitan Lima

Barrantes Lingán, Alfonso. Former mayor of Lima for Izquierda Unida. Lima, 16 November 1991.
Barrera, Soledad. Director-general of the Oficina General de Participación Vecinal (General Office for Neighborhood Participation) of the municipality of Metropolitan Lima. Lima, 20 April 1994.

Chirinos, Luis. Former member of the Oficina General de Participación Vecinal (General Office for Neighborhood Participation) of the municipality of Metropolitan Lima under Mayor Barrantes. Lima, 21 April 1992.

Guerrero, Elsi. Director in the Oficina General de Participación Vecinal (General Office for Neighborhood Participation) of the municipality of Metropolitan Lima. Lima, 23 October 1991.

Pease García, Henry. Former vice-mayor of Metropolitan Lima for Izquierda Unida. Lima, 16 April 1992.

Orrego, Eduardo. Former mayor of Metropolitan Lima for Acción Popular. Lima, 11 November 1991.

Zolezzi Chocano, Mario. Former director of the urban development secretariat of the municipality of Metropolitan Lima under Mayor Barrantes. Lima, 24 October 1991.

Other Interviews

Adrianzén, Alberto. Researcher at DESCO. Lima, 30 October 1991.
Ballón, Eduardo. Researcher at DESCO. Lima, 12 March 1992.
Bedoya, Susana. Researcher at IPADEL. Lima, 4 October 1991.
Calderón, Julio. Researcher at CENCA. Lima, 11 November 1991.
Dirmoser, Dietmar. Head of the Lima office of the Friedrich Ebert Foundation. Lima, 15 October 1991.
Joseph, Jaime. Researcher at Alternativa. Lima, 8 November 1991.
Olivera Cárdenas, Luis. Researcher at DESCO. Lima, 30 October 1991.

glossary of frequently used spanish terms

agencias municipales	municipal agencies
alcalde	mayor
asamblea popular	popular assembly
asentamiento humano	low-income "popular" settlement
asistencialismo	"assistentialism," denotes a relationship of dependency with public institutions, NGOs, etc.
autogolpe	"self-coup," refers to the closure of the Peruvian Congress by President Alberto Fujimori in 1992
autogobierno	self-government
barrio	neighborhood
cabildos abiertos	reunions between the municipal administration and representatives of popular organizations to inform and consult the population on municipal policy
capacitación	training
centralización	"centralization," refers to the process by which individual popular movements unite
cerro	hill
ciudadano	citizen
clubes de madres	mothers' clubs
co-gestión	joint management
comedor popular	communal soup kitchen
comisiones mixtas	mixed commissions, often comprising representatives of urban popular movements and the municipal administration
comité de gestión	management committee
comités comunales	neighborhood committees under the Decreto Ley No. 051

cono	cone, refers to one of the cone-shaped outskirts of Lima comprising low-income or "popular" districts
coordinadora	coordinating committee
democracia popular	popular democracy
desarrollo	development
directiva	see junta directiva
director municipal	municipal director, head of the municipal administration
dirigente	leader
emergencia	emergency, often in a social or economic sense
fiscalización	supervision, control
frente de defensa	defense front composed of different organizations, such as unions or neighborhood movements, responding to cuts in social services, the impact of economic adjustments programs, etc.
frente barrial	equivalent to frente de defensa, but limited to the neighborhood level
gestión	management
junta directiva	steering committee
junta de gobierno	steering committee, governing committee
juntas de vecinos	neighborhood committees under the Decreto Ley No. 051
lotización	demarcation of lots in a settlement
manzana	block
obras	public works
poblador	settler
poder popular	people's power
lo popular	the popular world
promotor	"promoter," community worker
protagonismo popular	attitude denoting sympathy with the concerns of popular movements and their social and political practices
pueblo	low-income or "popular" settlement
pueblos jóvenes	term coined by the Velasco government denoting urban squatter settlements
remodelación	process of restructuring a squatter settlement after the initial land occupation, including the remarking of individual plots
rondas campesinas	peasant self-defense leagues
taller	workshop
técnico	specialist
Vaso de Leche	glass of milk
vecino	neighbor
Zona Plana	central or "level" zone in the district of El Agustino, as opposed to those areas located in the hills

references

A Medio Camino. 1998. *Caretas*, no. 1538, 15 October (web edition).
Abers, Rebeca Neaera. 2000. *Inventing local democracy: Grassroots politics in Brazil.* Boulder, Colo.: Lynne Rienner Publishers.
Abregú, V. 1992. Interview by author. Lima, 21 January. Tape recording.
Acosta, D. 1986. "Plan Integral de Desarrollo Urbano." Typescript.
Adrianzén, A. 1990. Tragedia e ironía del socialismo peruano. *Pretextos* 1 (1): 7–22.
Adrianzén, A., and E. Ballón, eds. 1992. *Lo popular en América Latina ¿una visión en crisis?* Lima: DESCO.
Allou, S. 1988. Gestion urbaine et démocratie: La expérience avec la Gauche Unie à Lima. *Economie et Humanisme* 303 (September–October): 17–30.
———. 1989. *Lima en cifras.* Lima: CIDAP/IFEA.
Althusser, L. 1965. *Pour Marx.* Paris: Maspero.
Althusser, L., E. Balibar, R. Establet, P. Macherey, and J. Rancière. 1965. *Lire "Le Capital."* 2 vols. Paris: Maspero.
Alvarez, S. E., E. Dagnino, and A. Escobar. 1998. Introduction: The cultural and the political in Latin American social movements. In *Cultures of politics, politics of cultures: Re-visioning Latin American social movements.* Boulder, Colo.: Westview Press.
Amin, S. 1991. El problema de la democracia en el Tercer Mundo contemporáneo. *Nueva Sociedad* 112 (March-April): 24–39.
Arnao Rondán, R., and M. Meza Carey. 1990. *Economías municipales en la provincia de Lima: Retos de un problema nacional.* Lima: Fundación Friedrich Ebert/Instituto de Investigaciones Económicas (IECOS-UNI).
Arnillas, F. 1986. El movimiento popular urbano. Algunos puntos para el debate. *Nuevos Cuadernos Celats* 9:29–43.
Assies, Willem. 1993. Urban social movements and local democracy in Brazil. *European Review of Latin American and Caribbean Studies* 55 (December): 39–58.

Astiz, C. 1969. *Pressure groups and power elites in Peru.* Ithaca: Cornell University Press.
Atúncar, J. 1991. "El Agustino: Aquí se forjan las MIADES." Typescript.
———. 1992. Interview by author. Lima, 14 January. Tape recording.
Ballón, E. 1986a. Movimientos sociales y sistema político: El lento camino de la democratización: síntesis nacional. In *Movimientos sociales y democracia,* ed. E. Ballón. Lima: DESCO.
———. 1990. Movimientos sociales: Itinerario de transformaciones y lecturas. In C. R. Balbi, E. Ballón, M. Barrig, M. Castillo, J. Gamero, T. Tovar, and A. Zapata, *Movimientos sociales: Elementos para una relectura.* Lima: DESCO.
———. 1992. Actores sociales y populares: Orientaciones y cambios. In *El nuevo significado de lo popular en América Latina,* ed. A. Adrianzén and E. Ballón. Lima: DESCO.
———, ed. 1986b. *Movimientos sociales y crisis: El caso peruano.* Lima: DESCO.
———, ed. 1986c. *Movimientos sociales y democracia: La fundación de un nuevo orden.* Lima: DESCO.
Ballón, E. and A. Filomeno. 1981. Los movimientos regionales: ¿Hacia dónde van? *Quehacer* 11:96–103.
Barnet, C., and A. Collazos. 1992. Interview by author. Lima, 21 January. Tape recording.
Barrantes Lingán, A. 1983a. ¿Cuán alto vuela el cuervo? Interview. *Caretas,* 17 October, pp. 28–30, 40.
———. 1983b. ¡Adiós a Lenin! Interview. *Caretas,* 21 November, pp. 28–31.
———. 1984. *Sus propias palabras (entrevistas).* Lima: Mosca Azul Editores.
———. 1986. *Memoria, 1984–1986.* Lima: Municipalidad de Lima.
———. 1991. Interview by author. Lima, 16 November. Tape recording.
Barrantes puede ganar. 1983. *Quehacer* 25 (November): 8–12.
Barrenechea, C. 1989. *Izquierda Unida, gobiernos locales y protagonismo popular.* Cuzco: Mosoq Suyo.
Barrig, M. 1986. Democracia emergente y movimiento de mujeres. In *Movimientos sociales y democracia: La fundación de un nuevo orden,* ed. E. Ballón. Lima: DESCO.
———. 1989. The difficult equilibrium between bread and roses: Women's organizations and the transition from dictatorship to democracy in Peru. In *The women's movement in Latin America,* ed. J. Jaquette. Boston: Unwin Hyman.
———. 1990. Quejas y contentamientos: Historia de una política social, los municipios y la organización femenina an Lima. In C. R. Balbi, E. Ballón, M. Barrig, M. Castillo, J. Gamero, T. Tovar, and A. Zapata, *Movimientos sociales: Elementos para una relectura.* Lima: DESCO.
Barros, R. 1986. The Left and democracy: Recent debates in Latin America. *Telos* 68:49–70.
Bennett, V. 1992. The evolution of urban popular movements in Mexico between 1968 and 1988. In *The making of social movements in Latin America.*

Identity, strategy, and democracy, ed. A. Escobar and S. Alvarez. Boulder, Colo.: Westview Press.

Bernales, E. 1983. 50 años después. *Quehacer* 26 (December): 84–86.

Boisier, S. 1987. Decentralization and regional development in Latin America today. *CEPAL-Review* 31:133–44.

———. 1991. La descentralización: Un tema difuso y confuso. In *Descentralización política y consolidación democrática. Europa-América del Sur,* ed. D. Nohlen. Caracas: Editorial Nueva Sociedad.

Borja, J. 1975. *Movimientos sociales urbanos.* Buenos Aires: Ediciones Siap-Planteos.

———. 1988a. La descentralización del estado: Balance crítico y cuestiones de método. In *Estado y ciudad. Descentralización política y participación,* ed. J. Borja. Barcelona: Promociones y Publicaciones Universitarias.

———. 1988b. Participación ¿para qué? *Urbana* 9 (November): 25–44.

———. 1989a. Descentralización del estado y democracia local. In *Estado, descentralización y democracia,* ed. J. Borja. Bogotá: Ed. Foro Nacional por Colombia.

———. 1989b. Descentralización: Una cuestión de método. In *Estado, descentralización y democracia,* ed. J. Borja. Bogotá: Ed. Foro Nacional por Colombia.

Bottomore, T. 1992. Citizenship and social class, forty years on. In T. H. Marshall and Tom Bottomore, *Citizenship and social class.* Chicago: Pluto Press.

Bourricaud, F. 1970. *Power and society in contemporary Peru.* New York: Praeger.

Brand, K.-W., ed. 1985. *Neue soziale Bewegungen in Westeuropa und den USA: Ein internationaler Vergleich.* Frankfurt am Main: Campus.

Brand, K.-W., D. Büsser, and D. Rucht. 1986. *Aufbruch in eine neue Gesellschaft: Neue soziale Bewegungen in der Bundesrepublik Deutschland.* Frankfurt am Main: Campus.

Burt, J.-M. 1997. Political violence and the grassroots in Lima, Peru. In *The new politics of inequality in Latin America,* ed. D. Chalmers, C. Vilas, K. Hite, S. Martin, K. Priester, and M. Segarra. Oxford: Oxford University Press.

Burt, J.-M., and J. López Ricci. 1994. Peru: Shining Path after Guzmán. *NACLA Report on the Americas* 28 (4).

Cáceres, I. 1992. Interview by author. Lima, 15 January. Tape recording.

Calderón Cockburn, J. 1980a. Elecciones municipales, izquierda y movimientos de pobladores. *Quehacer* 6:50–59.

———. 1980b. *El Agustino: 33 años de lucha.* Lima: SEA.

Calderón Cockburn, J., and L. Olivera Cárdenas. 1989. *Municipio y pobladores en la habilitación urbana (Huaycán y Laderas del Chillón).* Lima: DESCO.

Calderón Cockburn, J., and R. Valdeavellano. 1991. *Izquierda y democracia. Entre la utopía y la realidad.* Lima: Instituto de Desarrollo Urbano (CENCA).

Calhoun, C. 1991. The problem of identity in collective action. In *Macro-micro linkages in sociology,* ed. J. Huber. London: Sage.

Cameron, M. 1991. Political parties and the worker-employer cleavage: The impact of the informal sector on voting in Lima, Peru. *Bulletin of Latin American Research* 10 (3): 293–313.

———. 1997. Political and economic origins of regime change in Peru: The eighteenth brumaire of Alberto Fujimori. In *The Peruvian labyrinth: Polity, society, economy,* ed. Maxwell A. Cameron and Philip Mauceri. University Park: Pennsylvania State University Press.

Cameron, M., and P. Mauceri. 1997a. *The Peruvian labyrinth: Polity, society, economy.* University Park: Pennsylvania State University Press.

———. 1997b. Conclusion: Threads in the Peruvian Labyrinth. In *The Peruvian labyrinth: Polity, society, economy,* ed. Maxwell A. Cameron and Philip Mauceri. University Park: Pennsylvania State University Press.

Cancho, E. 1992. Interview by author. Lima, 23 January. Tape recording.

Caravedo, B. 1988. *Descentralización y democracia.* Lima: GREDES.

Carbajo, J. L. 1986. El reto de la educación y la cultura. *Tarea* 16 (December): 40–43.

———. 1990. Comités de gestión distrital de la emergencia. Protesta con propuesta y gestión. *Tarea* 25 (December): 10–15.

Carbonetto, D., J. Hoyle, and M. Tueros. 1988. *Lima: Sector informal.* 2 vols. Lima: Centro de Estudios para el Desarrollo y la Participación (CEDEP).

Cardoso, F. H. 1971. Comentario sobre los conceptos de sobrepoblación relativa y marginalidad. *Revista Latinoamericana de Ciencias Sociales* 1/2.

Cardoso, R. 1983. Movimentos sociais urbanos: Balanço critico. In *Sociedad e Política no Brasil pós 64,* ed. B. Sorj and M. de Almeida. São Paulo: Brasiliense.

———. 1992. Popular movements in the context of the consolidation of democracy in Brazil. In *The making of social movements in Latin America. Identity, strategy, and democracy,* ed. A. Escobar and S. Alvarez. Boulder, Colo.: Westview Press.

Carlessi, C. 1989. The reconquest. *NACLA* 23 (4): 15–21.

Carr, B., and S. Ellner, eds. 1993. *The Latin American left: From the fall of Allende to Perestroika.* Boulder, Colo.: Westview Press.

Carroll, T. F. 1992. Capacity building for participatory organizations. In *Participatory development and the World Bank,* ed. B. Bhatnagar and A. C. Williams. Washington, D.C.: World Bank.

Casanova, J. 1991. Interview by author. Lima, 26 November. Tape recording.

Castañeda, J. 1993. *Utopia unarmed: The Latin American left after the cold war.* New York: Alfred A. Knopf.

Castells, M. 1977. *The urban question: A Marxist approach.* Cambridge: MIT Press.

———. 1978. *City, class, and power.* Basingstoke: Macmillan.

———. 1983. *The city and the grass-roots.* Berkeley and Los Angeles: University of California Press.

Castells, M., and J. Borja. 1988. Urbanización y democracia local en América Latina. In *La ciudad de la democracia,* ed. M. Castells et al. Santiago de Chile: Vector.

Castro-Pozo Díaz, H., and A. Delgado Silva. 1989. *Manual del regidor.* Lima: IPADEL/DESCO.

Castro-Pozo Díaz, H., P. Iturregui Byrne, and M. Zolezzi Chocano. 1991. La gestión urbana. In *Construyendo un gobierno metropolitano: Políticas municipales, 1984–1986*, comp. H. Pease García. Lima: IPADEL.
CELATS. 1983. *Manual de organización y funciones de comedores populares de El Agustino*. Lima: CELATS.
CENCA and SEA. [1991]. Las Microáreas de Desarrollo en El Agustino: Municipio y pobladores. In *Gestión popular del habitat. 7 Experiencias en el Perú*. Lima: Comisión Habitat.
Centralización del movimiento popular. Asamblea Nacional Popular. 1987. *Sur* 10 (109): 4–15.
Chalmers, Douglas, Scott B. Martin, and Kerianne Piester. 1997. Associative networks: New structures of representation for the popular sectors? In *The new politics of inequality in Latin America*, ed. Douglas Chalmers et al. Oxford: Oxford University Press.
Chamberlain, F. 1992. Interview by author. Lima, 13 February. Tape recording.
Cheema, G. S. 1983. The role of voluntary organizations. In *Decentralization and development: Policy implementation in developing countries*, ed. G. S. Cheema and D. Rondinelli. Beverly Hills, Calif.: Sage.
Cheema, G. S., and D. Rondinelli. 1983. *Decentralization and development: Policy implementation in developing countries*. Beverly Hills, Calif.: Sage.
Chilcote, R. 1990. Post-Marxism: The retreat from class in Latin America. *Latin American Perspectives* 17 (2): 3–24.
Chirinos, L. 1980. *Elecciones municipales: Un debate más allá de lo electoral*. Lima: CIDAP.
———. 1984. *Tipología de organizaciones populares en barrios*. Lima: CIDAP.
———. 1986. Gobierno local y participación vecinal: El caso de Lima Metropolitana. *Socialismo y Participación* 36:1–27.
———. 1991. La participación vecinal. In *Construyendo un gobierno metropolitano. Políticas municipales 1984–1986*, comp. H. Pease García. Lima: IPADEL.
———. 1992. Interview by author. Lima, 21 April.
Cohen, J. 1985. Strategy or identity: New theoretical paradigms and contemporary social movements. *Social Research* 52 (4): 663–716.
Cohen, Jean L., and Andrew Arato. 1995. *Civil society and political theory*. Cambridge: MIT Press.
Collier, D. 1976. *Squatters and oligarchs*. Baltimore: Johns Hopkins University Press.
Confluencia Socialista. 1991. "Primer encuentro socialista de El Agustino. Documentos." Typescript.
Conyers, D. 1983. Decentralization—The latest fashion in development administration? *Public Administration and Development* 3 (2): 97–109.
———. 1984. Decentralization and development: A review of the literature. *Public Administration and Development* 4 (2): 187–97.
———. 1986. Future directions in development studies: The case of decentralization. *World Development* 14 (5): 593–601.

Coraggio, J. L. 1989. La propuesta de descentralización: En busca de un sentido popular. In *Descentralización del Estado. Requerimientos y políticas en la crisis,* ed. E. Laurelli and A. Rofman. Buenos Aires: Centro de Estudios Urbanos y Regionales (CEUR) / Fundación Friedrich Ebert.

Cornelius, W. 1974. Urbanization and political demand-making: Political participation among the migrant poor in Latin American cities. *American Political Science Review* 58 (September): 1125–46.

Cosecha roja. 1991. *La República,* 3 November 1991, pp. 5–6.

Cotler, J. 1978. *Clases, estado y nación en el Perú.* Lima: Instituto de Estudios Peruanos (IEP).

———. 1986. Military interventions and "transfer of power to civilians" in Peru. In *Transitions from authoritarian rule,* ed. G. O'Donnell, P. Schmitter, and L. Whitehead. Baltimore: Johns Hopkins University Press.

———, ed. 1987. *Para afirmar la democracia.* Lima: Instituto de Estudios Peruanos (IEP).

Crabtree, John, and Jim Thomas. 1998. *Fujimori's Peru: The political economy.* London: Institute of Latin American Studies, University of London.

CTIC (Comité Coordinador Técnico Intercentros). [1991]. *Plan Integral de Desarrollo de El Agustino (Versión Resumida).* Lima: CTIC.

Cuadros, C. 1992. Interview by author. Lima, 8 January. Tape recording.

Dahl, R. A. 1989. *Democracy and its critics.* New Haven: Yale University Press.

Dahl, R. A., and E. R. Tufte. 1973. *Size and democracy.* Stanford: Stanford University Press.

Dalton, R., and M. Kuechler. 1990. *Challenging the political order: New social and political movements in western democracies.* Cambridge: Polity Press.

de Althaus Guarderas, J. 1986. *Realidad de las municipalidades en el Perú. Bases para una política de descentralización y fortalecimiento municipal.* Lima: Instituto Latinoamericano de Promoción Comunal y Municipal / FFE.

———. 1987. *El desarrollo hacia adentro y anemia regional en el Perú.* Lima: Fundación M. J. Bustamante de la Fuente.

de la Cruz, J. 1992. Interview by author. Lima, 20 January. Tape recording.

de Mattos, C. 1989a. Falsas expectativas ante la descentralización. Localistas y neoliberales en contradicción. *Nueva Sociedad* 104:118–33.

———. 1989b. La descentralización, ¿una nueva panacea para impulsar el desarrollo local? *Socialismo y Participación* 46 (June): 23–42.

de Tocqueville, A. 1945 [1835]. *Democracy in America.* 2 vols. New York: Vintage Books.

Degregori, C., C. Blondet, and N. Lynch. 1986. *Conquistadores de un nuevo mundo. De invasores a ciudadanos en San Martín de Porres.* Lima: Instituto de Estudios Peruanos (IEP).

Degregori, C., and R. Grompone. 1991. *Elecciones 1990. Demonios y redentores en el nuevo Peru. Una tragedia en dos vueltas.* Lima: Instituto de Estudios Peruanos (IEP).

Delgado Silva, A. 1982a. Estado, municipios y lucha por la democracia. *Tarea* 6 (March): 5–8.

———. 1982b. *Municipio, descentralización y movimiento popular. Las alternativas de la izquierda.* Lima: Editora INGRAF Peruana.

———. 1991. Economía municipal. In *Construyendo un gobierno metropolitano. Políticas municipales 1984–1986*, comp. H. Pease García. Lima: IPADEL.

———. 1994. Autocracia y régimen local. *Socialismo y Participación* 65 (March): 31–40.

Delgado Silva, A., and L. Olivera Cárdenas. 1983. De que municipio hablamos. *Quehacer* 22 (May): 98–102.

Delgado, C. 1975. *Revolución peruana: Autonomía y deslindes*. Lima: Librería Studium.

Delpino, N., and L. Pásara. 1991. El otro actor en la escena: Las ONGs. In *La otra cara de la luna. Nuevos actores sociales en el Perú*, ed. L. Pásara, N. Delpino, R. Valdeavellano, and A. Zarzar. Lima and Buenos Aires: CEDYS.

Democratization and class struggle. 1988. *Latin American Perspectives* 15 (3): 3–150 (Special Issue).

Derpich, V. 1986. Decisión y democratización. In *El poder municipal. Elecciones 86*, ed. M. del Pilar Tello. Lima: Universidad del Pacífico and Fundación Friedrich Ebert.

DESAL. 1968. *Tenencia de la tierra y campesinado en Chile*. Buenos Aires: Ediciones Troquel.

———. 1969. *Marginalidad en América Latina. Un ensayo de diagnóstico*. Barcelona: Editorial Herder.

Díaz Palacios, J. 1990. *Municipio: Democracia y desarrollo*. Lima: CIDAP / IPADEL / LABOR-Ilo / TAREA.

Dietz, H. 1980. *Poverty and problem-solving under military rule: The urban poor in Lima, Peru*. Austin: University of Texas Press.

———. 1985. Political participation in the barriadas. An extension and reexamination. *Comparative Political Studies* 18 (3): 323–55.

———. 1989. Political participation in the barriadas. A research update. *Comparative Political Studies* 22:122–30.

———. 1991. Some political ramifications of urban informality in Lima, Peru. Paper presented at the 1991 conference of the Latin American Studies Association (LASA), Washington, D.C.

———. 1998. *Urban poverty, political participation, and the state. Lima 1970–1990*. Pittsburgh: University of Pittsburgh Press.

Dietz, Henry, and Gil Shidlo, eds. 1998. *Urban elections in democratic Latin America*. Wilmington, Del.: Scholarly Resources.

Diez Canseco, J. 1983. IU: Camino se hace al andar. *Quehacer* 26 (December): 87–89.

———. 1987. Partido Unificado Mariateguista, PUM (Peru). *Nueva Sociedad* 91 (September-October): 80–81, 89.

———. 1990. La agenda de la Izquierda Unida. *Debate* 12 (60): 30–34.

———. 1992. La izquierda en el Perú el problema nacional y la democracia. *Nueva Sociedad* 117 (January-February): 77–87.

Domenack, H. 1987. "Determinación de Microáreas en el Distrito de El Agustino." Typescript.

Driant, J. C. 1991. *Las barriadas de Lima*. Lima: DESCO.

Eckstein, S., ed. 1989. *Power and popular protest: Latin American social movements*. Berkeley and Los Angeles: University of California Press.

El Pulso Municipal. 1998. *Caretas*, no. 1535, 24 September (web edition).
Ellner, S. 1989. The Latin American left since Allende: Perspectives and new directions. *Latin American Research Review* 24 (2): 143–67.
Escalante, C. 1992. Interview by author. Lima, 9 January. Tape recording.
Escobar, A., and S. Alvarez, eds. 1992a. *The making of social movements in Latin America. Identity, strategy, and democracy.* Boulder, Colo.: Westview Press.
———. 1992b. Introduction: Theory and protest in Latin America today. In *The making of social movements in Latin America: Identity, strategy, and democracy*, ed. A. Escobar and S. Alvarez. Boulder, Colo.: Westview Press.
Esman, M. J., and N. H. Uphoff. 1984. *Local organizations: Intermediaries in rural development.* Ithaca: Cornell University Press.
Espinoza, Gustavo. 1996. Ser socialista en el Perú. *Socialismo y Participación*, no. 75 (September): 61–65.
Estrada, L. 1992. Interview by author. Lima, 27 February. Tape recording.
Evers, T., C. Müller-Plantenberg, and S. Spessart. 1979. Stadtteilbewegung und Staat. Kämpfe im Reproduktionsbereich in Lateinamerika. *Lateinamerika— Analysen und Berichte* 3:118–70.
Fadda, G. 1988. Revisión crítica del concepto de participación como base para la formulación de un instrumento de analisis. *Urbana* 9 (November): 109–26.
Fals Borda, O. 1986. El nuevo despertar de los movimientos sociales. *Revista Foro* 1 (1): 76–83.
Fernández V., J., and B. Núñez Deza. 1986. *Aunque nos desalojen mil veces.* Lima: La Rueda, Colectivo de Educación Popular.
Ferree, M. 1992. The political context of rationality: Rational choice theory and resource mobilization. In *Frontiers in social movement theory*, ed. A. Morris and C. Mueller. New Haven: Yale University Press.
Figueroa, Adolfo. 1998. Income distribution and poverty in Peru. In *Fujimori's Peru: The political economy*, ed. John Crabtree and Jim Thomas. London: Institute of Latin American Studies, University of London.
Fisette, J. 1990. *La décentralisation dans les pays en développement. Points de repères méthodologiques.* Montréal: Urbanization and Development, Montreal Interuniversity Group (Discussion Paper, no. 10-90).
FitzGerald, E.V.K. 1983. State capitalism in Peru: A model of economic development and its limitations. In *The Peruvian experiment reconsidered*, ed. C. McClintock and A. F. Lowenthal. Princeton: Princeton University Press.
Flores Galindo, A. 1981. Región y regionalismo en el Perú. In *Lecturas sobre regionalización*, ed. C. Amat y León et al. Lima: Centro de Investigación de la Universidad del Pacífico.
Fontes, Breno Augusto Souto-Maior. 1997. Gestión urbana y participación popular. ¿Utopía o reingeniería política? *Nueva Sociedad*, no. 149 (May-June): 178–89.
Foss, D., and R. Larkin. 1986. *Beyond revolution: A new theory of social movements.* South Hadley, Mass.: Bergin and Garvey.
Foweraker, J. 1990. Popular movements and political change in Mexico. In *Popular movements and political change in Mexico*, ed. J. Foweraker and A. L. Craig. Boulder, Colo.: Lynne Rienner Publishers.

———. 1995. *Theorizing social movements.* Boulder, Colo.: Pluto Press.
Fox, J. 1994. Latin America's emerging local politics. *Journal of Democracy* 5 (2): 105–16.
Franco, C. 1979. *Peru: Participación popular.* Lima: Centro de Estudios para el Desarrollo y la Participación (CEDEP).
———. 1983. Las limitaciones del enfoque y las estrategias participativas. In *El Perú de Velasco,* ed. C. Franco et al. Lima: Centro de Estudios para el Desarrollo y la Participación (CEDEP).
———. 1991. *Imágenes de la sociedad peruana: La otra modernidad.* Lima: Centro de Estudios para el Desarrollo y la Participación (CEDEP).
Frías, C. 1986. Luces y sombras en la relación gobierno local y organización popular. *Tarea* 16 (December): 44–48.
Galín, P., J. Carrión, and O. Castillo. 1986. *Asalariados y clases populares en Lima.* Lima: Instituto de Estudios Peruanos (IEP).
Gamson, W. A., and D. S. Meyer. 1996. Framing political opportunity. In *Comparative perspectives on social movements: Political opportunities, mobilizing structures, and cultural framings,* ed. D. McAdam, J. D. McCarthy, and M. N. Zald. Cambridge: Cambridge University Press.
García de Chu, Inés, and María del Carmen Piazza. 1998. *Sociedad y gobierno local: Espacios de concertación y democracia.* Lima: DESCO.
Gay, R. 1990. Neighborhood associations and political change in Rio de Janeiro. *Latin American Research Review* 25 (1): 102–18.
Germani, G. 1980. *Marginality.* New Brunswick, N.J.: Transaction Books.
Giraldo, Y., and J. Berna. 1992. Interview by author. Lima, 8 January. Tape recording.
Goldrich, D., R. Pratt, and C. R. Schuller. 1976. The political integration of lower-class urban settlements in Chile and Peru. In *Peruvian nationalism: A corporatist revolution,* ed. D. Chaplin. New Brunswick, N.J.: Transaction Books.
Gonzales de Olarte, E. 1989. Regionalización y descentralización en el Perú. In *¿Hacia un nuevo orden estatal en América Latina?* vol. 5. Buenos Aires: CLACSO.
González, E. 1986. Una experencia educativa de masas. *Tarea* 16 (December): 33–39.
Gorz, A. 1980. *Adieux au prolétariat: Au delà du socialisme.* Paris: Editions Galilée.
Graham, C. 1991. The APRA government and the urban poor: The PAIT programme in Lima's pueblos jóvenes. *Journal of Latin American Studies* 23:91–130.
———. 1992. *Peru's APRA: Parties, politics, and the elusive quest for democracy.* Boulder, Colo.: Lynne Rienner Publishers.
Grompone, R. 1990. Las lecturas políticas de la informalidad. In A. Bustamante, E. Chávez, R. Grompone, S. Machacuay, and G. Ríofrío, *De marginales a informales.* Lima: DESCO.
———. 1995. Nuevos tiempos, nueva política. In *Nuevos tiempos, nueva política. El fin de un ciclo partidario,* ed. Romeo Grompone and Carlos Mejía. Lima: Instituto de Estudios Peruanos (IEP).

Grompone, Romeo, and Carlos Mejía. 1995. *Nuevos tiempos, nueva política. El fin de un ciclo partidario.* Lima: Instituto de Estudios Peruanos (IEP).
Guerra García, F. 1983. SINAMOS y la promoción de la participación. In *El Perú de Velasco,* ed. C. Franco et al. Lima: Centro de Estudios para el Desarrollo y la Participación (CEDEP).
Guerrero, E. N.d. "Egresos, estructura orgánica municipal y elementos de diagnóstico para su mejoramiento." Typescript.
Gurr, T. R. 1970. *Why men rebel.* Princeton: Princeton University Press.
Guzmán, A. 1988. La entrevista del siglo. Habla el Presidente Gonzalo. Interview by L. Arce Borja and J. Talavera. *El Diario,* 24 July, pp. 2–47.
Haak, R. 1987. El programa del Vaso de Leche. In *Estrategias de vida en el sector urbano popular,* ed. R. Haak and J. Díaz Albertini. Lima: FOVIDA/DESCO.
Haber, P. L. 1996. Identity and political process: Recent trends in the study of Latin American social movements. *Latin American Research Review* 31 (1): 171–87.
Habermas, J. 1987. *Theorie des kommunikativen Handelns.* Frankfurt am Main: Suhrkamp.
Harris, R. L. 1983. Centralization and decentralization in Latin America. In *Decentralization and development: Policy implementation in developing countries,* ed. G. S. Cheema and D. Rondinelli. Beverly Hills, Calif.: Sage.
Haworth, N. 1993. Radicalization and the Left in Peru, 1976–1991. In *The Latin American Left: From the fall of Allende to Perestroika,* ed. B. Carr and S. Ellner. Boulder, Colo.: Westview Press.
Haya de la Torre, Agustín. 1996. La izquierda: viejas y nuevas ideas. *Socialismo y Participació*n, no. 75 (September): 67–71.
Hellman, J. A. 1992. The study of new social movements in Latin America and the question of autonomy. In *The making of social movements in Latin America. Identity, strategy, and democracy,* ed. A. Escobar and S. Alvarez. Boulder, Colo.: Westview Press.
Henríquez, N. 1986. Notas y tesis sobre los movimientos regionales en el Perú. In *Movimientos sociales y crisis: El caso peruano,* ed. E. Ballón. Lima: DESCO.
Henry, E. 1978. *La escena urbana. Estado y movimiento de pobladores 1967–1976.* Lima: PUC.
———. 1981. La centralización barrial entre 1979 y 1980. In *Movimiento de pobladores y centralización.* Lima: CIDAP (Series: Cuadernos CIDAP, no. 3).
———. 1982. Pérou: La dynamique des secteurs populaires urbains. *Notes et Etudes Documentaires* 4653/4654:119–46 (Series: Problèmes d'Amérique Latine, no. 63).
Herman, E., and J. Petras. 1985. "Resurgent democracy": Rethoric and reality. *New Left Review* 154 (November/December): 83–98.
Herrera, G. 1983. El triunfo de Izquierda Unida. *Quehacer* 26 (December): 89–91.
Herzer, H., and P. Pirez. 1991. Municipal government and popular participation in Latin America. *Environment and Urbanization* 3 (1): 79–97.

Hirsch, J., and R. Roth. 1986. *Das neue Gesicht des Kapitalismus*. Hamburg: VSA-Verlag.
Iguiñiz, J., V. Paniagua, C. Vásquez, and P. Tábory. 1986. El descentralismo en las propuestas de plan de gobierno 1985–1990. In *Descentralización y desarrollo regional*, ed. Asociación Nacional de Centros de Investigación, Promoción Social y Desarrollo (ANC). Lima: ANC / Fundación Friedrich Ebert.
Illy, H. F., E. Kaiser, and K. Schimitzek. 1988. *Lokale Verwaltungsinstitutionen und Selbsthilfemaßnahmen in Entwicklungsländern*. Köln: Weltforum Verlag.
Iturregui Byrne, P. 1990. Las Juntas Interdistritales de Planeamiento. In *Lima, crisis y alternativas. La carta de Lima*. Lima: CIPUR / Fundación Friedrich Ebert.
Iturregui Byrne, P., and J. Zavaleta Alegre, comps. 1988. *Hacia un nuevo gobierno municipal: La participación popular*. Lima: Fundación Friedrich Ebert.
Izquierda Unida. 1983. *Programa de gobierno municipal*. Lima: Comisión de Plan de Gobierno de Izquierda Unida.
―――. 1985. *Plan de gobierno de Izquierda Unida: Peru 1985–1990*. Lima: Comisión de Plan de Gobierno de Izquierda Unida.
Jaquette, J. 1989a. Conclusions. In *The women's movement in Latin America*, ed. J. Jaquette, Boston: Unwin Hyman.
―――, ed. 1989b. *The women's movement in Latin America*. Boston: Unwin Hyman.
Jelin, E. 1996. Citizenship revisited: Solidarity, responsibility, and rights. In *Constructing democracy: Human rights, citizenship, and society in Latin America*, ed. E. Jelin and E. Hershberg. Boulder, Colo.: Westview Press.
―――, ed. 1990. *Women and social change in Latin America*. London: Zed Books.
Jenkins, J. C. 1983. Resource mobilization theory and the study of social movements. *Annual Review of Sociology* 9:527–53.
Kärner, H. 1983. Los movimientos sociales. Revolución de lo cotidiano. *Nueva Sociedad* 64:25–32.
Katznelson, I. 1986. Working-class formation: Constructing cases and comparisons. In *Working-class formation: Nineteenth-century patterns in Western Europe and the United States*, ed. I. Katznelson and A. Zolberg. Princeton: Princeton University Press.
Kaufmann, M., and H. Dilla Alfonso, eds. 1997. *Community power and grassroots democracy: The transformation of social life*. London: Zed Books.
Kay, C. 1989. *Latin American theories of development and underdevelopment*. New York and London: Routledge.
Kebir, S. 1991. *Antonio Gramscis Zivilgesellschaft*. Hamburg: VSA-Verlag.
Keck, Margaret. 1992. *The Workers' Party and democratization in Brazil*. New Haven: Yale University Press.
Kim, Sung Han. 1992. The political process of decentralization in Peru, 1985–1990. *Public Administration and Development* 12 (3): 249–65.
Klandermans, B. 1991. New social movements and resource mobilization: The European and the American approach revisited. In *Research on social movements*, ed. D. Rucht. Boulder, Colo.: Westview Press.
Kuechler, M., and R. Dalton. 1990. New social movements and the political order: Inducing change for long-term stability? In *Challenging the political*

order: New social and political movements in western democracies, ed. R. Dalton and M. Kuechler. Cambridge: Polity Press.
La Batalla de Lima. 1992. *Caretas*, 24 February, pp. 33–37, 40, 84–85.
Laclau, E. and C. Mouffe. 1985. *Hegemony and socialist strategy—towards a radical democratic politics*. London: Verso.
———. 1987. Post-Marxism without apologies. *New Left Review* 166:79–106.
Lechner, N. 1985. De la revolución a la democracia. El debate intelectual en América del sur. *Opciones* 6:57–72.
———. 1991. The search for lost community: Challenges to democracy in Latin America. *International Social Science Journal* 129 (August): 541–53.
———, ed. 1982. *¿Qué significa hacer política?* Lima: DESCO.
Leeds, A. 1969. The significant variables determining the character of squatter settlements. *America Latina* 12 (4): 44–86.
Leeds, A., and E. Leeds. 1978. Accounting for behavioural differences: Three political systems and the responses of squatters in Brazil, Peru and Chile. In *The city in comparative perspective*, ed. J. Walton and L. Masotti. New York: John Wiley and Sons.
Letts, R. 1981. *La izquierda peruana: Organizaciones y tendencias*. Lima: Mosca Azul.
Libia, G. 1992. Interview by author. Lima, 22 January. Tape recording.
Lo, C. 1992. Communities of challengers in social movement theory. In *Frontiers in social movement theory*, ed. A. D. Morris and C. McClurg Mueller. New Haven: Yale University Press.
Lobo, S. 1982. *A house of my own: Social organization in the squatter settlements of Lima, Peru*. Tucson: University of Arizona Press.
Lojkine, J. 1977. *Le marxisme, l'état et la question urbaine*. Paris: Presses Universitaires de France.
Lowder, S. 1992. Decentralization in Latin America: An evaluation of achievements. In *Decentralization in Latin America: An evaluation*, ed. A. Morris. New York: Praeger.
Lowe, S. 1986. *Urban social movements: The city after Castells*. London: Macmillan.
Lowenthal, A. F., ed. 1975. *The Peruvian experiment*. Princeton: Princeton University Press.
Lummis, C. D. 1996. *Radical democracy*. Ithaca: Cornell University Press.
Lynch, N. 1989. ¿Anomía de regresión o anomía de desarrollo? *Socialismo y Participación* 45 (March): 19–27.
———. 1996. Resignificar el socialismo en el Perú. *Socialismo y Participación*, no. 75 (September): 73–83.
———. 1997. New citizens and old politics in Peru. *Constellations* 4 (1): 124–40.
Mainwaring, S. 1987. Urban popular movements, identity, and democratization in Brazil. *Comparative Political Studies* 20 (2): 131–59.
———. 1989. Grassroots popular movements and the struggle for democracy: Nova Iguaçu. In *Democratizing Brazil*, ed. A. Stepan. New York: Oxford University Press.
Mainwaring, S., and E. Viola. 1984. New social movements, political culture and democracy: Brazil and Argentina in the 1980s. *Telos* 61:17–54.

Maraví, Y. 1992. Interview by author. Lima, 27 February. Tape recording.
Mariátegui, J. 1971. *Seven interpretive essays on Peruvian reality.* Austin: University of Texas Press.
Marshall, T. H. 1992 [1950]. Citizenship and social class. In T. H. Marshall and T. Bottomore, *Citizenship and social class.* Chicago: Pluto Press.
Matos Mar, J. 1977. *Las barriadas de Lima 1957.* Lima: Instituto de Estudios Peruanos (IEP).
———. 1988. *Desborde popular y crisis del estado.* Lima: CONCYTEC.
Mawhood, P. 1987. Decentralization and the third world in the 1980s. *Planning and Administration* 14 (1): 10–22.
McAdam, D. 1996. Conceptual origins, current problems, future directions. In *Comparative perspectives on social movements: Political opportunities, mobilizing structures, and cultural framings,* ed. D. McAdam, J. D. McCarthy, and M. N. Zald. Cambridge: Cambridge University Press.
McAdam, D., J. McCarthy, and M. N. Zald. 1988. Social movements and collective behavior: Building macro-micro bridges. In *Handbook of Sociology,* ed. N. Smelser and R. Burt. Beverly Hills, Calif.: Sage.
McAdam, D., J. D. McCarthy, and M. N. Zald, eds. 1996. *Comparative perspectives on social movements.* Cambridge: Cambridge University Press.
McCarthy, J., and M. Zald. 1977. Resource mobilization and social movements: A partial theory. *American Journal of Sociology* 82 (6): 1212–41.
McClintock, C. 1983. Velasco, officers, and citizens: The politics of stealth. In *The Peruvian experiment reconsidered,* ed. C. McClintock and A. F. Lowenthal. Princeton: Princeton University Press.
McClintock, C., and A. F. Lowenthal. 1997. Foreword. In *The Peruvian labyrinth. Polity, society, economy,* ed. Maxwell A. Cameron and Philip Mauceri. University Park: Pennsylvania State University Press.
———, eds. 1983. *The Peruvian experiment reconsidered.* Princeton: Princeton University Press.
McCormick, G. 1992. *From the sierra to the cities: The urban campaign of the Shining Path.* Santa Monica, Calif.: The Rand Corporation.
Mejía Navarrete, J. V. 1990. *Estado y municipio en el Perú.* Lima: Consejo Nacional de Ciencia y Tecnología.
Melucci, A. 1985. The symbolic challenge of contemporary movements. *Social Research* 52 (4): 789–815.
———. 1988. Getting involved: Identity and mobilization in social movements. *International Social Movement Research* 1:329–48.
———. 1989. *Nomads of the present: Social movements and individual needs in contemporary society.* Philadelphia: Temple University Press.
Méndez, J. L. 1990. La reforma de descentralización en Perú, 1978–1989. *Foro Internacional* 31 (1): 88–119.
Mendoza, E. 1992. Interview by author. Lima, 22 February. Tape recording.
Michels, R. 1957 [1925]. *Zur Soziologie des Parteiwesens in der modernen Demokratie. Untersuchungen über die oligarchischen Tendenzen des Gruppenlebens.* Stuttgart: Alfred Kröner Verlag.

Midgley, J. 1986. Community participation: History, concepts and controversies. In J. Midgley et al., *Community participation, social development, and the state*. London: Methuen.
Moisés, J. 1982. O estado, as contradições urbanas, e os movimientos sociais. In *Cidade, Povo e Poder*, ed. J. Moisés et al. Rio de Janeiro: Paz e Terra.
Montes, O. 1987. El comedor popular: De la gestión individual a la participación colectiva. In *Estrategias de vida en el sector urbano popular*, ed. R. Haak and J. Díaz Albertini. Lima: FOVIDA/DESCO.
Morales, A. 1991. La tenaza senderista. *La República*, 1 September, pp. 2-6.
Morris, A., ed. 1992. *Decentralization in Latin America. An evaluation*. New York: Praeger.
Munck, R. 1989. *Latin America. The transition to democracy*. London: Zed Books.
———. 1990. Farewell to socialism? A comment on recent debates. *Latin American Perspectives* 17 (2): 113-21.
Municipalidad de Lima. [1986]. *Tres años de gestión municipal. Una promesa largamente cumplida*. Lima: Municipalidad de Lima.
NACLA. 1995. Report on local politics: Introduction to hope—the Left in local politics. *NACLA: Report on the Americas* 24 (1): 14-44.
Nef, J. 1986. Redemocratization in Latin America or the modernization of the status quo? *NS Canadian Journal of Latin American and Caribbean Studies* 11 (21): 43-55.
———. 1988. The trend toward democratization and redemocratization in Latin America: Shadow and substance. *Latin American Research Review* 23 (3): 131-53.
Neira, H. 1984. Le processus de légitimation de la gauche au Pérou. *Notes et Etudes Documentaires* 4768:63-103 (Series: Problèmes d'Amérique Latine).
———. 1987. Violencia y anomía. *Socialismo y Participación* 37 (March): 1-13.
Nickson, A. 1995. *Local government in Latin America*. Boulder, Colo.: Lynne Rienner Publishers.
Nieto, J. 1983. *Izquierda y democracia en el Perú 1975-1980*. Lima: DESCO.
Nohlen, D., ed. 1991. *Descentralización política y consolidación democrática. Europa—América del Sur*. Caracas: Editorial Nueva Sociedad.
North, L. 1983. Ideological orientations of Peru's military rulers. In *The Peruvian experiment reconsidered*, ed. C. McClintock and A. Lowenthal. Princeton: Princeton University Press.
Nun, J. 1969. Superpoblación relativa, ejército industrial de reserva y masa marginal. *Revista Latinoamericana de Sociología* 5 (2): 178-236.
Nylen, William. 1995. The Workers' Party in rural Brazil. *NACLA Report on the Americas* 34 (1): 27-32.
———. 1997. Reconstructing the Workers' Party (PT): Lessons from North-Eastern Brazil. In *The new politics of inequality in Latin America*, ed. Douglas Chalmers et al. Oxford: Oxford University Press.
O'Donnell, Guillermo. 1994. Delegative democracy. *Journal of Democracy* 5 (January): 55-69.

O'Donnell, G., and P. Schmitter. 1986. Tentative conclusions about uncertain democracies. In *Transitions from authoritarian rule: Prospects for democracy*, ed. G. O'Donnell, P. Schmitter, and L. Whitehead. Baltimore: Johns Hopkins University Press.

Offe, C. 1987. Challenging the boundaries of institutional politics: Social movements since the 1960s. In *Changing boundaries of the political*, ed. C. Maier. Cambridge: Cambridge University Press.

Olivera Cárdenas, L., M. del Carmen Piazza, and R. Vergara. 1991. *Municipios: Desarrollo local y participación*. Lima: DESCO.

Olson, M. 1965. *The logic of collective action*. Cambridge: Harvard University Press.

¿Ordenanza con contrabando? 1984. *Expreso*, 28 June.

Ordenanza objetable. 1984. *El Comercio*, 3 July.

Oxhorn, P. 1991. Class formation or class deformation? The popular sectors and the concept of class in Latin America. Paper presented at the Sixteenth International Congress of the Latin American Studies Association, Washington, D.C.

———. 1995. *Organizing civil society: The popular sectors and the struggle for democracy in Chile*. University Park: Pennsylvania State University Press.

Palma, D. 1988. *La informalidad, lo popular y el cambio social*. Lima: DESCO.

Palmer, D., ed. 1992. *The Shining Path of Peru*. New York: St. Martin's Press.

Panfichi, Aldo. 1997. The authoritarian alternative: "Anti-politics" in the popular sectors of Lima. In *The new politics of inequality in Latin America*, ed. Douglas Chalmers et al. Oxford: Oxford University Press.

Panfichi, Aldo, and Cynthia Sanborn. 1996. Fujimori y las raíces del neopopulismo. In *Los enigmas del poder: Fujimori, 1990–1996*. Lima: Fundación Friedrich Ebert.

Parodi, J. 1986. La desmovilización del sindicalismo industrial peruano en el segundo Belaundismo. In *Movimientos sociales y crisis: El caso peruano*, ed. E. Ballón. Lima: DESCO.

Pásara, L. 1991. Ambivalencia en los nuevos actores sociales. La experiencia peruana. *Nueva Sociedad* 115 (September-October): 56–68.

Pásara, L., and A. Zarzar. 1991. Ambigüedades, contradicciones e incertidumbres. In *La otra cara de la luna. Nuevos actores sociales en el Perú*, ed. L. Pásara, N. Delpino, R. Valdeavellano, and A. Zarzar. Lima and Buenos Aires: CEDYS.

Pásara, L., N. Delpino, R. Valdeavellano, and A. Zarzar. 1991. *La otra cara de la luna. Nuevos actores sociales en el Perú*. Lima and Buenos Aires: CEDYS.

Pease García, H. 1977. *El ocaso del poder oligárquico. Lucha política en la escena oficial 1968–1975*. Lima: DESCO.

———. 1979. *Los caminos del poder. Tres años de crisis en la escena política*. Lima: DESCO.

———. 1983a. Vanguardia iluminada y organización de masas. ¿Que significa hacer política? *Nueva Sociedad* 64:33–38.

———. 1983b. Testimonio de parte. *Quehacer* 26 (December): 27–32.

———. 1984. Movimientos populares, municipios y estado. *Pensamiento iberoamericano—Revista de Economía Política* 5a:127–39.
———. 1988. *Democracia local: Reflexiones y experiencias.* Lima: DESCO.
———. 1990. Participación ciudadana y gobierno local. In *Lima, crisis y alternativas. La carta de Lima.* Lima: CIPUR/Fundación Friedrich Ebert.
———. 1991. Lima es gobernable. Una gestión municipal popular y democrática. In *Construyendo un gobierno metropolitano. Políticas municipales 1984–1986,* comp. H. Pease García. Lima: IPADEL.
———. 1992. Interview by author. Lima, 16 April. Tape recording.
Pease García, H., et al. 1981. *América Latina 80: Democracia y movimiento popular.* Lima: DESCO.
Pease García, H., and P. Jibaja Vargas-Prada. 1989. Los gobiernos locales en el Perú. In *Descentralización y democracia. Gobiernos locales en América Latina,* ed. J. Borja et al. Santiago: CLACSO.
Perlman, J. 1976. *The myth of marginality: Urban poverty and politics in Rio de Janeiro.* Berkeley and Los Angeles: University of California Press.
Peterson, G. E. 1997. *Decentralization in Latin America: Learning through experience.* Washington, D.C.: The World Bank.
Petras, J. 1988. The metamorphosis of Latin America's intellectuals. *Latin American Perspectives* 17 (2): 102–12.
———. 1997. Latin America: The resurgence of the Left. *New Left Review,* no. 223 (May/June): 17–47.
Pickvance, C., ed. 1976. *Urban sociology: Critical essays.* London: Tavistock.
Piester, K. 1997. Targeting the poor: The politics of social policy reform in Mexico. In *The new politics of inequality in Latin America,* ed. D. Chalmers, C. Vilas, K. Hite, S. Martin, K. Priester, and M. Segarra. Oxford: Oxford University Press.
Piven, F., and R. Cloward. 1979. *Poor people's movements: Why they succeed, how they fail.* New York: Vintage.
Pomar Ampuero, Nelly. 1997. Gobierno local, ciudadanía e izquierda in Lima Metropolitana: Independencia y Villa El Salvador. In *Lima. Aspiraciones, reconocimientos y ciudadanía en los noventa,* ed. Carmen Rosa Balbi. Lima: Pontífica Universidad Católica del Perú.
Ponce, A. 1989. ¿Quienes son los líderes naturales de las organizaciones populares de Lima Metropolitana? *Debates en Sociología* 15:217–22.
Portes, A. 1985. Latin American class structures: Their composition and change during the last decades. *Latin American Research Review* 20 (3): 7–39.
Portocarrero, Felipe. 1991. El Fondo Metropolitano de Inversiones (INVERMET). In *Construyendo un gobierno metropolitano. Políticas municipales 1984–1986,* comp. Henry Pease García. Lima: IPADEL.
Poulantzas, N. 1971. *Pouvoir politique et classes sociales.* Paris: Maspero.
Powell, S. 1976. Political participation in the barriadas: A case study. In *Peruvian nationalism: A corporatist revolution,* ed. D. Chaplin. New Brunswick, N.J.: Transaction Books.
Przeworski, A. 1985. *Capitalism and social democracy.* Cambridge: Cambridge University Press.

Quijano, A. 1974. The marginal pole of the economy and the marginalized labor force. *Economy and Society* 3:393–428.
Quintanilla, J. 1987. "El Agustino. Una experiencia con participación popular." Typescript.
———. 1988. Estamos gestando las bases del poder popular. *El Agustino: Boletín Municipal* 26 (June): 4–7.
———. 1991. Interview by author. Lima, 6 November. Tape recording.
Rankin, A. 1998. Why are there no local politics in Uruguay. In *Urban elections in democratic Latin America*, ed. Henry Dietz and Gil Shidlo. Wilmington, Del.: Scholarly Resources.
Reid, M. 1985. *Peru: Paths to poverty*. London: Latin America Bureau.
Reilly, C., ed. 1995. *New paths to democratic development in Latin America*. Boulder, Colo.: Lynne Rienner Publishers.
Rénique, J. L. 1995. The Latin American Left: Epitaph or new beginning? *Latin American Research Review* 30 (2): 177–94.
Rhodes, Sybil Delaine. 1998. Explaining innovation in local governance. An in-depth look at Porto Alegre, 1989–1997. Paper presented at the 1998 meeting of the Latin American Studies Association (LASA), Chicago Ill., 24–26 September 1998.
Roberts, Kenneth M. 1995. Neoliberalism and the transformation of populism in Latin America: The Peruvian Case. *World Politics* 48 (October 1995): 82–116.
———. 1996. Economic crisis and the demise of the legal Left in Peru. *Comparative Politics* 29 (1): 69–92
———. 1997. Beyond romanticism: Social movements and the study of political change in Latin America. *Latin American Research Review* 32 (2): 137–51.
———. 1998. *Deepening democracy? The modern Left and social movements in Chile and Peru*. Stanford: Stanford University Press.
Rochabrún, G. 1988. Crisis, democracy, and the Left in Peru. *Latin American Perspectives* 15 (3): 77–96.
———. 1989. Gestión popular o neomutualismo (interview). *Cuadernos Urbanos* 23 (April): 20–25.
———. 1992. Del mito proletario al mito popular (notas sobre el caso peruano). In *El nuevo significado de lo popular en América Latina*, ed. A. Adrianzén and E. Ballón. Lima: DESCO.
Rodrigo, J.-M. 1990. *Le sentier de l'audace. Les organisations populaires à la conquête du Pérou*. Paris: L'Harmattan.
Rodríguez Rabanal, C. 1989. *Cicatrices de la pobreza. Un estudio psicoanalítico*. Caracas: Nueva Sociedad.
Rojas Huaroto, C. 1982. Trabajo municipios: Táctica y estrategia. *Tarea* 6 (March): 12–13.
Rojas Julca, J. A. 1989. *Gobierno municipal y participación ciudadana. Experiencias de Lima Metropolitana 1984–1986*. Lima: Fundación Friedrich Ebert.
Rojas Samanez, A. 1991. *Los partidos y los políticos en el Perú*. 8th ed. Lima.
Romero, C. 1987. Violencia y anomía, comentarios sobre una reflexión. *Socialismo y Participación* 37 (March).

Romero, R. 1992. Interview by author. Lima, 15 January. Tape recording.
Roncagliolo, R. 1989/1990. Elecciones en Lima: Cifras testarudas. *Quehacer* 62:12–20.
Rondinelli, D. 1990. Decentralization, territorial power and the state: A critical response. *Development and Change* 21 (3): 491–500.
Rondinelli, D., and P. Wilson. 1987. Linking decentralization and regional development planning: The IRD project in Peru. *Journal of the American Planning Association* 53 (Summer): 348–57.
Rondinelli, D., J. McCullough, and R. W. Johnson. 1989. Analysing decentralization policies in developing countries: A political-economy framework. *Development and Change* 20 (1): 57–87.
Ruiz de Somocurcio, J., M. Llona, G. Riofrío, J. Huamán, and F. Portocarrero. 1987. *Procesos urbanos homogéneos en los distritos de San Martín de Porras y El Agustino.* Lima: Alternativa.
Sagasti, Francisco, Pepi Patrón, Nicolas Lynch, and Max Hernández. 1996. *Democracia y buen gobierno. Proyecto Agenda: Perú.* Lima: Editorial Apoyo.
Salcedo, J. M. 1981. ¿Adónde va Izquierda Unida? *Quehacer* 10 (March-April): 64–97.
Salman, T. 1990. Between orthodoxy and euphoria. Research strategies on social movements: A comparative perspective. In *Structures of power, movements of resistance: An introduction to the theories of urban movements in Latin America,* ed. W. Assies, G. Burgwal and T. Salman. Amsterdam: CEDLA.
Samoff, J. 1990. Decentralization: The politics of interventionism. *Development and Change* 21 (3): 513–30.
Sassoon, A. Showstack. 1987. *Gramsci's politics.* London: Hutchinson.
Saunders, P. 1981. *Social theory and the urban question.* London: Hutchinson.
Schmidt, G. 1989. *Donors and decentralization in developing countries: Insights from AID experience in Peru.* Boulder, Colo.: Westview Press.
Schönwälder, Gerd. 1997. New democratic spaces at the grassroots? Popular participation in Latin American local governments. *Development and Change* 28 (4): 753–70.
———. 1998. Local politics and the Peruvian left: The case of El Agustino. *Latin American Research Review* 33 (2): 73–102.
Schwartz, M., and P. Shuva. 1992. Resource mobilization versus the mobilization of people: Why consensus movements cannot be instruments of social change. In *Frontiers in social movement theory,* ed. A. D. Morris and C. McClurg Mueller. New Haven: Yale University Press.
Schydlowsky, D. M., and J. Wicht. 1983. The anatomy of an economic failure. In *The Peruvian experiment reconsidered,* ed. C. McClintock and A. F. Lowenthal. Princeton: Princeton University Press.
Scott, A. 1991. *Ideology and social movements.* London: Allen and Unwin.
Servicios Educativos El Agustino (SEA). 1989. "Micro Areas de Desarrollo: Proyecto Popular." Typescript.
Serrano, C. 1987. La calificación y adjudicación de lotes: Una experiencia democrática-participativa. In *Estrategias de vida en el sector urbano popular,* ed. R. Haak and J. Díaz Albertini. Lima: FOVIDA/DESCO.

Servicios Educativos El Agustino (SEA). 1995. *Hablan los dirigentes vecinales. Entrevistas a 27 dirigentes de El Agustino.* Lima: Servicios Educativos El Agustino.

———. 1996. *Hablan las mujeres dirigentes. Testimonios de 28 dirigentas de El Agustino.* Lima: Servicios Educativos El Agustino.

Shidlo, Gil. 1998. Local urban elections in democratic Brazil. In *Urban elections in democratic Latin America,* ed. Henry Dietz and Gil Shidlo. Wilmington, Del.: Scholarly Resources.

Slater, D. 1989. Territorial power and the peripheral state: The issue of decentralization. *Development and Change* 20 (3): 501–31.

———. 1990. Debating decentralization—a reply to Rondinelli. *Development and Change* 21 (3): 501–12.

———. 1991. Regionalización en una época de crisis social: Peru, 1985–1990. *EURE (Revista Latinoamericana de Estudios Urbano-Regionales)* 17 (51): 33–41.

———, ed. 1985. *New social movements and the state in Latin America.* Amsterdam: CEDLA.

Smelser, N. 1962. *Theory of collective behavior.* New York: Free Press.

Smith, B. C. 1985. *Decentralization—the territorial dimension of the state.* London: Allen and Unwin.

Smith, M. 1992. Taking the high ground: Shining Path and the Andes. In *The Shining Path of Peru,* ed. D. S. Palmer. New York: St. Martin's Press.

Stein, S., and C. Monge. 1988. *La crisis del estado patrimonial en el Perú.* Lima: Instituto de Estudios Peruanos (IEP) / University of Miami.

Stepan, A. 1978. *The state and society: Peru in comparative perspective.* Princeton: Princeton University Press.

Stiefel, M., and A. Pearse. 1982. UNRISD's popular participation programme: An inquiry into power, conflict, and social change. *Assignment Children,* no. 59/60: 145–62.

Stokes, S. 1995. *Cultures in conflict. Social movements and the state in Peru.* Berkeley and Los Angeles: University of California Press.

Tanaka, Martín. 1998. *Los epejismos de la democracio. El colapso del sistema de partidos en el Perú.* Lima: IEP.

Távara, J. 1983. Participación popular en el gobierno local. In *Lima una metrópoli / 7 debates,* ed. A. Sánchez-León and L. Olivera Cárdenas. Lima: DESCO.

Tavares, Ricardo. 1995. The PT experience in Porto Alegre. *NACLA Report on the Americas* 34 (1): 29.

Taylor, L. 1990. One step forward, two steps back: The Peruvian Izquierda Unida, 1980–1990. *The Journal of Communist Studies* 6:108–19.

Thompson, E. P. 1978. The poverty of theory. In *The poverty of theory and other essays,* ed. E. P. Thompson. London: Merlin

Touraine, A. 1984. *Le retour de l'acteur.* Paris: Fayard.

———. 1985. An introduction to the study of social movements. *Social Research* 52 (2): 749–87.

Tovar, Jesús. 1996. *Dinámica de las organizaciones sociales.* Lima: Servicios Educativos El Agustino (SEA).

Tovar, T. 1982a. *Movimiento popular y paros nacionales*. Lima: DESCO.
———. 1982b. *Movimiento barrial organización y unidad (1978–1981)*. Lima: DESCO.
———. 1982c. 1968–1975 Movimiento popular: Otra historia prohibida. *Quehacer* 16:68–75.
———. 1985. *Velasquismo y movimiento popular: Otra historia prohibida*. Lima: DESCO.
———. 1986a. Vecinos y pobladores en la crisis (1980–1984). In *Movimientos sociales y crisis: El caso peruano*, ed. E. Ballón. Lima: DESCO.
———. 1986b. Barrios, ciudad, democracia y política. In *Movimientos sociales y democracia*, ed. E. Ballón. Lima: DESCO.
———. 1991. El discreto desencanto frente a los actores. Modernidad, revolución y anomia en los sectores populares. *Páginas* 111 (October): 25–39.
Tovar, T., and A. Zapata. 1990. La ciudad mestiza. Vecinos y pobladores en el 90. In C. R. Balbi, E. Ballón, M. Barrig, M. Castillo, J. Gamero, T. Tovar, and A. Zapata, *Movimientos sociales: Elementos para una relectura*. Lima: DESCO.
Tuesta Soldevilla, F. 1983. *Elecciones municipales: Cifras y escenario político*. Lima: DESCO.
———. 1985. *El nuevo rostro electoral. Las municipales del 83*. Lima: DESCO.
———. 1989. *Pobreza urbana y cambios electorales en Lima*. Lima: DESCO.
———, ed. 1996. *Los enigmas del poder. Fujimori 1990–1996*. Lima: Fundación Friedrich Ebert.
Turner, R. H., and L. M. Killian. 1972. *Collective behavior.* 2d ed. Englewood Cliffs, N.J.: Prentice-Hall.
Ugarte Ubilluz, O., and R. Haak. 1991. Alimentación y salud: Los niños y el millón de vasos de leche. In *Construyendo un gobierno metropolitano. Políticas municipales 1984–1986*, comp. H. Pease García. Lima: IPADEL.
United Nations Development Programme (UNDP). 1993. *Human development report*. Oxford: Oxford University Press.
Valdeavellano, R. 1981. *Historia del movimiento barrial (segunda parte)*. Lima: DESCO.
Vanden, H. E. 1986. *National Marxism in Latin America: José Carlos Mariátegui's thought and politics*. Boulder, Colo.: Lynne Rienner Publishers.
Vargas Valente, V. 1990. *The women's movement in Peru: Rebellion into action*. The Hague: ISS (Working Paper Sub-Series on Women, History and Development: Themes and Issues, no. 12).
———. 1992. The feminist movement in Latin America. *Development and Change* 23 (3): 195–214.
Vilas, Carlos. 1997. La izquierda en América latina: presente y futuro (notas para la discusión). *Socialismo y Participación*, no. 77 (March): 93–106.
Villarán, J. L. 1991. La administración municipal. In *Construyendo un gobierno metropolitano. Políticas municipales 1984–1986*, comp. H. Pease García. Lima: IPADEL.
Weffort, F. 1989. Democracia y revolución. *Cuadernos Políticos* 56 (January–April): 5–18.

Willis, E., C. Garman, and S. Haggard. 1999. The politics of decentralization in Latin America. *Latin American Research Review* 34 (1): 7–56.
Wilson Salinas, P., and J. M. Garzón. 1985. Prospects for political decentralization: Peru in the 1980s. *Journal of Urban and Regional Research* 9 (3): 330–40.
Winn, P. 1995. Frente Amplio in Montevideo. *NACLA Report on the Americas* 24 (1): 20–26.
Winn, Peter, and Lilia Ferro-Clérico. 1997. Can a leftist government make a difference? The Frente Amplio administration of Montevideo, 1990–1994. In *The new politics of inequality in Latin America*, ed. Douglas Chalmers et al. Oxford: Oxford University Press.
Wise, Caroline. 1997. State policy and social conflict in Peru. In *The Peruvian labyrinth. Polity, society, economy*, ed. Maxwell A. Cameron and Philip Mauceri. University Park: Pennsylvania State University Press.
Woy, S. 1978. Infrastructure of participation in Peru: SINAMOS. In *Political participation in Latin America*, vol. 1, ed. J. A. Booth and M. A. Seligson. New York: Holmes and Meier.
Zolezzi Chocano, M. 1988. Asamblea Nacional Popular. Parto en el arenal. *Quehacer* 50 (January-February): 8–15.
———. 1991. Interview by author. Lima, 24 October. Tape recording.
Zolezzi Chocano, M., and A. Sánchez León. 1979. *Municipalidad y gobierno local: El D.L. 22250 en el tapete*. Lima: DESCO.
Zúñiga, Z. 1992. Interview by author. Lima, 11 February. Tape recording.

index

Abregú, Victor, 107–8, 157, 171
Acción Popular (AP, Popular Action Party)
   boycotts Constituent Assembly, 69, 104
   against decentralization, 95–96 n. 6
   discredited, 64
   economic policies, 74
   1978 elections, 69, 104
   1980 elections, 70, 91 n. 1, 93, 104
   1983 elections, 114, 117
   1998 elections, 197 n. 10
   on power of local government, 124 n. 12
   provincial government of Lima, 106 n. 17, 106
   support dwindles, 111
   today, 199
Acuerdo Socialista, 161, 167, 182 n. 15
agrarian reform
   of 1969, 63
   role of SINAMOS, 65
agricultural cooperatives, 63
Alianza Popular Revolucionaria Americana (APRA, American Popular Revolutionary Alliance)
   clientelism, 139, 145
   constitutional negotiations, 69–70
   control of regional governments, 38 n. 5
   corruption, 167
   discredited under Velasco, 64
   dominance, 114 n. 1
   1983 elections, 114, 114 n. 1
   1985 elections, 114
   1986 elections, 53, 147, 150, 150 n. 28, 151, 153, 161, 162, 165 n. 9
   1998 elections, 197
   2001 elections, 198–99
   in Lima during IU rule, 120
   PAD program, 143–44 n. 24, 154
   PAIT program, 30, 30 n. 22, 79, 143–44 n. 24, 145, 154
   resumes importance, 69, 90, 91 n. 1
   structure, 57
alliances
   and autonomy, 20–22, 25, 33
   based on respect, 192
   in Chile, 25–26
   under democratization, 36
   multiple, 54, 72, 190
   nonhierarchical nature, 26
   among political parties, 151
   among popular movements, 54, 72, 109, 162–66, 173, 180–81
   between popular movements and the Left, 25, 47–49, 53, 57–59, 99, 100–102, 108, 148–49, 162, 170, 177, 181, 183–84, 188–89
   possibilities today, 199
   rarely equal, 188–89, 190
   value to popular movements, 14, 30–32, 49, 51 n. 16, 183, 192
American Popular Revolutionary Alliance. *See* Alianza Popular Revolucionaria Americana
Ames, Rolando, 99 n. 10, 167
Andrade, Alberto, 194, 194 n. 6, 197 n. 10
AP. *See* Acción Popular
APRA. *See* Alianza Popular Revolucionaria Americana
Arenal de Canto Grande, Peru, 137–38

Arequipa, Peru, 113, 116
Argentina, 52–53
Asamblea Nacional Popular (ANP), 78
Asociación de Municipalidades de Perú, 194
Asociación de Pobladores, 139
associative networks, 33
Ate-Vitarte, Lima, 81, 104, 161 n. 7
autonomy
  as key issue, 10
  of popular movements, 10, 10 n. 1, 19–22, 32–33, 40, 48, 51, 54, 110, 148–49, 184
  relative, 20–21, 20 n. 13
Aylwin, Patricio, 38 n. 4
Azcueta, Michel, 167, 196

Ballón, Eduardo, 84, 87
banking sector reform (1970), 63
Barnet, Carmen, 77, 172
Barrantes, Alfonso
  administration finances, 128–29, 131
  administrative reforms, 134
  1983 elections, 114, 114 n. 3, 161
  1986 elections, 151
  1990 election, 167–68
  financial policies, 194
  intergovernmental conflicts, 125–26
  as mayor of Lima, 100, 115, 117, 119, 123, 127, 167
  on political freedom of Vaso de Leche program, 143–44
  political views, 115 n. 4, 116–17, 117 n. 7, 167
  and popular participation, 121, 121 n. 11, 132
  significance, 118, 118 n. 8
  splits from IU, 99 n. 10, 167–68, 182 n. 15
  on unions, 129
Belaúnde Terry, Fernando
  boycotts Constituent Assembly, 69
  economic policies, 74, 94
  1980 elections, 70, 93, 104
  World Bank loan for Lima, 128
Belmont, Ricardo, 91 n. 1, 196
Bernales, Enrique, 99 n. 10, 167, 182 n. 15
Blanco, Hugo, 99 n. 10
Blancos (party), 202
Boisier, Sergio, 49
Borja, Jordi, 49, 133 n. 17
Brazil
  decentralization, 37 n. 2, 202 n. 13

  freedom of urban popular movements, 32
  popular participation, 200–202
bureaucrats as allies, 19, 49

Cáceres, Irene, 159
Callao, Peru, 93 n. 4
Canto Grande, Peru, 81 n. 19
Carabayllo, Lima, 104, 108, 110
Cárdenas, Cuauhtémoc, 30 n. 22
Casanova, Julio, 175
Castells, Manuel, 12, 24, 25, 25 n. 17, 66 n. 3
centralization
  under APRA, 153–54
  of neighborhood movements, 71–72, 72 n. 9
  of popular movements, 78–79
Centro de Investigación y Promoción Popular (CENDIPP), 169
CG. See Comité de Gestión Distrital
Chamberlain, Francisco, 178
Chile
  decentralization, 38 n. 4
  squatter movements, 25–26
Chirinos Segura, Luis, 105, 109 n. 18, 131 n. 15, 132
Church
  support of CG, 174, 176
  support of survival movements, 32, 159–60, 173
citizen identity. See *ciudadano* identity
citizenship rights, 28, 28 n. 20, 78, 120
ciudadano identity
  defined, 27–28
  emergence, 78
  significance, 28
class
  basis of social movements, 17, 25 n. 17, 26
  defined, 17–18 n. 11
  effect of decentralization, 43, 46–47
  effect of economic crisis, 74–75
clientelism
  defined, 27
  eliminates autonomy, 51, 51 n. 15
  entrenched, 29–30
  in El Agustino, 157–58, 172, 179
  in neighborhood movements, 62
  and *poblador* identity, 27
  returns after 1986 election, 153
coalitions. See alliances
Collazos, Amanda, 77, 173

Collier, David, 23–24
Colombia, 37 n. 2
Colorados (party), 202
Comando Unitario de Lucha, 69
Comas, Lima, 104, 108
Comisión de Saneamiento Físico-Legal, El Agustino, 137 n. 21
Comité de Coordinación y Lucha Barrial (CCLUB), 69
Comité de Gestión Distrital (CG), El Agustino
curtailed by Sendero Luminoso, 161 n. 7
emergence, 166, 173
funding, 176, 182
leadership, 174
objectives, 173, 175–76, 181
rivalry with MIADES, 174, 176–77, 177 n. 12, 179–80
Comunidad Autogestionaria de Villa El Salvador (CUAVES), 162
Confederación General de Pueblos Jóvenes (CGPP), 72
Consejos Transitorios de Administración Regional (CTARs), 193–94 n. 5
conservative view of decentralization, 37
Constituent Assembly, Peru, 69–70, 73, 104
Constitution (1979), 70, 73 n. 10, 90, 92, 106–7, 124–25
Constitution (1993), 93 n. 4, 192, 193 n. 5
Convergencia Socialista, 99 n. 10
cooperatives movement, 65
coordinating program, 77–78, 143
culture, 73, 129
Cuzco, Peru, 113

Dammert, Manuel, 99 n. 10
decentralization
and administrative reform, 45–47
in Brazil, 202 n. 13
as centralist concept, 94 n. 5
in Chile, 38 n. 4
crucial to popular participation, 191
effect on political institutions, 36
effect on popular movements, 36, 39–40
espoused by international organizations, 37–38, 42, 43
forms, 39 n. 6
in Mexico, 39 n. 8
in Peru, 57, 93–96, 202 n. 13
political approach, 44–50
political implications, 43, 43 n. 11, 50
political obstacles, 46, 95–96 n. 6
as political plank, 36–38, 89, 122
potential to reduce popular participation, 39 n. 7
pragmatic approach, 41–44, 50
as strategy, 38–39, 38 n. 5
universal model, 42–43
in Uruguay, 202–3
decision-making
in alliance between Left and popular movements, 48, 101
industrial, 63
in local government, 92, 133–34, 146, 187
through MIADES, 162–63
by popular movements, 105, 120–21, 131, 149, 187
popular participation, 41, 49, 95, 105, 120, 146–48
prerogative of the elected, 49–50
by shantytown dwellers, 65
deconcentration
Chile, 38 n. 4
defined, 39 n. 6
delegation, defined, 39 n. 6
democracy
decentralization as tool, 44–45, 47, 50, 95
differing views among leftists, 96–98, 100–103, 111, 115 n. 5, 154, 180 n. 13
enhanced by popular movements, 187
history in Peru, 56–57, 56 n. 1, 69–70, 72
popular, 47
democratization
effect of popular movements, 22–23, 30
effect on popular movements, 30–33, 73–74
of elections, 92
furthers political stability, 45
late 1970s/early 1980s, 35–36, 69–70, 115 n. 5
led to *ciudadano* identity, 27–28
at local level, 33, 38, 50, 119, 133, 133 n. 17, 146–48
demonstrations
under Barrantes, 116, 143, 143 n. 23
under Belaúnde, 108
for MIADES funds, 165
under Morales, 68
as strategy for change, 189
under Velasco, 68 n. 6

developing countries, 42, 44
development corporations, 94
development organizations, regional, 94
devolution, 39 n. 6
Dietz, Henry, 24, 104 n. 14, 188 n. 2, 198 n. 9
Diez Canseco, Javier, 99–100, 99 n. 10, 100 n. 11, 117, 118
education
    addressed by popular movements, 73
    funding, 129
    system reform (1971), 63
El Agustino, Lima
    Comité de Gestión Distrital, 173–80
    effects of intraleftist struggles, 168–70
    1980 elections, 104
    1989 elections, 182 n. 15
    history and characteristics, 155–57
    MIADES project, 162–73
    popular movements, 107, 157–60, 161 n. 7, 184
    popular participation, 161–62, 170–73
    Sendero Luminoso, 161 n. 7
    Vaso de Leche program, 144, 171
    women's movements, 77, 158–60
El Cercado, Lima, 122, 135, 146–48
elections
    democratic, 92
    of mayors, 114 n. 2, 160 n. 5
    1978, 91, 103, 104, 160
    1980, 70, 91, 91 n. 1, 93, 96, 103–4, 104 n. 14, 113, 160
    1983, 76, 111, 113–15, 114 nn. 1–3, 116–17, 128, 161
    1985, 114, 114 n. 1, 117, 150
    1986, 53, 147, 150–51, 150 n. 28, 153, 154, 161, 162, 165 n. 9, 167
    1989, 161, 167, 168–69, 170, 182 n. 15
    1990, 118 n. 8, 167–68, 169, 192, 196
    1993, 161, 161 n. 6
    1995, 192–93, 194 n. 6, 196
    1998, 194 n. 6, 197, 197 n. 10
    2000, 194, 198
    2001, 198–99
ELECTROPERU, 126
emergency relief funds, 77
employment movements, 18
Encuentro Metropolitano de Organizaciones Vecinales, 78
England, 28 n. 20
environment, 15 n. 8

Erundina, Luiza, 201
Escalante, Carlos, 178
ethnicity, 28 n. 21

Federación de Centrales de Comedores Populares Autogestionarios de Lima y Callao, 195 n. 7
Federación de Pueblos Jóvenes y Urbanizaciones Populares (FEDEPJUP), 72
Federación Distrital de Pueblos Jóvenes y Urbanizaciones Populares de El Agustino, 158
Federación Popular de Mujeres de Villa El Salvador, 145 n. 25
Flores, Lourdes, 199
FOCEP. *See* Frente Obrero Campesino Estudiantil y Popular
FODECO. *See* Fondo de Desarrollo Comunal
Fondo de Compensación Municipal, 194, 195
Fondo de Desarrollo Comunal (FODECO), 164–65, 164 n. 8
Fondo de Inversiones Metropolitanas, Lima (INVERMET), 129, 194
Fondo Nacional de Desarrollo y Compensación Social (FONCODES), 195
foreign aid, 44 n. 12, 86
Fortaleza, Brazil, 201
FOVIDA program, 76
free-rider problem
    resource mobilization theory, 13 n. 5
    social movement theory, 30 n. 22
Frente Amplio, 202–3
Frente Obrero Campesino Estudiantil y Popular (FOCEP), 99 n. 10, 168
Frente Unico de Chillón, Peru, 137–38
Fujimori, Alberto
    centralist regime, 93 n. 4, 193–94
    economic programs, 37 n. 3, 173, 175, 192, 193, 193 n. 4
    1990 elections, 118 n. 8, 168, 192, 196
    1995 elections, 192–93, 196
    2000 elections, 198
    flees, 198
    media skill, 193, 196 n. 9
    rise, 91 n. 1, 168, 192, 196–97 n. 9
    self-coup, 56, 56 n. 1, 99 n. 10, 192, 193 n. 5

García, Alan
    brief economic upturn, 79

decentralization, 38 n. 5
1985 election, 114 n. 1, 150
1986 elections, 150
2001 election, 198–99
interjurisdictional conflicts, 126–27
regionalization, 193
supporters, 144 n. 24
gender, 28–29, 76–78
Giraldo, Yolanda, 144–45
Gortari, Salinas de, 30 n. 22
Gramsci, Antonio, 97, 97–98 n. 8
Guardia Civil, 67
guerrilla campaign. *See* Sendero Luminoso
guerrilla groups. *See also* Sendero Luminoso
MRTA, 98
Guzmán, Abimael, 80, 80 n. 18, 161 n. 7, 192

Haya de la Torre, Agustín, 69
Henry, Etienne, 66 n. 3
Herrera, Guillermo, 117
homeless people, 117
housing
  demands for better, 18
  popular settlements, 137–38
  shantytowns, 62, 65
Huaycán, Peru, 81 n. 19, 137–39, 149
human rights, 98
Hurtado, Jorge, 99 n. 10
Hurtado Miller, Juan Carlos, 194 n. 6, 197 n. 10

Icapuí, Brazil, 201
identities, collective, 14–18, 28
  as key issue, 10, 10 n. 1
  popular movements, 16–19, 26
  social movements, 14–16
  stronger in contemporary movements, 31
  successive and various types in Peru, 27–29
identity
  ciudadano, 27–28, 78
  poblador, 27–28, 68, 157–58
  vecino, 27–28, 68
illiterates (suffrage), 73 n. 10
indigenous people, 28, 28 n. 21
individualist strategies. *See also* self-help strategies, 29–30
industrial reform (1970), 63
interest groups, 11, 13
International Monetary Fund, 67, 74
international organizations

assistance, 44 n. 12, 86, 126–28, 130
espouse decentralization, 37–38, 42, 43
structural adjustment, 67, 74
International Petroleum Company, 63
INVERMET. *See* Fondo de Inversiones Metropolitanas
Izquierda Socialista, 99 n. 10, 118 n. 8
Izquierda Unida (IU)
  approach to local government, 101, 102–3, 119–24, 134, 148, 150–51
  Barrantes' plans, 115
  breakup, 99 n. 10, 100, 118 n. 8, 161, 167–68
  1980 elections, 103–4, 160
  1983 elections, 76, 111, 113–14, 114 n. 3, 116, 161
  1985 elections, 114
  1986 elections, 53, 150–51, 150 n. 28, 154, 161, 167
  1989 elections, 161, 168–69, 182 n. 15
  1989 national congress, 167
  1990 elections, 118 n. 8, 169
  formation, 103–4, 166
  internal tensions, 116–18, 118 n. 8, 167–70
  on popular movements, 131, 131 n. 16
  and PUM, 100
  radical-democratic orientation, 99 n. 10, 118–21, 148, 181–82
  reformist orientation, 99 n. 10
  revolutionary orientation, 98–99 n. 10, 110–11, 180–81
  social emergency program, 119, 140
  support increases, 111
  Vaso de Leche program, 140–46, 143–44 n. 24

Laderas del Chillón, Peru, 137–39
land
  development programs, 135–40, 156, 157–60, 162–64
  reforms, 63
  rights, 18, 27, 62, 70–71, 120–21, 135–40, 136 n. 19, 137 n. 20
Latin America
  application of new social movement theory, 26
  democratization, 45, 115 n. 5, 203
  disagreements among leftists, 96–97, 98 n. 8
  history of popular movements, 18–19, 56
  identity paradigm, 15 n. 8, 16

Latin America *(cont'd)*
  marginality theory, 23
  movements under democracy, 21–22, 26–29, 33
  social movements, 11, 11 n. 3, 14, 16
  social rights, 28 n. 20
  strategy paradigm, 13 n. 5
Left
  alliances: with other actors, 97, 115, 117, 154, 177, 182–83; with popular movements, 25, 47–49, 53, 57–59, 89–91, 96, 99–102, 108, 148–49, 162–63, 170, 177, 181, 183–84, 188–89, 190, 199
  attempts to unite popular movements, 78
  in Brazil, 201
  as creators of popular movements, 86
  decline: in late 1970s, 70, 90–91, 96; in late 1980s, 151, 166–70, 182 n. 15, 199
  differing views: of democracy, 96–98, 100–103, 111, 119, 154; of violence, 98
  in El Agustino, 160–62
  1978 elections, 91, 103
  1980 elections, 91, 96, 103–4, 104 n. 14
  1983 elections, 113, 115, 116–17
  growing rift, 91, 154, 166–70, 181
  ideological transformation in 1980s, 48, 115 n. 5
  influence of popular participation, 186
  internal democracy, 168 n. 11
  as lead in decentralization, 47–48
  in Lima, 106–11, 114–15, 118–24, 148–51
  local government links and roles, 90, 92, 96, 99
  opposes Morales regime, 69
  in Peru, 98, 98 n. 10
  and political pluralism, 97, 101, 115 n. 4
  popular support, 114–17, 114 n. 3
  promotes decentralization, 38, 89, 122
  promotes popular participation, 38, 48–49, 89, 107–9, 116, 119, 120–23
  strategies of governance: radical-democratic approach, 99, 101–3, 109–11, 116–24, 117 n. 7, 148–50, 154, 182; revolutionary approach, 99–101, 103, 105, 107–10, 116, 154, 180–82; to win local power, 96, 98
  subdivisions, 98–99 n. 10
  in Uruguay, 202
  in Western Europe, 97–98 n. 8

legislation
  Constitution (1979), 70, 73 n. 10, 90, 92, 106–7, 124, 125
  Constitution (1993), 93 n. 4, 192, 193 n. 5
  D.L. No. 776 (31 December 1993), 194
  Edicto No. 021, Lima, 147
  land titles (D.L. No. 13517), 62, 136
  Ley del Financiamiento (D.L. No. 24030), 128, 130
  Ley Marco de Descentralización (D.L. No. 26922), 193–94 n. 5
  Ley Orgánica de Municipalidades (D.L. No. 051 of 1981), 105–8, 124 n. 12, 131, 131 n. 15, 133
  Ley Orgánica de Municipalidades (D.L. No. 23853), 106 n. 17, 114, 124–27, 130, 131–33, 131 n. 15, 135, 150
  Ordenanza No. 192, Lima, 132–33, 135, 150
  settlements (D.L. No. 22612), 70–71, 71 n. 8
  SINAMOS (D.L. No. 18896), 64
  SINAMOS (D.L. No. 19352), 66
  Vaso de Leche (D.L. No. 24059), 143 n. 23
liberalism
  interventionist school, 42 n. 9
  on local politics, 46 n. 14
Libia, Gloria, 158
Lima, Peru, 57
  attempts to unite popular movements, 78
  CGs, 176
  1980 elections, 103–4
  1983 elections, 111, 113–15, 128
  1986 elections, 53, 154, 165 n. 9
  1989 elections, 182 n. 15
  finances, 126–30, 127 n. 14
  government, 93 n. 4, 103–4, 106, 111, 115, 118–19, 126, 135, 153–54
  growing schism with country, 197
  history, 155–56; of popular movements, 57–58, 72
  municipal agencies, 122, 146–48
  political and economic center, 94
  popular districts, 155
  riots (1975), 67
  Sendero Luminoso, 81–83, 82 n. 20
  shantytowns, 24, 58, 68, 79–80 n. 14, 82 n. 20, 155, 156–57
  soup kitchens, 75–76, 79 n. 14, 142, 160
  survival movements, 76–78, 142

urban development, 135–40, 162
Vaso de Leche program, 76–77, 79 n. 14, 80 n. 15, 120–21, 140–46, 160
literacy programs, 158
living standards
  under economic crisis of early 1980s, 75, 79, 140
  as rights, 78
local government
  autonomy, 92, 106, 125, 125 n. 13, 127–28, 154
  Brazil, 32, 37 n. 2, 200–202
  clientelist strategies, 172, 179
  Colombia, 37 n. 2
  conflicts with other levels, 125–27, 149, 174
  democratization, 27–28, 33, 50, 92, 133
  differing views of Left, 96, 101–3, 115–18
  effect of decentralization, 38, 38 n. 5, 44, 45–46, 90, 95–96
  hierarchical structure, 133
  ideal vehicle for popular movements, 22–23, 28, 73
  institutional weakness, 124, 149
  leadership: by APRA, 153–54; by leftists, 99, 115–18, 119–24, 148–51
  meeting place between state and civil society, 46
  popular participation, 36, 38, 40, 45–46, 49, 95, 107–10, 120–22, 130–35, 148–50, 186–87
  resources and roles, 37, 45, 71 n. 8, 92, 92–93 n. 3, 106, 108, 117 n. 7, 121–23, 124–30, 131, 154, 164–65, 165 n. 9, 182, 194
  targeted by Left, 89, 91–92, 96, 105
  urban development, 135–40, 137–39, 137 n. 22, 149, 162–64

Maraví, Yolanda, 171
marginality theory, 23, 23 n. 15, 86
Mariátegui, José Carlos, 115 n. 4
Marxism
  Barrantes' views, 115 n. 4
  Latin American left moves away from, 97
  root of urban social movement theory, 25, 25 n. 17
  on socioeconomic structures, 17, 17–18 n. 11, 26
MAS. See Movimiento de Afirmación Socialista

mayors
  election, 114 n. 2, 160 n. 5
  Lima, 104, 107, 115, 124 n. 12
  power, 93 nn. 3–4, 109–10, 133–34
Mendoza, Enrique, 169
Mexico
  decentralization, 39 n. 8
  squatters, 52
  state-run public works programs, 30 n. 22
MIADES. See Micro-Areas de Desarrollo
Micro-Areas de Desarrollo (MIADES, Microareas of Development)
  curtailed by Sendero Luminoso, 161 n. 7
  funding, 164–65, 181
  growth, 163–65
  launched, 161–63
  objectives, 162–63, 179
  problems and decline, 165–66, 171–73, 175, 181
  rivalry with CG, 174, 176–77, 177 n. 12, 179–80
microentrepreneurs, 164, 173, 176
modernizers, 37
Monterrey, Mexico, 52
Montesinos, Vladimiro, 198
Montevideo, Uruguay, 202
Moquegua, Peru, 116
Morales Bermúdez, Francisco
  dismantles labor laws, 70
  economic policies, 67, 68, 94
  takes power, 67
  transition to democracy, 69, 69 n. 7
mothers' clubs, 158, 173, 176
Movimiento de Afirmación Socialista (MAS), 82, 99 n. 10, 145 n. 25, 169, 177, 180 n. 12
Moyano, María Elena, 82, 145 n. 25, 161 n. 7
multinational companies, 63–64
municipal agencies, 122, 146–48
municipal councillors
  head secretariats, 134
  Lima, 107, 119
  power, 93 n. 3, 109, 133

National Solidarity Program (PRONASOL), Mexico, 30 n. 22
National System for the Support of Social Mobilization. See Sistema Nacional de Apoyo a la Movilización Social

neighborhood movements
  centralization, 71–72, 72 n. 9, 78
  character and leadership, 62, 69, 72 n. 9, 77
  declining need for, 76
  division from other movements, 176–77
  early dominance, 27, 66
  in El Agustino, 158, 163–65, 171, 176–77
  formation, 62
  in land development programs, 139
  legal recognition, 132–33, 135
  link with SINAMOS, 65–66
  oppose Morales regime, 68–69
  participation, 79–80 n. 14, 109
  renewal in late 1970s, 70–72
neighbor identity. See *vecino* identity
neoliberals, 37
NGOs
  allies in popular movements, 19, 31, 76, 141, 173
  do not support municipal government, 173, 180 n. 14
  effect of popular movements, 10 n. 1
  foreign aid, 86–87
  support CGs, 178, 180
  support MIADES, 164–65
non-governmental organizations. See NGOs
North America, 10 n. 1, 13 n. 5
nutrition
  addressed: by popular movements, 73, 77; by the Left in Lima, 114, 120, 140–46
  problems under economic crisis, 75, 140

OBRAS movement, 161, 161 n. 6
Odría, Manuel, 62
Oficina de Promoción y Desarrollo (PRODES), 170–71
Oficina General de Participación Vecinal, 134–35, 147
Organismo Nacional de Desarrollo de Pueblos Jóvenes (ONDEPJOV), 65, 71
Orrego, Eduardo, 106 n. 17, 119 n. 9, 124 n. 12, 127, 136, 137 n. 20

PAD program, Peru, 143–44 n. 24, 154
PAIT program, Peru, 30, 30 n. 22, 79, 143–44 n. 24, 145, 154
Pampas de San Juan, Peru, 137–38
Pamplona land invasion, Lima, 64, 65 n. 2
Paniagua, Valentín, 198

Partido Comunista Peruano (PCP), 99 n. 10, 117, 167, 168
Partido Comunista Revolucionario (PCR), 99 n. 10, 116
Partido Mariateguista Revolucionario (PMR), 99 n. 10, 168, 170, 177, 180 n. 13
Partido Popular Cristiano (PPC), 69–70, 150 n. 28, 199
Partido Socialista Revolucionario (PSR), 99 n. 10, 116
Partido Unificado Mariateguista (PUM)
  dissension, 168, 169
  in El Agustino, 168, 170–72
  founded, 100
  leadership, 117
  local influence, 160
  MIADES project, 177, 179
  revolutionary orientation, 99 n. 10, 167
Pásara, Luis, 86–87
PCP. See Partido Comunista Peruano
PCR. See Partido Comunista Revolucionario
Pease, Henry, 100
  backs Barrantes, 117
  Christian influences, 100, 167
  on breakup of IU, 118 n. 8
  1989 elections, 167
  1990 election, 118 n. 8, 168
  on intergovernmental conflicts, 126, 128
  on reform methods, 99 n. 10, 102 n. 12, 117 n. 7
  on unions, 129
  on women's organizations, 141
Pérez de Cuellar, Javier, 100, 198
Peru
  decentralization, 57, 93–96, 202 n. 13
  demise of military regime, 32
  democratic history, 56–57, 56 n. 1, 69–70, 72–73
  economic crisis of 1980s, 74–75, 79, 140
  history of popular movements, 56–57, 61–62, 66, 68, 70–84
  military regime, 62–71, 63 n. 1
  political jurisdictions, 93 n. 4
  poverty relief programs, 37 n. 3
  public works programs, 30, 30 n. 22
  recent political history, 197–99
  regionalization of 1980s, 38 n. 5
  squatter settlements, 24, 58, 62
  state-run public works programs, 30
Perú Posible, 198–99

PMR. *See* Partido Mariateguista Revolucionario
poblador identity
  defined, 27
  end of, 68
  in El Agustino, 157–58
  significance, 28
political independents, 197–98
political institutions
  allies in popular movements, 31
  chaos under democracy, 98
  effect of decentralization, 39
  effect of popular movements, 10, 10 n. 1, 12, 31
  external actions by popular movements, 51–52, 189
  increasing accountability, 36, 37
  internal actions by popular movements, 52–53, 189–90
  participatory structures, 109–10
  views of the Left, 101, 114, 182
political opportunity structures, 21–22, 21 n. 14
political parties
  after 1979 Constitution, 22, 69–70, 73, 89–90
  alliances with popular movements, 19, 31, 47–48, 151, 192
  co-opt popular movements, 25–26
  disintegration under Fujimori, 193, 196, 196 n. 9
  effect of popular movements, 10, 10 n. 1
  growing dissatisfaction with, 161 n. 6, 182 n. 15
  penetration by popular movements, 52–53
  weakened under Velasco, 64
  working-class, 14 n. 6
politicians
  allies in popular movements, 19, 31
  leftist in Lima, 103–4, 107–11
  as representatives of popular movements, 52–53
politics, local. *See* local government
Popular Action Party. *See* Acción Popular
popular participation
  Brazil, 200–202
  clear mechanisms needed, 191
  crucial to decentralization, 42, 43–44
  defined, 40–41
  differing views of Left, 103, 105
  El Agustino, 161–62, 170–73
  as end in itself, 38, 41, 45, 47–48
  enhances popular movements, 39–40, 105
  impact on political institutions, 36
  increases government efficiency and responsiveness, 186
  increasingly politicized in 1980s, 154
  in land development programs, 138–40
  in local politics, 36, 38, 40, 45–46, 49, 95, 107–10, 120–22, 130–35, 148–50, 186–87
  as means to end, 37, 37 n. 3, 41
  through MIADES, 162–63
  under military regime, 65–66
  in municipal agencies, 122, 146–48
  new openings needed, 191
  openings and barriers under Barrantes, 130–35
  in Peruvian provinces, 57 n. 2
  as political plank, 36–38, 89
  potentially reduced by decentralization, 39 n. 7
  promoted by Left, 38, 48–49, 89, 107–9, 116, 119, 121 n. 11, 122–23
  and resources, 131
  today and future, 199–200, 203
  in Uruguay, 202–3
  in Vaso de Leche program, 140–46
popular sector theory, 16–17, 16 n. 10
Porto Alegre, Brazil, 201
poverty relief programs, 37 n. 3
PPC. *See* Partido Popular Cristiano (PPC)
Prado, Manuel, 94
privatization, 37
Programa de Gobierno Municipal, Lima, 119
Programa Popular de Emergencia, Lima, 119, 140
PSR. *See* Partido Socialista Revolucionario
PT (Workers' Party), Brazil, 32, 200–202
public administration reform (1969), 63
public health
  addressed: by popular movements, 73, 77; by the Left in Lima, 114, 120–21
  emergence of movements, 18
  problems under economic crisis of 1980s, 75, 140
public policy
  effect of popular movements, 10, 31–32
  universal model of decentralization, 42–43

public services. *See* urban services
public works programs, 30, 30 n. 22, 37, 94, 120
PUM. *See* Partido Unificado Mariateguista

Quintanilla, Jorge, 162–63, 174, 178–79
Quixadá, Brazil, 201

Rafael Belaúnde, Carabayllo, 137
Raucana, Felix, 81 n. 19
regionalization
  blocked by Fujimori, 93 n. 4
  under 1993 Constitution, 93 n. 4
regional movements, 68–69
regions
  development aided by decentralization, 37, 42, 45–46
  development organizations, 94
  economic disparities, 93–94
  under Fujimori, 193–94 n. 5, 193
  political structures, 93 n. 4
resource mobilization theory
  free-rider problem, 13 n. 5
  group processes, 15 n. 9
  strategy paradigm, 10 n. 1, 13 n. 5
riots, Lima, 67
Rochabrún, Guillermo, 85–86, 87
Romero, Rosario, 169

Salta, Argentina, 52–53
San Juan de Lurigancho, Peru, 81 n. 19
San Martín de Porres, Lima, 104
Santiago de Chile, 25–26
São Paulo, Brazil, 200–201
SEDAPAL, 108, 126
self-help strategies. *See also* individualist strategies, 19 n. 12
  limited potential, 189
  popular movements as, 85, 86–87
  shantytowns, 65
Sendero Luminoso
  attacks on democratic institutions, 57, 80, 161 n. 7, 167
  claimed far Left terrain, 168
  exploited problems in movements, 81–83, 188
  fought by armed forces, 98
  fought by: Fujimori, 192; popular movements, 56
  inroads, 81 n. 19, 82
  terrorist tactics, 81–82, 145 n. 25, 161 n. 7, 195

Servicios Educativos de El Agustino, 178
settler identity. *See poblador* identity
shantytowns
  under authoritarian regimes, 23–24, 27
  in Chile, 25–26
  conditions, 18, 75, 140
  decision-making, 65
  effect of economic crisis, 75, 140
  first popular movements, 18, 62
  land rights, 18, 27, 62, 70–71, 120–21, 136
  in Lima, 24, 58, 68, 79–80 n. 14, 82 n. 20, 135–36, 155, 156–57
  marginality theory, 23
  in Mexico, 52
  role of SINAMOS, 65, 67–68
  self-help, 65
  Sendero Luminoso, 81, 82 n. 20
  taxes, 71, 71 n. 8
  urban services, 27, 71
Shining Path. *See* Sendero Luminoso
SINAMOS. *See* Sistema Nacional de Apoyo a la Movilización Social
Sistema Nacional de Apoyo a la Movilización Social (SINAMOS, National System for the Support of Social Mobilization)
  activities, 64–66, 65 n. 2
  decreasing support to settlers, 67–68
  dissolution, 71
  in El Agustino, 157–58
  established, 64
social movements. *See also* urban popular movements
  alliances, 14
  collective identity of participants, 14–16, 14–15 n. 8, 17
  defined, 11, 12 n. 4
  democratizing influence, 46
  dual logic, 14 n. 7
  group processes, 15, 15 n. 9
  in Latin America, 11, 11 n. 3, 14, 26
  need for and dangers of structure, 13–14, 14 n. 6
  noninstitutionalized action, 12–14
  participation in local politics, 45–46
  potential impact, 11–12
  in Western Europe, 11, 14–15 n. 8, 24–25
social networks, 15–16, 15 n. 9
socioeconomic structures, 17
Socorro Popular, 81

Somos Perú, 194 n. 6, 197, 197 n. 10
soup kitchens
  El Agustino, 158–60, 163, 173, 176
  emergence, 18, 75, 142
  number of, 195 n. 7
  organizational structure, 7
  proliferation, 75–76, 79 n. 14, 160
  targeted by Sendero Luminoso, 82
  today, 195
  women's involvement, 28, 75
squatter settlements. *See* shantytowns
state
  focus of strategies of popular movements, 19, 25
  public works programs, 30, 30 n. 22
  relations with popular movements, 31–32
  responsibility for urban services, 19, 126
  use of decentralization as policy tool, 52
state agencies. *See* political institutions
Stokes, Susan, 84 n. 22
strategies
  clientelist, 29–30
  individualist, 29–30
  Latin American context, 13 n. 5
  popular movements, 10, 10 n. 1, 19, 19 n. 12, 21–22, 50–54, 189–90
  resource mobilization theory, 10 n. 1, 13 n. 5
  social movements, 21–22
street vendors, 173, 176
strikes
  under Barrantes, 129
  under Morales, 68, 69, 70–72, 160
  under Velasco, 64, 67
students, 116–17
survival movements
  El Agustino, 159, 163–65
  emergence, 18–19, 30, 75, 142
  organizational structures, 77–78
  participation in local politics, 109, 132, 149
  proliferation and power, 76, 78
  reduced participation rates, 188
  targeted by Sendero Luminoso, 82
  women's involvement, 28, 76–77

Tacna, Peru, 116
Távara, José, 110
taxes, 71, 71 n. 8, 130, 194
Toledo, Alejandro, 198–99
Touraine, Alain, 12 n. 4
Tovar, Teresa, 66, 66 n. 3, 85, 87

Unidad Nacional, 199
Unidad Popular alliance, Chile, 25
Unión Nacional de Izquierda Revolucionaria (UNIR), 99 n. 10, 160, 168
Unión para el Perú, 100
unions
  allies in popular movements, 19
  attempts to unite popular movements, 78
  bureaucratic tendencies, 14 n. 6
  lead opposition against Morales regime, 68–69, 160
  municipal, 129
  weakened under Morales, 70
UNIR. *See* Unión Nacional de Izquierda Revolucionaria
United Left. *See* Izquierda Unida
urban popular movements. *See also specific types*
  alliances: and autonomy, 20–22, 25, 33; with each other, 54, 72, 109, 162–66, 173, 180–81; with Left, 25, 47–49, 53, 57–59, 99, 101, 108, 148–49, 162, 170, 177, 181, 183–84, 188–89; multiple, 190–91; need for, 14, 30–32, 49, 51 n. 16, 183, 192; with NGOs, 19, 31, 76, 141, 173; with political parties, 19, 31, 47–48, 151, 192; with politicians, 19, 31; rarely equal, 188–89, 190; with unions, 19
  attacked by Sendero Luminoso, 161 n. 7, 195
  autonomy, 10, 10 n. 1, 19–22, 32–33, 40, 48, 51, 110, 148–49, 184
  centralization, 71–72, 72 n. 9, 78–79
  changes over time, 9–10
  defined, 10, 11
  democratic potential, 22–23, 25 n. 17, 30, 31, 36, 40, 85, 87–88, 187, 191
  differ from other social movements, 11, 16–17, 19
  effect of: decentralization, 39–40; economic crisis, 74–80, 84; Velasco reforms, 66, 66 n. 3
  in El Agustino, 157–60, 162, 172, 180–81, 184
  emergence in 1970s, 72
  under Fujimori, 194–95
  history in: Latin America, 56–57; Peru, 56–58, 61–62, 66, 68, 70–84
  identity of participants, 10, 10 n. 1, 16–19, 26–29
  inherent weaknesses, 187–88, 190, 191–92

urban popular movements *(cont'd)*
  leadership, 52–53, 79–80, 80 n. 15, 82–83
  legal recognition, 131–32
  participation rates, 79, 79 n. 14, 195 n. 7
  political freedom under democratization, 35–36
  potential to influence change, 84–88, 84 n. 21
  power in local government, 105, 120–22, 131–33, 183
  problems, 30
  risk of co-optation, 19–22, 30, 48, 51, 54, 79, 154, 183–84, 190–91
  strategies, 10, 10 n. 1, 19, 19 n. 12, 21–22, 50–54, 189–90
  today, 31, 195–96, 199, 200 n. 12
  types, 10
urban services
  improved under decentralization, 37–38
  in Lima, 114, 125–27, 129
  popular movements, 18, 25, 177
  prerogatives of local government, 106–7, 125, 126
  prerogatives of state, 19, 126
  shantytowns, 27, 62, 71
Uruguay, 202–3

Vamos Vecino, 197 197 n. 10
Vanguardia Revolucionaria (VR), 117
Vargas Llosa, Mario, 168
Vaso de Leche program
  in El Agustino, 163–64, 171, 173, 176
  established, 120–21, 140, 160
  limitations, 144–45
  number of committees, 76, 79 n. 14, 142
  organizational structure, 76, 77, 140–42, 143–44, 145–46
  participation rates, 195 n. 7
  practical difficulties, 142
  success, 142–44, 149
  today, 195
  viewed as state service, 80 n. 15
Vázquez, Tabaré, 202
vecino identity
  defined, 27
  emergence, 68, 131
  significance, 28

Velasco Alvarado, Juan
  deposed, 67
  moves toward right, 67 n. 5
  promotes popular participation, 66
  reformist policies, 24, 27, 56, 63, 66, 70–71
  takes power, 62
Venezuela, 200
Villa El Salvador, Lima, 65 n. 2, 68, 68 n. 6, 81 n. 19, 82, 155, 161 n. 7
Villa Hermosa, Lima, 173
violence, 51, 51 n. 15, 97, 98
voluntary organizations, local, 42

welfare state, 15 n. 8
Western Europe
  identity paradigm, 14–15 n. 8
  leftists, 97–98 n. 8
  new social movement theory, 11, 14–15 n. 8, 24–25, 84
women
  empowered through survival movements, 74, 76–77, 80 n. 15, 142, 144–45
  killed by Sendero Luminoso, 82, 82 n. 20, 145 n. 25, 161 n. 7
  lead survival movements, 18, 28, 75–76, 80 n. 15, 141–43
  in politics, 29, 77, 82, 159
  in popular movements, 195 n. 7
  in workforce, 28
women's movements
  in El Agustino, 158–59, 163–65, 171, 176
  emergence, 28–29, 76–78, 142
  in Latin America, 76 n. 12
  participation in local politics, 109, 132
women's rights, 28–29, 77
workers' movement, 66 n. 3, 70
Workers' Party (PT), Brazil, 32, 200–202
World Bank, 126–27, 128, 130

Yoshiyama, Jaime, 194 n. 6
youth groups, 164, 171, 173

Zolezzi Chocano, Mario, 140
Zúñiga, Zenaida, 159